My Rocky Road and Beyond

My Rocky Road and Beyond

MARY MURIEL HALL

My Rocky Road and Beyond

All Rights Reserved. Copyright © 2014 Mary Muriel Hall

No part of this book may be reproduced or transmitted in any form or by any means, graphic, electronic, or mechanical, including photocopying, recording, taping or by any information storage or retrieval system, without the permission in writing from the copyright holder.

Spiderwize
Remus House
Coltsfoot Drive
Peterborough
PE2 9BF

www.spiderwize.com

The views expressed in this work are solely those of the author and do not necessarily reflect the views of the publisher, and the publisher hereby disclaims any responsibility for them.

ISBN: 978-1-908128-49-2

Table of Contents

Foreward vii
Acknowledgements ix

Chapter 1: St Flannon's Terrace 1
Chapter 2: Doora Bridge 12
Chapter 3: Escape to Ballyglass 16
Chapter 4: Home to Ennis 28
Chapter 5: Almost Normal 39
Chapter 6: Potato Picking in Ballyglass 56
Chapter 7: The Woods 60
Chapter 8: Where is my doll? 70
Chapter 9: Grandad Goes to Cork 76
Chapter 10: Dad Returns 81
Chapter 11: Florrie and the Low-flying Beachball! 92
Chapter 12: Shhhh! Mams Got a Job! 97
Chapter 13: And We All Come Back! 103
Chapter 14: Martin'w Washing Disaster 116
Chapter 15: Dad's Final Journey 122
Chapter 16: Where Did You Put the Winkles? 128
Chapter 17: At the End of the Rocky Road 138
Chapter 18: A New Start In England 145
Chapter 19: Homesick and Feeling Alone 152
Chapter 20: New Hobbies and Interests 158
Chapter 21: Martin's Here At Last 161
Chapter 22: Martin's Disasters Continue 165

Chapter 23: Grandad Comes to England 167
Chapter 24: Mam Gets Married 177
Chapter 25: My Convent Experience 188
Chapter 26: The Garden Fête 193
Chapter 27: The School Holidays 200
Chapter 28: Reminiscing 221
Chapter 29: Grandad Passes Away 227
Chapter 30: Prize Giving 234
Chapter 31: My Holidays in Ennis 242
Chapter 32: A Nice Christmas 262
Chapter 33: My New Job 270
Chapter 34: Learning to Dance 278
Chapter 35: Moving Again 295
Chapter 36: Meeting Arthur 309
Postscript: (by Jane McGregor, Muriel's daughter) 314

Foreword

For the last few years of her life, Muriel (as she was known to family and friends) was in poor health. As part of a therapeutic process, a consultant had suggested she reflect upon her life and put these reflections down in words. Muriel decided to do so and start with her earliest memories, and some these reflections are contained in this book.

It starts from her earliest memory at the age of two-and-a-half years and describes the hardship and joy she and her family endured throughout the 1940's in Ennis, County Clare, Ireland. She wrote the book very much through the eyes of the child she was at the time and it describes her life with mam, dad, three brothers and her granddad. Consequently, the language and style of writing reflects both the period and how a child would interpret the events described. Therefore, in finalising the text for the book, it was decided to leave it as Muriel intended it to be.

Personally, I feel it helps set the context for what is an emotionally powerful story and helps the reader see the unfolding events as they were intended—through the eyes of a child. I hope you agree and enjoy the book.

Alan Hall
13th May 2007

Acknowledgements

As stated in the Foreword, the writing of this book was started as part of a therapeutic process. Therefore, I would like to thank the consultant who made the suggestion to write these memoirs, Dr. J Flowerdew of Ailsa Hospital who not only encouraged Muriel to start these memoirs, but also to continue writing them.

Finally, I would like to thank all family and friends for their patience, encouragement and support in the completion this book in memory of Muriel.

Alan Hall
13th May 2007

Chapter 1:
St Flannon's Terrace

I was born in Ennis, a small market town in the west of Ireland on the 18th Feb 1939 and lived at a house in St Flannon's Terrace. The house had four rooms, one was the kitchen and the other three used as bedrooms, two small patches of garden at the front of the house and a step up to the front door. In the house was a small hall with a bedroom at each side, and straight ahead there was another door which led into the kitchen and the other bedroom, which was to the right, off the kitchen. When you went out the back door there was a yard and an outside lavatory, a small shed which was used to keep the turf and logs in, and next to the lavatory was a back gate that led onto a dirt road that went along the back of the houses. We had a lot of big rocks that were embedded into the ground which we could sit on and a dirt path up the side of one of them led up our back garden that seemed to go on for ever. That path led on to another little dirt road which went to a gate that led onto the Clare Road and this was the main road leading out of Ennis towards Clare Castle.

I lived in the house with my mam, dad, and granddad, who was my mother's father and had lived with us for as long as I can remember and my three brothers. Of my brothers, Ray was five years older than I, Martin was three and a half years older, and Patrick was two years younger.

My first memory was when I was two and a half years old; I was stood out in the road in front of our house waiting for my mam coming from the train station, where she had gone to meet my uncle Bert who was coming to visit us for the first time. I watched them coming up the road. He was tall with dark hair and wearing a gabardine coat; he had a bag in one hand and a brown paper parcel tied with string in the other. My mother had a brown coat on; her hair was way down below her waist, and she looked very happy. When they got in the house my uncle Bert gave me the brown paper parcel and when I opened it, it was a small doll's pushchair and a rag doll; I can't remember anything else about the visit.

My next memory was when I was about three and a half and was sitting on the kitchen floor playing with some beads; the floor was concrete and there was a ragged-mat in front of the range, a big kitchen table and two wooden chairs in the centre; a big sideboard and a big square sink and my mother's friend was sitting on one chair with my mother on the other. Her friend was saying how beautiful my brothers were with their lovely curly hair and their lovely smiles. My mother then looked at me and said, "Yes, she's the ugly duckling of the family."

I didn't know what it meant so I went to ask my granddad who was sitting in his bedroom, which was my first memory of him. My granddad took me by the hand back into the kitchen; and he started shouting at my mother that if she ever said that to me again there was going to be trouble, but by then it was too late. The seed was planted. I was an ugly duckling.

A short time after that I got very ill, and the doctor was sent for; he told my granddad he didn't think I would last the night. I felt terrible; every part of my body felt sick. My granddad lit a fire and I remember thinking I must be ill if we are having a fire in the bedroom; I didn't know where my mam was. The next thing I knew, the bedroom door flew open. It was my parents and this was the first-memory of my dad. He had hold of my mam by the hair and her head was pulled back; she looked very frightened. He was calling her a whore and a bitch; and said, "Your daughter is dying". He tried to push her into the room but she got away from him; I was too ill to cry. I remember thinking what a lovely dress she had on; it had lovely coloured squiggles all over it. I spent a whole week in that room. I never saw my mam or dad; but every time I opened my eyes my granddad was there. He'd wrap me up in my mams navy blue apron ready for when the doctor came; I remember it had little flowers all over and hung down to my ankles and gaping big holes for my arms to go through.

A few days later I began to feel a little bit better and it was then that my granddad started to give me drinks of this black stuff; it would be several years later before I knew this were called Stout. He used to put a red-hot poker into it and give it me to drink; it tasted horrible; but he said it would make me better, so I drank it. One morning I woke up and my granddad was asleep on the top of the bed. The poor man must have been exhausted. I started jumping up and down on the bed; he woke up and I told him I was better and that I wasn't going to die. He said, "That's my wee ducksey". He always called me that.

When I was four, I started school and I remember my mam standing me over the big stone sink and washing my face and hands with cold water and washing soap. I had poker straight hair, looked like a beanpole, and was pigeon-toed. On top of all that, I had a stutter and even when I did get the words out I couldn't pronounce them properly. I used to say "dix, dope and devon", when what I was really trying to say was, six, soap and seven; my brothers were always teasing me about it.

My mam was trying to put a ribbon in my hair but my hair was that fine it kept falling out which would lead to a hunt around the house to find hairgrips, So there I was, with my ribbon in place, and loads of grips to hold it on and off I went to school. I liked school for the first couple of months as all you did was draw on a slate with chalk and make little figures out of Marla (Plasticine). The thing I liked best was the free lunches; all the poor children got these. We had a bread bun with a glazed top that tasted sweet, and a mug of cocoa; I could never forget the taste of that bread bun; it was lovely.

My dad never went to work and he was always drunk. We used to dread the night time; he'd come home drunk and start cursing and shouting at my mam, then he would start beating her; she was always covered in bruises. The four of us children slept in a double bed in one room. Patrick and I were terrified and we would scream for it to stop, I would cuddle him and then he'd put his hands over his ears. Ray and Martin would lie there looking terrified and we would all fall asleep sobbing.

This carry-on happened most nights but it seemed to get worse as the days went by. Ray and Martin started to go out into the kitchen and try to help my mam but my dad was like a madman. One night it got so bad my brother Ray went next door to get help. He told Mr Riedy, our neighbour, that my dad was going to kill our mam. When he came in we were all in the kitchen crying and trying to get my dad away from her. Mr Riedy was a tall man, always had a cap on, and he wore small thick glasses. He walked into the kitchen with another man who was wearing a dark coat; I don't know who he was but Mr Riedy told my dad that if he didn't let her go he'd have both of them to deal with and dad let her go and went through to the bedroom without saying a word; at last all was quiet.

When my dad got up the next morning he told my mam he was going to stop drinking and that he was going to go to England to get a job and he'd send her money every week to keep us. About a week later, just like my other friends dads, he went off to England looking for work.

After my dad went away the house was nice and peaceful and my granddad would look after us a lot. I remember asking him about the big lump he had hanging from under his right arm just above his wrist; I asked why the Doctor didn't cut it off? He told me that when he was in the war, the First World War, he was hit with shrapnel, and they couldn't take it out because it would be too dangerous.

No money wire came from my dad and week after week we waited. My granddad had a small pension from the army once a month. I think his pension kept us all from starving. One week little Patrick came running from the back of the house all excited; he was shouting "Mam' its here its here!" He brought his hands from behind his back and gave her a long piece of wire; he was too little to understand. When we ran out of turf for the fire, we would all go down the Crags to collect rotten wood; as there was lots of it there, but it burnt away very quickly and you needed an awful lot to bake bread and cook a meal.

My mam used to buy a sheep's head because they were very cheap; she would make a sort of broth with it that would last a couple of days. I never liked it but I ate it. Ray would take the eyes out and chase us round the house with them. Sometimes we got a pig's head but they cost more money; mam would roast this and it tasted a lot nicer than the sheep's head and when it was cold you could make a sandwich with it. We also had pig's feet, which were also nice, but they didn't fill you up; they were mostly bone and gristle and sometimes when Mr Riedy next door got a few rabbits he would give us one for our dinner, which we were very grateful for.

As the weeks went by and the weather was getting warmer, we only needed wood for cooking so we would play down at the crags a lot more. There were great big rocks down there, three times the size of us. One was called the fairy rock and we would climb all over them and play all sorts of games. The flat rocks would become tables and chairs; we'd gather bits of broken bottles to put on them, competing to see who had the best-decorated table. Not just us though, all the children loved it down there.

My godmother Florrie had a goat in the Crags. Florrie was always a happy woman and she was big and fat and you could hear her laugh half a mile away. Every day she would come to milk the goat, sometimes letting us have a go. Once she'd just finished milking and bent over to pick up the milk and the goat butted her right on the backside, knocking her to the floor and throwing the milk everywhere. As we all tried to pull her up, all she could do was laugh about it.

One Sunday we went to see my Nana and Granda Burns, my dad's parents who lived about five minutes away from our house. My Nana was small with grey hair tied back in a bun; and my Granda was well built with a long bright white moustache that he'd play with and twiddle the ends into neat little points, he never spoke to us; he just nodded his head when we went in. Both were devout Catholics, and my Nana's first words would be, "Have you all been to mass this morning?" I don't think she would've let us in the house if we hadn't been. Mass was one of those things we'd be too frightened to ever miss; it was drummed into us that it was a mortal sin, and if you missed mass you would go to Hell and burn.

My Nana would give us a penny each and we'd play outside her house for a while, then Ray would go off with his friends, leaving Martin as the eldest in charge of about six of us. There was a lane across the road from nana's; it was called Scabby Lane and we were never allowed to go down there, but I didn't know why. We were all a bit frightened, but went anyway. What could all the fuss be about? It seemed okay at the time! About three quarters of the way down we saw a tramp. I'd never seen anyone that looked quite like him before. I was closest to him and he smelt terrible. His hands were filthy with long black fingernails, his hair was long to match his black beard and he wore a ragged coat tied with string around his waist; I couldn't stop staring at him. Next thing Martin shouted to us "Run", so they all ran, but the tramp caught hold of me and pulled me toward him, He pulled my pants down and put his fingers up my front passage, I screamed with the pain; it felt as though someone was pulling my insides out, I screamed and screamed.

The next thing I could hear was all the footsteps running back towards me and when he heard them, the tramp ran off the other way; Martin got back to me first; he was shouting, "What happened? I thought you were running behind me?" I told him what the tramp had done to me, and that I was hurting; He cuddled me and said I would be all right but I wasn't to tell my mam or anyone else because we would get a good hiding for going down the lane when we were told not to. He said if Patrick knew what the tramp had done to me he would tell mam, so when Patrick came up to me, and asked why I was crying, Martin told him I had fallen and hurt myself. We made our way home and I was sore for days.

A few days later my mam was in the town and met one of my nana's neighbours and she told her she had seen us go down Scabby Lane. So we all got a good hiding and I was so sore again, but I didn't tell her about the tramp.

Not long after that, we were told my dad was coming home. I think my mam couldn't have had more than two money wires in the five months he'd been away, she had been able to make a few shillings here and there by doing a lot of sewing for other people; she could make anything out of anything but it was hard getting the money off some people, they would say, "Tell your mam we'll give it to her next week", and so it went on, but at least there were some good payers amongst them.

My dad arrived home drunk and he had a pal with him. I can remember them sitting at the kitchen table and they had bottles of beer. My dad lifted me on his knee and asked me to sing a song for them. I can still remember the words of that song, although I can't remember the title.

My family (left to right, top to bottom): Me aged 2½ and my earliest memory; my brothers Martin and Patrick; Ray with my dad; Granddad, my mum and my uncle Bert (Paddy).

My mam was standing near the kitchen window; she seemed to be on edge all the time. Then he suggested to his pal, that they went to the pub for a couple of pints of beer, then mam went over to him and asked him for some money, he gave her some, and off they went.

My mam went up the town and did a lot of shopping and we helped her carry it home, I'd never seen so much food in all my life. When we got home she started to make bread, a fruitcake that she always called a bit of old cake; apple pies, and a big piece of beef. I think it was pickled beef; it was a reddish colour when it was cooked and she called it corned beef. When the meat was cooked she put it on the sideboard to cool. She told us not to touch it as it was for Sunday lunch, but as soon as she turned her back, we would all have a pick at it. The meat was getting a bit lopsided so we thought we'd better stop picking. I think she was watching us out of the corner of her eye but never said anything; she had a little smile on her face and I'd never seen her look so relaxed. We all went to bed with a full belly and happy that night.

We were all fast asleep when we were woken up with mam screaming; my dad was hitting and swearing at her. Martin went to look through a crack in the door; he came and told us dad had turned the table over and all mam's baking was all over the floor and the two chairs had been thrown across the kitchen. He was shouting at her, saying he wanted the money back, and mam was trying to tell him she'd spent it on food and she had ordered and paid for a load of Turf for the fire to be delivered on Monday. He was breaking everything he could get his hands on. The funny thing was he never broke the holy pictures and statues or never tried to sell them; so if he didn't break or sell them, he must have known what he was doing to mam.

Poor little Patrick had his hands over his ears again. My dad went back out again. I don't know where he went, but he wasn't there the next morning. All was quiet again; all we could hear was my mam sobbing.

The next morning my granddad got us up for mass; he was a Protestant, but he always made sure we went to mass, would stand over us while we got washed and would polish our shoes or boots until you could see your face in them; and he gave us a penny each for the collection plate.

Patrick didn't want to go without his mam, but she couldn't go with us as she was covered in bruises. My granddad told him he was to be a big boy because he was starting school on Monday. I remember thinking, as we were going up the path, I hope nothing happens to mam until she goes to confession or she would go to hell for not going to mass.

I took Patrick to school with me on Monday. He had to go to the convent school, as he wasn't old enough to go to the brothers' school; he carried on all the way there. He was saying, "I don't want to go to school. I want to go to the brothers", and I had to drag him along. I told him if we were late we would get into trouble. I got him there, eventually, but we were late. The big iron gates were locked so I had to ring the bell. A nun came and opened the gate and we went to my classroom. Sister Mary told Patrick to sit down and me to come up to her desk and hold my hand out. She then hit me with the cane three times for being late. I was trying not to cry so as not to upset Patrick, but the tears were running down my cheeks and I couldn't control them.

Suddenly Patrick jumped up from his chair and ran at the nun; he was shouting at her, "Don't you hit my sister you bastard." He was kicking at her but he couldn't find her legs because of the long habit she was wearing. Then he started calling her a whore and a bitch; all the things he had heard my dad call my mam. Eventually I got him settled down and I told him not to talk to me or she would give me the cane again, that was the longest day of my life.

The next day I begged him to be good and he said he would and we got to school on time. We were sat in the classroom and Patrick kept talking to me, but I didn't answer him because Sister Mary was watching me all the time and I knew she would cane me again if I talked to him. The next thing, Patrick burst into song; "She'll be coming round the mountains when she comes". All the girls in the class were dying to laugh but they daren't. Sister Mary came over and grabbed Patrick by the neck and stood him in a corner. He started swearing at her again; "I don't want to stay here you old bitch, I want to go to the brothers". Her face was red with anger and she called me up to her desk, thinking I was going to get the cane again, but I didn't. She just told me to take him home and I was never to bring him back to that school again.

Patrick was over the moon at not having to go back to the girl's school; he would have to wait until he was five now to go to the brothers. Patrick got a good telling off from my mam; he told her he would never say those bad words again. It would have been better if mam could have taken him to school, but she couldn't, because she was still covered in bruises.

Patrick went off to play with his little friend; he was called Joe, and he was deaf and dumb but they played together all the time; we often wondered how they got through to each other; but they did. Patrick had my old red coat on; it was too small for me but he was plump and the coat wouldn't fasten on him. He would put his hands in the sleeves and hold the flaps of the coat up, and pretend to be, Captain Marvel; him and Joe would run up and down the road with their arms out laughing; the wind blowing their coats out, I would always remember them that way.

Our road was a very quiet one; all the children used to play on it. We used to play hopscotch, skipping, and piggy in the middle. The boys used to play Hurley as you hardly ever saw any traffic on the road, although there was the odd horse and cart, the rag and bone man, and a woman with a handcart selling sea grass and periwinkles. Sometimes mam would get a penny's worth of each for us to share. I liked the sea grass best.

We carried on with our lives the best we could but the rows went on. Then Ray got ill. He had awful pains in his side, so mam sent for the Doctor. He came and thought it was his appendix; he told mam to get him to the hospital as soon as possible. Mam had to walk Ray to the hospital and he was in agony; he collapsed in the hospital corridor and Ray had his appendix out. The day he was coming home we were all told not to make him laugh, because he would be sore. Martin couldn't resist trying to make him laugh though; he got a fit of the giggles, and that started me off. Then Ray tried to laugh too but it was hurting him. Patrick sat there his face all serious and told us to stop it or Ray would have to go back to hospital.

Patrick loved Ray; he followed him all over like a little puppy; he missed him when he was in hospital, and didn't want him to go back there. The two great loves in Patrick's life was Ray and his little pup that he called Bran. Ray wasn't getting over his operation like he should have been and was very pale and had dark circles under his eyes; mam took him back to the Doctor, who said he was very run down and gave him a tonic. He told mam that he could do with some country air and some peace and quiet. Even the doctor knew he wouldn't get any peace in our house.

Mam took Ray away to the country; she had friends that lived on a farm in Ballyglass, about five miles from the town of Westport. I don't know where she got the money from for the train fare. My granddad was looking after us while mam and Ray were away as my dad was always in the pub. One day, after we'd had our tea; Martin said, "Let's play, hide and seek". The nights were beginning to draw in and granddad said to us, "It'll be dark soon so don't stay out to long." Patrick was saying, "I want to go and play with them", and granddad said no at first; but Patrick could twist him round his little finger and eventually he gave in and let him go. Granddad told me to watch him all the time, as he was a little monkey for running off. I told him I would, and off we went. We could hear all the children laughing down the road and when we caught up with them; I asked them who it was hiding! They said it was Martin; so we all went looking for him.

Patrick let go of my hand and ran off. I got into a panic and I was shouting to the others, "Have you seen Patrick?" Nobody had and I climbed up onto this high wall to see if I could see him. There was a car coming up the road. It passed me where I was sitting on the wall and I saw the shadow of Patrick run across the road; I screamed out his name but it was too late, the car had hit him, people were coming out of their houses and were all stood around the car and all I could hear was them saying, "Its young Patrick; I think he's dead; God Rest his Soul". The ambulance came and took him to hospital and I was still sat on the wall, I seemed to be frozen to it. I don't know how long I was sat there or how I got down but the next thing I know I was sat in our back lane; I daren't go in the house and all I could do was cry.

My granddad had been looking for me in the road where it had happened and went back in the house. Then I could hear footsteps in the yard. He opened the back gate and found me and picked me up in his arms and cuddled me to him; he said "It's not your fault, my wee Ducksey."

Martin was sent to find dad; he didn't know which pub he went in so he had to try them all; he found him eventually. Dad came in the house and was shouting at my granddad, "How did this happen, you were supposed to be looking after them?" I wanted to scream at him; it wasn't granddad's fault. It was mine. Granddad hushed me up and told my dad to get to the hospital, we were told to go to bed; but we couldn't sleep.

Next morning when we got up dad was in the kitchen. He told us Patrick wasn't dead but was very ill. We asked if we could go to see him, but he said no because he was too poorly. Dad had sent mam a telegram and hoped she'd be home today and the waiting seemed to go so slowly. It was nearly dusk when we saw her walking up the road, a suitcase in one hand and was holding Ray with the other; my dad came out to the gate. Granddad was with him. No one ran to meet them as we were still in shock and waited by the gate until they got to us. Then dad was shouting, "Where've you been? It can't have taken you this long to get here." Then he was saying, "If you had been here to look after your children this wouldn't have happened." Mam never said a word; she just stared at him.

Granddad took her arm and lead her into the house. Ray was just standing there; I'll never forget the look on his face. He was pale before he left but now he looked like a ghost; not a word was said. Martin got hold of one arm and I the other; we took him inside. Mam had gone in the house, dropped the suitcase and gone out the back door and up to the hospital. She stayed there all night.

The next morning Patrick had spoke to her; he'd asked her if she would get him a green shirt. She went to the shops and bought him one. When she went back and gave it to him; he smiled at her, and then he died. We went to the mortuary to see him laid out. His little head was bandaged down to his eyebrows and they hadn't put his arms out as they were too badly damaged. I gave him a kiss and told him I was sorry. Martin was there but he didn't go up to him. He just sat on a chair, looking very sad and Ray didn't go, because he wasn't well enough and was still in shock.

The day after that, Patrick's little friend Joe knocked at the door. He was standing there with tears streaming down his face and making a noise in his throat; he held his hand out and he gave mam a couple of marbles; they must have been Patrick's. Mam told him he could keep them; she then gave him Patrick's red coat; which he took and hugged; he gave a little smile and left.

The man who was driving the car that knocked Patrick down had only one arm. It was said he was teaching his daughter to drive and I thought that maybe if he had two arms he would have been able to stop in time. I think they paid forty pounds in compensation to my mam and dad for the accident, but dad took a good bit of the money. Mam paid for Patrick's funeral, some turf for the fire, a lot of food and a good few clothes for us. Then she hid what was left behind the holy picture of Jesus, for emergencies!

We tried to get on with life the best we could; we were all missing Patrick. Patrick's little dog (Bran) was killed on the main road a week after he died.

Chapter 2:
Doora Bridge

Our neighbour on the other side of our house had a great big dog; it was called (Touser), but we always called him Touser Malone, although his owners name was Malloy. I used to sit on one of the big rocks in our back lane next to Mr. Reidy's pigsty; he didn't have any pigs in it, but he did at one time. Touser Malone would come and sit in front of me, and I would tell him all my problems. I think he understood and he would put his paw on my knee. He was my best friend.

Next door to Touser Malone, lived two old ladies and they were always dressed in black clothes. They had two German Shepherd dogs which were vicious. You never saw those old ladies out the front; we only ever saw them in their back yard with the dogs. Ray told me they were witches, so I was frightened of them.

Dad had kept a good bit of the money they had got from the compensation, but he was still drunk all the time. He came home one night and we were all in bed and could hear all the swearing and things being thrown about the house. You could hear granddad's voice. He was trying to get dad away from mam. Ray went out to help granddad and they were trying to drag him away from mam, but he was like a madman. Ray shouted to Martin and me to go and get the guards. The Garda station was a long way away and it was pouring down with rain and very cold. Martin and I ran out the front door. I only had my pants and vest on and Martin was only wearing short trousers and we had nothing on our feet. We ran all the way as fast as we could. We went through the middle of the town and there wasn't a soul about. It must have very late at night. When we got to the Garda station we went in and there was a big desk. Martin could just see over the top of it but I couldn't. There were two guards behind the desk and they both leaned over and asked us what was wrong. We told them our dad was killing our mam and Ray and granddad were trying to stop him. We asked them if they would come and help. They told us they couldn't interfere as it was a domestic row and to run along home, it would all be over when we got back. We ran all the way home and we were soaking wet and shivering with the cold. When we got to the house, it seemed very quiet. We didn't know whether to go in or not. Then the front door opened. It was Ray and he was just coming to look for us. He asked where the guards where? We told him what they had said and he took us in the house and mam's first words were, "Have they let you come home on your own?" We told her they had and she said even the guards were frightened of him.

Mam's nose was bleeding and one of her eyes was a lot bigger than the other granddad had a bleeding lip and Ray had a big red mark down the side of his face. Granddad had hit my dad with a pan; so dad had gone back up the path towards town, but my mam said he would be back again. She was trying to dry us off and we were still shivering. She told us to put as many clothes on as we could find. Mam and granddad were going round the house collecting blankets together. When they were ready we all went out the back door and through the back gate. Mam closed it behind her and we followed her into Mr Reidy's pigsty. You could feel there was straw all over the floor and mam was putting blankets down the best she could as it was pitch black. We were very cramped up together as I think it was only made for two pigs and there was five of us in there. Shortly after that we heard dad coming down the path, he was cursing and swearing and had to pass the pigsty to get to our back gate. Mam told us to be very quiet, he passed the pigsty and went through the gate into the house; we could all settle down for the night now or what were left of it.

Mam must have been in a lot of pain because I could hear her moaning and groaning every now and again. I was very cold but eventually I went to sleep. Very early the next morning mam took us back into the house, She lit the fire and we started to feel warm; we could hear dad snoring, when he did go to sleep, he slept the sleep of the dead. Everything was back to normal and we were told to get washed and ready for school. A few days later mam told us that granddad was going over to England to stay with Uncle Bert and his new wife. I felt very sad and I didn't want him to go as he was the only adult that cuddled me and told me stories. I loved him so much and would miss him. I found out later that dad had told him to go. I think it was because granddad had hit him with the pan.

Life was awful without Granddad. Dad was still coming home drunk, and he would pull mam out of her bed when she was asleep and knock her around the place. Mam got more and more depressed. One day when we arrived home from school; she gave us our tea and she said she was going out for a while. She was looking awful.

Dad came home early that night; he never came home until the pubs were shut, and it was only six o'clock and he was only half drunk. He asked us where mam was and we told him we didn't know; she had gone out over an hour ago, He didn't go back out. We waited and waited for mam to come home and I was getting a bit frightened. I was thinking she'd gone and left us. About ten o'clock, there was a knock at the front door, dad went to answer it and we all followed him. There was two guards standing there; one each side of my mam. They said she was on Doora Bridge. (Doora Bridge was a place where people went to commit suicide). They said she was going to jump in the fast flowing river but some people walking their dogs had grabbed her and had sent for the guards and, so they had brought her home. She looked half dead, and she never spoke a word. She had a vacant look on her face.

There was one good thing that came out of it all; it frightened my dad for the next few days; he couldn't do enough for her. It was nice to be in a house where there were no rowing, swearing or throwing things about; all the fight had gone out of mam; her eyes were dull and she didn't seem to care. Dad was sober for a whole week; he was quite a nice man when he was sober. Mam was looking a bit better by the end of the week; she seemed to be getting the fight back in her and she didn't look so vacant any more. Dad had started drinking again; he would come home ranting and raving at mam because of what she had tried to do. He would say it was a sin to try and commit suicide and you weren't thinking about your children and what if the neighbours found out about what you tried to do.

Mam said one day that she would have to teach him a lesson. She told us that she was going to stay with my cousin Maureen and her husband. They lived about eight doors up the road from us. She said we could go and see her every day when it got dark and we were to go one at a time. We were told we weren't to tell dad.

Dad couldn't go out on a night because there was no one to look after us; he had to be up for us in the mornings to see us off to school and he didn't like that. He was looking everywhere for her. He even went to Maureen's house but Maureen said she hadn't seen her.

An aunt of ours came over from limerick about four days later; (she was my dads sister) and visited our house, so he must of thought mam had gone to limerick, but she told him she hadn't seen or heard from her. My dad and my aunt were sitting in the kitchen asking me questions all the time, but I didn't tell. Then my aunt tried other ways to catch me out, she spoke to dad and said, "I know where she's gone! She's gone to England and left those poor children! What an awful thing to do." I jumped to mam's defence, and said, "No she hasn't left us; and she's up at Maureen's." I'd let the cat out of the bag.

Dad went to Maureen's house with my aunt and promised in front of them both that he would never touch a drink again if mam would come home. She did come home and it lasted about a week before dad was back on the drink. Dad was given a tip for a horse that was running that day. He won quite a bit of money and gave mam some of it and then he said he had to go and see someone, he came back drunk, and started hitting mam again.

Me, Mam and spot the dog. The building in the background is the Reidy's pigsty, where we slept some nights when dad came home drunk.

Chapter 3:
Escape to Ballyglass

A couple of days later; Mam got us all out of bed. It was pitch black outside and must have been about five o clock in the morning. She had laid out three sets of clothes and told us to put them on and took a pair of new socks out of a bag and lifted me up and sat me on the end of the kitchen table. She put the socks on me and pulled them up to my knees; they were a beige colour and she was feeling my toes and heels were in the right place and then she patted my legs. I think I felt closer to my mam at that moment than I had ever had. I will never forget the soft feeling on my legs; they felt lovely and warm.

We were all half-asleep and didn't know what was going on. When we asked her what it was all about she just told us to be very quiet and would explain later as she was picking up a big heavy suitcase and we all made our way out the front door and walked up towards the Clare Road. Mam had arranged with Jon Jo, a family friend to pick us up in his car and give us a lift to Limerick. We must have spent the day there because my next memory was getting on a train and it was dark again and I was very tired. When we had all settled down in the compartment, mam told us we were going to Westport, to stay with her friends Sue and Willie in Ballyglass. Martin and I had never been there before but Ray had when he was ill.

We arrived in Westport, and got off the train. It was about ten o'clock at night. Mam told us we would have to walk out of the town into the country to Ballyglass, to the farm where Sue and Willie lived. It was a five-mile walk. When we left the town there were no lights. It was pitch black and very cold. It was near the end of November. I remember because it was four weeks to Christmas.

The case was very heavy and mam would carry it for a while, then Ray and Martin would carry it between them. We all kept walking into the ditches at the side of the road. Mam said she wished she had bought a torch with us but it was too late now. We were all starting to moan a bit; in fact we were nearly in tears. Mam told us to sing as it would make the journey pass quicker. So we did, but it didn't make any difference. There didn't seem to be any end to the road but eventually we got there and had to knock Sue and Willie up out of their bed; they didn't know we were coming. We could see the oil lamp being lit through the little window in the cottage and then Willie answered the door. I will never forget the look on his face. "God in heaven," he said, "Where have you all come from in the middle of the night?" He took us inside into a big kitchen with a stone floor. The fireplace was a big square open space and had a black iron bar hanging down the middle of the chimney with hooks on it. Sue came out of the bedroom and welcomed us all, and said she would get the fire going and make a cup of tea.

She raked the ashes away until there was a red glow then put some turf on and it started to light; I was amazed at this! She told me if you put the ashes over the fire before you went to bed and raked it away in the morning the fire would light without any paper or sticks. She then got a cloth and put a big black kettle on one of the hooks and pushed it over the flames; it wasn't long before Sue made us a cup of tea and gave us some soda bread with butter and sugar on it. We ate it and got nice and warm by the fire.

Mam was telling Sue she couldn't take any more of my dad and was crying. Sue was trying to comfort her. Willie said, "Let's get these children to bed and then we can talk". Sue lit another little lamp and filled a stone hot water bottle with hot water from the kettle. We followed her into this bedroom; it was very tiny and beyond that was another little room with a double bed. Sue then got hold of the mattress and started shaking it, she explained that it was a straw mattress and if you shook it every day it would be nice and soft. She then put a sheet on and some blankets, there was also a small cupboard in the room and a tiny window with wire netting on the outside, I was a bit frightened of this as I thought if dad came looking for us, I wouldn't be able to get out and run. Sue explained that the two bedrooms used to be one room, and Willie put a partition in the middle of it; so we had to go through their bedroom to get in and out of ours; and the wire netting was to keep out the chickens and cats when the window was open. We went to bed and I remember putting my sore feet on the hot water bottle and I was out like a light.

When I woke up the next morning I wondered where I was for a few minutes, and I was bursting for the lavatory. Sue had put a chamber pot under the bed the night before and said if we needed it during the night or in the morning we were to use it. My two brothers were still asleep and I hoped they would stay that way until I'd used the pot.

I made my way out through Sue's bedroom and into the kitchen; mam and Sue were making bread while they were talking. Sue was saying she would take mam to the school on Monday and see if they could take us children in. We were going to stay in Ballyglass. I was hoping we didn't have to walk five miles to school every day! Sue started to lay the table for breakfast; she set the table with a knife, small plate, a teaspoon, and an eggcup, mam told me to go and get my brothers up. They came into the kitchen still half-asleep and Sue told Ray to go to the barn and get Willie for his breakfast. We all sat down to the table and Sue gave us all a boiled egg each and in the middle of the table was a big plate full of hot bread and a big slab of butter. We were told to help ourselves. We weren't used to anything like this; it was like heaven.

After breakfast, Sue gave us a bucket each and told us to go and get water from the well; Ray knew where it was because he had been here with mam a few months previous. I thought we were never going to get there. It must have been a quarter of a mile away and when we got there I asked Ray why we couldn't get water out of a tap like we did at home. Ray told us there were no taps here, so if we wanted a drink of water it had to come from the well. He also told us there were barrels all round the cottage for collecting rainwater and that was used for washing clothes, dishes and washing ourselves, but he said we were never to drink from them. Sue had given me a little bucket to fill but the water kept spilling out on the way back; I hardly had any left and all the water splashing about was making me want to go to the lavatory. I asked Ray where the lavatory was, he said there wasn't one; you had to go in the field! I nagged on at him, but what if someone sees me! He said no one is going to see you out in the middle of nowhere; so it was either the field or wet yourself. I picked the field I was going to use, looking round all the time, in case someone was watching me.

Sue showed us how to feed the hens; She said we had to shout, "Here' chucky chucky' chucky", and the hens would come running and we got a fit of the giggles.

She gave us the feed and told us when they came running we had to scatter the feed round the place. She said if it were all in one place the hens would start fighting. We felt silly standing there shouting, "Here, chucky' chucky' chucky", then all the hens came running from all different directions. It was a bit frightening with all those hens coming towards you. We scattered the feed as quickly as we could and the hens didn't fight and we felt really proud of ourselves.

A bit later on, Sue gave us a basket, and asked us to go collecting the eggs that the hens had laid; we were to look in the barn, under the hedges, and in the orchard. She told us to put them in the basket very gently, so as not to crack them. The first egg we found was in the hen house and we all got very excited. By the time we finished we had collected about twenty eggs and took them in to Sue. Then we heard a lot of noise coming from the barn and we ran out to see what it was. Willie was walking out of the barn holding a chicken by its legs. He said we are going to have a chicken for Sunday dinner, and it wasn't even Christmas.

We got up on Sunday morning and had our breakfast. Sue and Willie got ready to go to church. They were Protestants, and they had to go into Westport to their church. We got ready to go to mass; the church was about a mile and a half away. Willie got the pony and trap out and they gave us a lift to the crossroads. They went straight to Westport and we turned right and walked along the road for a while. Then mam said we turn left here, up a big steep hill; when we got to the top, in the distance there stood a lovely little church. I had never seen a church so small, and we all went in to mass. When we came out all the farmers were talking to us; they were all very friendly.

We started walking back to the cottage; it seemed a long way but I didn't mind today. Sue and Willie got back about an hour after us and got changed into their working clothes; you didn't get a day off when you had a farm. There was a great big black pot sitting on the kitchen floor with three stumpy legs on it, I'd never seen such a big pot and it was full of potatoes, at the side of it there was a smaller one; I didn't know what was in that; it had a lid on. Willie lifted the pots and put them on the black hooks that were hanging from the chimney. There were black beams on the kitchen ceiling with half a pig with no head hanging off one of them. At the right hand side of the fireplace was a big wooden box. One side was higher than the other; on the high side there was an old gramophone and two records. One of the records was called, Dear Doctor John, and the other, The Little Black Moustache Man. On the lower side of the box there were two hinges, and when you opened it there was a big scoop and the box was full of flour, when you put the lid down it was used as a seat. Behind the wooden box was a small pantry; it was used for storing sacks of grain, pig meal; and other bits of things. Next to the pantry was a wooden dresser with plates standing up on display and hooks for hanging the cup's on. Just past the dresser was a little back door and at the other side of the fireplace was an old armchair; behind the armchair was a small window with a wireless sitting on the windowsill. Next to that was a kitchen table and four chairs, and then you came to the front door which led straight into the kitchen from outside. Behind the front door there was a small door that led to a very small parlour. The parlour was used to keep buckets of milk, cream, and the churn for making butter, and other odds and ends. All the doors in the cottage were very small and Willie was forever bending his head going from one place to another.

Martin kept on about the big pot of potatoes and how were we going to eat all those! I started to get worried and then mam had told us we had to eat what was put in front of us. I knew we would never be able to eat all those potatoes! Dinner was ready and we sat down to the table. Sue put a plate in front of us all, there was chicken, cabbage, and a couple of potatoes on the plates. I gave a sigh of relief, but then she put a big bowl of potatoes in the middle of the table and a big slab of butter, then she said help yourselves if you want more! After dinner, Sue put the kettle on for the washing up. There was no sink in the cottage; Sue used two bowls, one for the washing up, and the other to drain the pots in. She went outside with one of the bowls and half filled it with water out of a barrel. Then she topped it up with hot water from the kettle. Willie emptied the potatoes out of the big black pot into a bucket, he asked us to come over to him and to roll our sleeves up and put our hands into the bucket and squash all the potatoes in between our fingers; while we were doing that he went to the pantry and brought out some pig meal and started adding it to the potatoes, now he said we can go and feed the pigs. After the pigs were fed, Willie told us to go back into the cottage as he had to go and milk the cows.

When we got back in the cottage Sue was lighting the oil lamps and mam was doing a bit of washing. She hung it on a little line across the fire just under the mantelpiece. We asked Sue if we could play the gramophone and she said we could and showed us what to do. We had never seen one before so it was all very exiting. I got first go to wind the handle and put a record on. It was going fine at first and then the song started to go slower and slower. I though I'd broken it and looked over at mam and Sue. They burst out laughing together and told me I hadn't wound it up enough! I let out a sigh of relief.

Willie came in from the cowshed with buckets of milk and put them on the kitchen table, he messed about with them for a while then he put them in the parlour, Willie asked us to turn the gramophone off as he wanted to listen to the news on the wireless. It was only put on twice a day; once in the morning, and once in the evening for the news. We were told not to touch it as it took a big battery and they were very expensive to buy. I liked to listen to the news; I didn't understand it but I thought it was magic hearing people talking out of this square thing that was sitting on the windowsill. A bit later Sue gave us a cup of milk, and a slice of bread and butter, when we had finished we were told to get ready for bed. I was dreading the morning as I still couldn't talk properly and was frightened the other children would make fun of me.

We got up on Monday morning, and had our breakfast, we were still getting a boiled egg and this was sheer luxury, if we were at home we would be getting a slice of bread and jam if we were lucky. Sue said she would pack us some sandwiches and a bottle of milk in case they said we could start today. She wrapped the sandwiches in greaseproof paper and gave us a bottle of milk each. The milk was still warm from this mornings milking.

The school was over a mile away if we followed the road, but Sue said we could go down through their fields as it was a short cut. The fields were all downhill and you had to dig your heels in, to stop yourself from running. When we got to the road at the bottom we turned to the right for a short distance and then turned left. There was one house on the road and we passed that and walked for a while longer. Then we came to the school on the left-hand side; it was a very small building. We went into the school. There was a long narrow hallway and Sue told us to wait there while they went to see the teacher and after about ten minutes they came out. We were to start today and Mam said we were to be good and we were to come home the way we had come this morning. I was hoping my brothers remembered the way home because I couldn't!

The teacher beckoned us to follow him. He was a very tall man. At least he looked tall to me, and I had never seen a man teacher before. He wore a long black jacket with a woollen scarf round his neck, and had gloves on with no fingers in them.

We went to the classroom and he told me to sit at the front of the class and my brothers were told to go to the back. When I looked round, I saw all the bigger children at the back of the class, so there must only be one classroom. The classroom looked very old and dark with a fireplace sat about two feet from the floor and a black grate in front of it; the room was also very cold. The teacher put some turf on the fire and said we could keep our coat's on if we wanted to. The teacher kept his coat on, and his scarf and gloves. I wondered what the nuns at home would think, with us all sitting there with our coats on. I think we would all have got the cane.

The morning passed quickly and the bell went for lunchtime and we all went out into the playground. There were only about twenty of us in the whole school. The boys stood at one side of the little playground, and the girls at the other. One of the girls came over to me, she said her name was Bridget; we stood there together and had our lunch. I had blackberry jam in my sandwiches and they tasted lovely. I drank my bottle of milk which had gone very cold. We were told to bring the bottle and greaseproof paper back home with us so it could be used again tomorrow. I told Bridget I needed to go to the lavatory and asked if I had to go in the field. She laughed and said no, she would take me and show me where it was in the yard. I went in and it smelled awful but it was much better than having to go in a field.

The bell rang after lunch and we all went back to the classroom. The teacher still had his coat on and he said us younger children were going to do addition. We had a slate and chalk; he said we were to write down the numbers he called out. We wrote them down, two and two, three and three, three and four and so on. While we were doing our sums, he went down to the back of the class. He was doing other work with the older children. While he was at the back of the class, Bridget told me the teacher was always toasting his backside at the fire and that the only time you got a look at the fire, was when he was down the back. He came back up to the front of the class, "Well let's see how we are getting on up here". He asked some of the children questions, and then he came up to me, "What does two and two make?" I told him "Four." "Good!" he said. "Now what does three and four make?" I started stuttering a bit, but I got it out and said, "Devon". Then he asked me what eight and eight was. I said, "Dixteen." By this time I was shaking and he put my slate back on the desk. "You have got them all right!" and put his hand on my shoulder and said, "Look child, you are not to worry about the words you can't say. They will all come in their own good time." I thought what a very kind man he is, and I wouldn't mind if he toasted his backside all day long. None of the children had laughed at me because I couldn't speak properly, so I felt very happy.

The bell rang for home time; Martin and I made a dash for the lavatory to save us going in the field and then we started for home. We went back along the road we had come up this morning; we saw the one house and walked past it to the end of the road to the crossroads. Ray said we turned right; the field was a short way along. If we turned left, it was the long way home. We walked a short way along the road, but there were lots of fields and Ray couldn't remember which field we came down. He told us to look for footprints, but we couldn't find any, so he took a chance and climbed over this fence. Martin had a good idea, he said tomorrow; we would have to take a bit of rag and tie it on the fence, then we'd know which field to go up. We thought it was a good idea too, but it wasn't much help to us today. Martin was proud of himself for thinking about that, he had a big grin on his face. Ray said we had better get started; so we followed him. Ray and Martin had to keep stopping and wait for me and they told me to keep up. I was near to tears when I caught up with them, and they told me again that if I didn't keep up, they were going to leave me and that was it. I burst into tears and shouted at them, "Its all right for you, you got free boots and I didn't!"

Every winter all the poor people got dockets to get their children free boots. Ray and Martin got them, and there was loads of studs put in the soles and heels to make them last the winter. Mam got a docket for me as well but she knew the man in the shoe shop and asked him, if he would take the docket and she would pay a bit extra if I could have a pair of shoes. He said yes, so that was why I had shoes. But my shoes kept slipping on the hard ground, my two brothers put their arms around me, saying they were only joking and didn't mean it, but they told me not to tell mam. We got to the top of the first field; Ray said he was sure it was the right one. We went into the second field. It wasn't anywhere as steep as the first one and we kept walking. Then we saw a gate and we all ran to it. Martin got there first. He was shouting at us that we had come to Willie's. Boreen and mam was walking up towards the gate. "I was getting worried about you all," she was saying. But everyone was talking at the same time; Martin was saying we couldn't find the field, Ray was saying we were looking for footprints, then Martin was telling her about his good idea, and I was asking if I could have free boots. She looked at me and said, "Have you been crying"?

Martin butted in before I could answer, "She fell", he said, "Have you hurt yourself?", "No. I'm all right. But my shoes kept slipping on the hills, so please can I have some free boots?" Mam snapped at me, "Will you shut up about free boots? Do you want everyone to know our business? I don't want to hear those two words ever again!" I followed her into the cottage but I was thinking to myself; everyone knows what free boots looked like, they were like orange peel with all little dints in them; but they were black, but I kept my mouth shut.

After Willie had finished the milking he put his buckets in the parlour and sat down in his armchair, he lifted me onto his knee. "Now I want to hear all about your day at school." I told him about the very kind teacher, and that he hadn't caned one child all day, and about Bridget saying the teacher toasted his backside all day, the lavatory in the yard that smelt awful, and not being able to find the field to get back home. He laughed long and loud. When I told him about my shoes slipping coming up the steep hill, Mam gave me a warning look, and I didn't mention those two words. After Willie listened to the news he got up and went into the little pantry, he came out with a shoe last and told me to take my shoes off. He put one on the last and hammered some studs in the sole and heel. Then he did the other and I was over the moon. He was such a lovely man. I went to bed that night a very happy child.

My extended family in Ballyglass: Sue and Willie with Spot (Top) and again with Neddy (Bottom).

We set off for school on Tuesday and Willie walked us to the gate of the field. There was a great big hill in the distance and I asked Willie how far away it was. He told me to ask the teacher, and he would tell me all about it. The teacher would be pleased that we are taking an interest in this part of the country. Willie went off to mend his broken fences, saying good-bye to us and he'd see us after school. We made our way down the fields to the road. Martin tied his bit of rag to the fence and we made our way to school.

We asked the teacher about the big hill and he told us, it wasn't a big hill it was a mountain and it was six miles away, about 2500 ft high and was called Croagh Patrick, that pilgrims came from all over Ireland and other countries and climb to the top. Saint Patrick is said to have prayed and fasted there. He also told us lots of people climbed the mountain without any shoes on and their feet would be all cut and blistered. If they made it to the top, there was a little stone built church where they could go and pray. There was a pilgrimage on the last Sunday of July every year, and it was called Reek Sunday. We were very pleased to learn all this and the teacher was glad that we were showing an interest in their part of the country. When we got home we were telling them about, Croagh Patrick, but they already knew all about it so we were a bit disappointed. The rest of the week past very quickly and then on Friday, when we got home from school, mam seemed very tense.

After we'd had our tea she took a letter out of her pocket, and was showing it to Willie, It was from my dad. My heart sank. He knew where we were. I was frightened and Willie noticed the way I was looking and told me not to worry about it. He said he wouldn't come near the farm, but I did worry every time I heard a noise and my heart would start racing.

Saturday came and we all had our jobs to do. We fed the hens, Ray went to the well to get water and Martin and I went to collect eggs from under the hedges and the barn. Sue was making butter and we all had a go at turning the handle of the churn. It looked easy but made your arm ache. Ray got the cows into the cowshed ready to be milked and then Willie went along and milked them. When he had finished he saw to his buckets and put them in the parlour. Sue told us there were some people coming round later tonight for a bit of a shindig and I wondered what a shindig was but I didn't ask. After we'd had our tea four people arrived; there was two men and two women, one man had a violin the other had a concertina. They sat down and had a cup of tea and a natter and they then started playing Irish music. Sue, Willie and mam started dancing some sort of reel. I couldn't believe mam could dance like that. I had never seen her dance before; they were all having a great time and we children enjoyed watching them.

There was a knock on the door and my heart missed a beat again, I thought it was dad, but it wasn't. It was a couple of men from the next two farms down the road and they came in and joined the others. They were all singing Irish songs, and then they all took a turn singing on their own and there was a lot of laughing and clapping. They stopped and had another cup of tea and a bit of mam's old cake as she called it. After that break, they asked us to do a dance. Ray wasn't having any of it, but Martin said he would do a dance. Martin was a great dancer! When mam had a bit of money after Patrick died, she sent Martin and me to Mrs White's School of dancing, although it was just a house really, and we learned to dance in her front room. Martin picked it up straight away, but I had no confidence in myself at all. Mam was very proud of Martin and she even got some lino for the kitchen floor so he could practice. Martin took his boots off and started dancing; and was doing a jig. He did it great and everyone was clapping, Martin was very pleased with himself. They asked me to do a dance, but all I could do was a little bit of Martins jig. They clapped me but I knew I hadn't done very well. Mam was saying to them all, "She hasn't got the legs for it; she's that skinny her legs are like matchsticks". Willie lifted me on his knee and said, "Well I think she has lovely legs, and from now on that's what I am going to call her." Willie called me lovely legs for as long as I can remember. I was a bit upset with mam for talking about me as though I wasn't there; she always seemed to do it. The night came to an end; everyone went home flushed and happy. I thought to myself so that's a shindig! Wait till I tell my friends back home.

We set off for school on Monday morning. Ray didn't go with us as mam said she needed him on the farm. Martin said she was keeping him off school so he could run and get Willie if dad turned up. There was another letter from dad, and one from my aunt in limerick. Dad wrote that he hadn't had a drink since we left, and he was never going to drink again if we would just come home. He didn't threaten us in this letter like he did in the last one. My aunt wrote that she had been over to see dad two or three times and dad had been sober and she though he had learned his lesson. Mam didn't know what to do. She knew we couldn't stay here forever and it wasn't fair on Sue and Willie as they hadn't been married that long, but they were sharing everything with us. Mam was very lucky to have such good friends.

The third week came along and there was another letter from dad. He said he'd got all us children presents and wanted us all to be together for Christmas, and he would never drink again. Mam had heard it all before, but we would have to go back, there wasn't anywhere else to go. The little school broke up for the Christmas holidays. Martin and I said good-bye to everyone. We were very sad to be leaving. Ray hadn't been back to school since that first week and he was missing his friends and I think he was glad we were going home. Mam decided we were to go home on Christmas Eve.

It was awfully hard saying good-bye to Sue and Willie as we'd been so happy with them. Willie said we could come for a holiday in the summer when the weather was better. Before we left, Sue gave mam a ten-shilling note. She didn't want to take it, but Sue said she might need it. She also gave mam some eggs wrapped up in newspaper and a big slab of butter. Willie took us to the train station in Westport, but this time we didn't have to walk as we went in the pony and trap. Willie wished us all a Happy Christmas and hoped everything went well for us.

Chapter 4:
Home to Ennis

We arrived home in Ennis about half past three in the afternoon and dad met us off the train and he was sober. He took the suitcase from mam's hand. Not a word was spoken all the way home.

It was getting dark, and when we got in the house and dad switched the light on. We all blinked as we were that used to the dim light from the oil lamp. I couldn't wait any longer and I asked dad if I could see my presents. He opened the food cupboard and he gave me a small bag of toffees and a packet of Rolos. He gave the same to Ray and Martin. I was very disappointed, but at least we got some sweets. He was maybe keeping the presents for Christmas morning. Mam pulled the cupboard doors open and they were bare. There wasn't one thing in them. She turned to dad, "Where is the food?" He said he didn't have any money to get any. Mam was going mad and she was shouting at him, "Its Christmas Eve! How am I supposed to feed the children?" She told us to unwrap the eggs very carefully and put them in a dish and keep the newspaper they were wrapped in. She went out the back door and up the path. She didn't even look at my dad. Dad didn't have a full time job; no one would employ him, as he was always drunk. He did odd jobs here and there, he spent all the money he got on drink, and so mam never got any. He was supposed to have stopped drinking for the last four weeks, but he still had no money. I couldn't understand this. I thought he must have spent all the money on our presents.

Mam came back from the town; she had got what she could with the bit of money she had. She had some sausages, potatoes and a turnip, some flour and some dripping. There was an awful atmosphere in the house that night. We were all cutting newspapers into squares and threading string through it to put in the lavatory in the yard. We got up on Christmas morning and although there were no presents, we did have our boiled egg with bread and butter. We all set off to mass together and we were all very quiet. There was no Christmas sprit. I was glad to get in the church, and at least we would be able to sing Christmas carols. After mass we went out to play for a while. All the other kids were playing with the bits of things that they had got for Christmas. They hadn't got a lot, but at least they got something. We went back into the house and had our Christmas dinner of sausages, potatoes and turnip. Mam gave us an extra dab of butter on our potatoes. I was wishing I was back with Sue and Willie.

January came and dad got bits of work here and there, but now he was giving mam the money he made. He hadn't been drunk once since we got home. Near the end of January I got the mumps and I got them really bad. Mam took me to the church to have my throat blessed, but it didn't make me any better. Dad suggested she took me to Westport for a few days. He said he had a job to do and he would make enough money for mam's fare and mine, but the boys would have to stay home with him. Although mam wasn't too happy about it, we went.

It was lovely to get back to Ballyglass. Sue was very pleased to see mam again. They seemed to talk for hours and you wouldn't think it was only four weeks since they had seen each other! I sat up at the table with Willie. He was doing his books. I told Willie I was going to be Devon in a couple of weeks, he said you mean seven, I said yes. Willie looked down at his books and he said, "I have six hens here, and they all laid an egg this morning. How many eggs have I got?" I said, "Dix". "No," he said. "How many eggs have I got?" I said, "Dix." He asked me again and again and I was getting all flustered. All of a sudden, it came out. I shouted, "Six!" Willie looked at me and laughed, "I knew you could do it." I was half laughing, half crying. "Six, six, six!" I said. "Now," he said, "how old are you going to be in a couple of weeks?" I said, "Seven." and then he said, "What do you wash your hands and face with?" "Soap." I said. There was so much excitement I wanted to go home that minute, so I could tell my brothers that I could speak properly!

We arrived back in Ennis a couple of days later. When we got to our street, I could see my brothers playing outside our house. I let go of mam's hand and ran to them, I was so excited, I was shouting at them. "I can say six, soap and seven." I was saying it over and over again. My brothers said they were very pleased for me, but it was a shame they wouldn't be able to tease me any more. Martin asked me how I had learnt to say the words and I told him I wasn't sure. I told him about Willie and how I was helping him do his books and he kept on about hens laying eggs. He had kept on and on about eggs and it just came out. Or it could have been when mam took me to have my throat blessed, when I had the mumps. Maybe it was a miracle that took a little bit longer to happen. I went in the house to my parent's bedroom. I had a little Altar in there. I had a statue of the Virgin Mary, stood on a piece of white rag, and I had holy pictures around the back and sides. I had two jam jars, one each side of the statue. There were no flowers at this time of the year, so I put evergreen hedge in them. I said a prayer to my little statue of the Virgin Mary to thank her for letting me talk proper, I was so happy.

It started to snow that night. We were all excited and couldn't wait for the morning. Mam got us up early and said we were going to early mass, because she had a lot of things to catch up on with being away. We were glad we were going to early mass that meant we would be able to play in the snow all day. After mass we had our breakfast of some bread and dripping and a cup of tea, and then we got ready to go out. Mam was putting this woolly hat on my head. The hat went to a point at the top, and it tied under my chin and she called it a pixie hat. She made me mittens as well. The hat was dark brown and I hated it. I had wanted a blue one, but there was no blue wool. She had to unpick an old brown jumper with holes in it to get the wool. Mam said I was very ungrateful and I was lucky to have a pixie hat no matter what colour it was.

Just across the road from our house, there was a high wall. If you walked up the road a bit further the wall was lower, with a field on the other side. We all went in the field and we started playing snowballs. When we got fed up with that, we decided to build a snowman. We started rolling a big snowball down the hill and by the time it got to the bottom of the hill it was huge. We made a head for it and put stones for its eyes nose and mouth. Martin found a stick that had a knob at the end, he put it in the snowman's mouth, and it looked like a pipe we had no hat to put on its head. Then Martin wanted my pixie hat and he was trying to pull it off my head, but I kept a tight hold of the ties so he couldn't get it off. By now my hands and feet were freezing, I started to cry with the pain in them and at that moment I hated the field. We were down at the bottom of the hill and a few yards away, there was another big hill going up the other side. I said to Martin it was as though something had fallen out of the sky and squashed the field into two hills, and I had to get up one of them. Martin told me not to be so silly and that we had to get going up the hill. There was a cowshed at the top. Martin said, "Just make it to the cowshed and we will be able to get the snow off your shoes".

We went in the shed. Martin told me to cross my arms and put my hands under my arms pits and to stamp my feet and he started stamping his feet. I said, "It all right for you, you have free boots to keep your feet warm I haven't". Martin got very cross with me. "Mam told you not to say those two words again" he said. "You won't tell her will you?" "I will if you don't stop crying so stamp your feet!" I did as I was told, but it didn't make my feet any warmer. I thought if only I could walk through the wall in the shed I would be home. Martin dragged me out of the cowshed. We walked along the field until we got to where the wall was lower, we climbed over the wall and onto the road, and Martin was dragging me by the hand to our front door. He pushed me up the hall and into the kitchen; Mam looked up from her sewing. "What's wrong with her?" she said. Martin told her I was crying because I was cold, he shut the kitchen door and he was off. Mam told me to take my shoes and socks off. She was going on about getting my shoes dry for school in the morning. "Just look at the state of you!" she said, "What's happened to your pixie hat?" I told her I didn't know, she was saying, "That pixie fitted you when you left this house, now it looks two sizes bigger. Take it off till I try and put it back into shape." I daren't tell her Martin nearly pulled my head off trying to get a hat for the snowman.

That Monday morning, I went off to school feeling a lot more confident than I had ever felt. I could say my words, so no one was going to make fun of me. I still stuttered a bit but I didn't mind that. At the end of the week, mam, Ray and I were in the kitchen. It was in the afternoon and we heard the front door go bang, then the kitchen door burst open, and Martin came in he said dad was coming up the road and he was drunk. Mam shouted at us all to run, we all ran up the back path, I looked round to see if he was coming after us and I fell. Before I could pick myself up he was there. He got hold of me and put me under his arm and carried me back towards the house, and I was trying to look back at my mam. I could see the three of them on the path, but they weren't running. They were all stood very still and looked like statues. It was as if they couldn't move. That picture of them would be with me for the rest of my life.

My dad took me in the kitchen, he pulled out a chair with his free arm, and he sat down and put me on his knee. My whole body was shaking; even my teeth were chattering. He lifted my face up to look at him, and he said, "Are you really that frightened of me?" I nodded I was and with that mam came in the back door followed by Ray and Martin. They all came in slowly and quietly and I felt as though it was all in slow motion. I thought I was about to pass out. Dad lifted me very gently off his knee and stood me on the floor; he looked at my mam and said; "I can't believe my little girl is so frightened of me that she is shaking from head to toe."

"That's it", he said, "I'm going to take the pledge." he walked into the bedroom and closed the door, very quietly. We all stood there looking at each other. I had hold of Martin's hand with my two hands and I was still shaking. I asked Martin what taking the pledge meant, he told me, it meant dad was going to stop drinking. "But dads always saying that." I said. Martin said, "This is different, he has to wear a badge, and it would be a sin if he takes a drink". Martin told me dad wasn't very drunk today, but he had a few pints. I thought it was strange that dad had come in the front door, because he never came in the front door when he was drunk, and he hadn't hit my mam. So he can't have been drunk.

A few days later it was my birthday, and although I didn't get any presents, mam told me my granddad was coming back to stay with us in a week or so. That was the best present I could have had! Dad came in and told my mam, he was taking me to see my Nana. I was a bit frightened to go with him on my own. Mam said it would be all right, so off we went. My Nana was pleased to see us as dad didn't go very often and he seemed different in nanas house, as though he was frightened of her, or he was worried that I would say something that he didn't want her to know. We were all warned not to tell Nana anything. Nana came over to me, "Well child you are seven today, you are getting to be a big girl. You will be going to make your first Holy Communion in a few months". She told me to say my prayers; and learn my catechism and I said I would. She then put her hand in her apron pocket and she gave me sixpence. I couldn't believe it! A whole sixpence! She never gave me more than a penny before. Nana was talking to dad and she was pointing to a big picture that hung on the wall just inside my nana's living room door. It was a picture of Nana's daughter. She had died when she was seventeen. Nana took my hand and she looked up at the picture and said, "Look child. You look like auntie Biddy." Nana looked very sad and I felt very sorry for her.

We left nana's and walked towards home. We got half way there when dad stopped and asked me if he could have the sixpence as he needed it. I didn't know what to do. I didn't know how much beer cost or how much backing horses cost. I thought if I gave him the sixpence and he goes home drunk, mam will kill me. I was holding the sixpence that tight it was making a mark in the palm of my hand, then dad said, "Look, I need the money to get five woodbines." I wasn't letting go of the money in case he got drunk, but I went to the little shop across the road and asked for five woodbines and I think I got a penny change. I gave him the woodbines and he told me to run along home and not to tell mam. He said he would give me the money back when he got work, but I knew I would never see it again. I went home and mam said, "What did Nana say to you?" I told her she said I looked like my aunt Biddy. Ray and Martin were in the kitchen and they heard what I said, and for the rest of my childhood when they wanted to tease me they would call me Biddy Burns!

That week seemed to drag; I couldn't wait for my granddad to come home. After school one day, some of the girls went into the shop to buy balloons, they were a penny each and I didn't have any money, so I was walking past the church and I decided to go in. I said a prayer for Patrick's soul; also a prayer to god because he was going to send my granddad back to me. As I was walking back down the aisle there was a penny on the floor. I bent down and picked it up. I almost ran out of the church! Instead of going home down the Clare Road, I went another way, which was down past the Old Ground Hotel and turned right into Ard-Na-Greine where there was a shop that sold everything. I think it was a post office as well. I asked the woman behind the counter for a balloon, she asked me what colour I wanted and I replied, "A blue one." She gave me the balloon and I said, "Thank you.", and left the shop. I sat on the steps outside the shop and started to blow up the balloon but there was a hole in it, I took it back into the shop and told the woman. She said, "There was no hole in it when I sold it to you", I tried to tell her there was, but she wasn't having any of it, she said, "Away with you or I will send for the guards!" I ran all the way home looking behind me, all the time to see if there were any guards after me. When I got in the house, there was no one in. I was glad of that because mam would be asking why I came the front way from school. I got a needle and cotton, and started to sew the hole in the balloon. Ray came in and asked me what I was doing. I told him the story about the balloon and he started to laugh. "You can't sew a hole in a balloon." He said. I asked him why not and he told me, "Every time you put the needle through the balloon you are making more holes!" He couldn't stop laughing at me. I burst into tears as I was fed up with this day.

My granddad came back to us the following week and I was so happy to see him. I was trying to tell him everything at once! I was telling him I was seven years old now, and I could say my words and that dad had taken the pledge. Granddad lifted me on his knee and said; "Oh, how I have missed you my wee ducksey!" He cuddled me to him and I felt safe again. Things went back to normal. Granddad was up in the mornings, and had our boots and shoes shining ready for school. He cut the boys hair. He would put a bowl on their head, and cut around it and then he would cut their fringes very short. The boys hated a haircut the way granddad cut it. He was a lot stricter with them than he was with me.

Dad and granddad only spoke to each other when they had to, but they did go and dig the big garden at the back of the house together; they planted potatoes and carrots. Dad got a job, and there was a bit of money coming in and it helped with granddad's pension. Easter came, and we all went to mass on Easter Sunday. After mass, we were all allowed to eat two boiled eggs each and everyone was happy. We usually went bare feet in the warmer weather, but with dad working, mam bought Martin and me new sandals for Easter and Ray got new shoes. I took mine off when we came from mass, because they had given me a blister. I went out to play with my friends and we were just about to climb over the wall to go down the crags, when I saw Martin coming towards us. He looked odd with sandals on, they looked too big for him, but they weren't. I think it was the white crape soles on the brown sandals. He didn't have any socks on, and his trousers were down below his knees and it made his feet look huge. He was walking with his hands behind his back, and he kept looking down at his feet. He was very proud of his sandals.

We asked him if he was coming down the crags, but he said no, because mam had told him not to get his sandals scuffed. We told him to take them off. He took them off and climbed over the wall. There was a crevice in the wall and Martin decided to put his sandals in there and cover them up. He said he would pick them up on the way back. We came back a couple of hours later and Martin went to the wall to get his sandals, but they were gone. Mam went mad, she gave him a good hiding and Martin was barefooted again and the sandals were never found.

I will always remember that spring and summer. My little altar in the bedroom looked beautiful with one flower after another coming into bloom. First it was the daffodils then the bluebells, primroses and the cowslips. June came and I was to make my first Holy Communion. My godmother Florrie took me to town and bought me a pair of white shoes and socks. She let me pick them myself and said that was her present to me. Mam was making my dress and headdress and I was to borrow a vale and basket. Now it was time to go and make my first confession, and I was scared stiff. It was dark in the confession box, but I was glad it was as there was less chance of the priest seeing who I was. I said, "Bless me father for I have sinned." my mind went blank I couldn't remember one sin. Then I remembered about finding the penny on the church floor and buying a balloon with it. I didn't know if it was a sin or not, but I told him anyway. It must have been a sin because he gave me three Hail Mary's, one our father and a glory be to the father, for my penance.

When I got back home, Mam and Florrie were in the kitchen, filling the tin bath with water. Florrie looked up as I came in and said, "Well? Did you tell all your sins?", and started laughing. Florrie was always laughing. I was told to get in the bath. Mam washed my hair and I was getting an extra good scrubbing tonight. Then she was drying my hair, rubbing it that hard I thought my head would fall off! Now the dress had to be tried on again to make sure it fitted me. Mam put the vale and the head dress on me and they were both looking at me. Mam turned to Florrie and said, "It doesn't look right. It's her hair. It's too straight and fine. The head dress won't sit right." They took them off me; and the pair of them started cutting rags into strips; and with one each side of me, they were twisting the rags round my hair. I had a terrible time trying to get to sleep with all the rags in, and I was warned not to take them out.

When I got up next morning, mam was doing my basket with flowers and it looked very pretty. It had lots of little white flowers in it called snow in summer and they grew out in our back lane. Every time I see those little flowers I think back to that day. Mam finished the basket tying a big white bow on the handle of it. She made me a little white bag to carry. It was made out of the same material as my dress and she was taking all the rags out of my hair. She was determined I was going to have curls and curls I had. They were sticking up all over the place. She put my dress on and combed my hair this way and that way until she got it right. Then she put my vale and headdress on me. I looked about six inches taller with all the curls on top of my head and then the big headdress. Everyone was saying how lovely I looked and it made me feel good. When I was kneeling at the altar in the church, my tummy was rumbling and my mouth was dry. When the priest came to me and said, "Body of Christ." and he put the bread on my tongue, I tried to swallow it but it got stuck on the roof of my mouth. I tried to dislodge it with my tongue, but it wouldn't budge. I had to put my finger in my mouth and tried to move it. I thought I was going to be sick; it came loose and I swallowed it, then I felt better. We all went to have our photo taken and Florrie was paying for mine to be done. We all went home and had our communion breakfast. I remember a big juicy brown sausage, and the other thing I remember about that day was that my dad was sober.

About a week later, before we broke up for the summer holidays, the teacher gave us questions out of the catechism and said we had to learn them off by heart. I went out to play after school and forgot all about my homework. Next morning we all set off for school. I left my brothers at the top of the Clare road and they went across the road to their school. I went past the church and just as I was about to cross the road, I got cold feet. I knew if I went to school, I would get the cane for not doing my homework. So I turned right down past the Old Ground Hotel, and I ran until I reached the train station. There were a few people about so I went across the road and climbed over the wall and hid. I stayed there all day and I had no idea what time it was but my tummy was rumbling, and I was very thirsty. I was getting very frightened, but I daren't go home.

After what seemed like a lifetime, my dad stood in front of me. He didn't look cross and I was glad to see him. He took my hand, and we set off towards home. I asked him how he knew where to find me. He told me one of the railway workers had seen me, so he called at our house on his way home from work, and told them where I was. Dad told me everyone had been out looking for me, and that mam had been out of her mind worrying about me. I asked him if she was very cross and he said, "No, just worried. She has got you a bar of chocolate for when we get home." I couldn't wait to get home.

When we went into the kitchen they were all there; granddad, mam, and my two brothers. They didn't look cross, just relieved. My dad gave me a little cuddle and pushed me up to my mam. She said, "You have had us all worried sick, everyone was out looking for you." She didn't give me a cuddle, but she gave me a bar of Cadbury's chocolate. She got up off the chair and said she would make me a hot drink and something to eat. Everyone was making a fuss of me. My brothers were putting their arms around me and asking me if I was alright and granddad had me on his knee and was cuddling me. I had never had so much attention in my life and I was lapping it all up. Mam brought me a cup of tea and some brawn sandwiches. I went to bed that night and slept like a log.

We all set off for school next morning. I got as far as the church and decided I would do what I had done yesterday. So off I went to the train station, I went behind the wall and sat down and thought to myself no one will be worried about me today because they will know where to find me. I sat there until about lunchtime and then my dad appeared in front of me. "Home!" he said, and I followed him. I had to run to keep up with him. I asked him, "Has mam got me something?" "Oh yes, your mam has got something for you all right". I asked him what she had got me. "You will have to wait and see," he replied. When we got into the kitchen, I looked at mam and her face was like thunder. She grabbed hold of me, and put me over her knee, I didn't know what she was hitting me with but I thought it was never going to stop. I had never felt pain like it. I was put straight to bed with nothing to eat. My granddad was warned not to go near me. While I was in bed I got out my catechism, I learned the questions I was supposed to learn two days ago, as I didn't want to get the cane at school tomorrow. When I went to school next day, it was agony having to sit at my desk. I wouldn't be playing truant from school again as it just wasn't worth it!

Chapter 4: Home to Ennis

My family again: My dad with Martin (Top Left), Granddad (Top Right) and me (centre) with Raymond, Mam and Martin (Left to right).

My First Communion with my basket of flowers, the outfit Mam made and the socks and shoes Florrie bought me.

Chapter 5:
Almost Normal …

We broke up for the summer holidays. Martin said I could join his gang; if I could run fast and jump trenches like the boys and I told him I could. He said, "All right, then you can be in the gang." He had to let me anyway because every time he went out of the house mam would say, "And take her with you!" Poor Martin had to drag me everywhere with him, but he never complained as we were soul mates, Martin and I.

We all set off one day to go swimming and took a picnic with us. Martin and I had rhubarb jam sandwiches and a bottle of water. I hated rhubarb, but it grew in our back garden. Mam would make jam, and pies with it so it was eat it or go without, so I ate it. We made our way down to the railway track, and we walked on the sleepers in our bare feet. If there was a train coming we would have to jump off and wait at the side of the track until it passed. It took us about half an hour to get there. I couldn't swim so I stayed at the shallow end, but the boys went to the deep end, and they would be diving off the rocks, one trying to out do the other. There was lots of laughing and cheering. After a while we would all go and sit on the rocks and have our picnic and it was a lovely day out.

Another day we would go to Clare Abbey, which was an old ruin. It was some sort of battleground of years gone by. We would play there for hours, and there were plenty of trenches to jump. I fell in a few times, but in the end I could jump as good as the boys.

Sometimes after mass on a Sunday, we would walk to this little place called Clare Castle on gala day. It was two or three miles away, but it was a lovely little place. We would sit on this little bridge and watch the boats, and the men that were walking the greasy pole and falling in the water. The only thing I didn't like was the walk back home as it seemed to take twice as long coming back. But as I saw St Flannon's College, I knew I was nearly there.

Another day we were down the crags playing. It was a very hot day and we played all morning, but our tummies were telling us it was time to go for something to eat. We set off for home, we climbed over the wall on to the road, and we noticed all the women were standing at their doors talking to each other and some of them were fanning themselves with newspapers. When we got in the house the back door was open. We could see mam in the back yard, and she had the tin bath full of washing. She was rubbing the clothes up and down on the scrubbing board, she looked very flushed and the sweat was pouring of her. She shouted that there was food on the table. We tucked into thick wedges of bread and dripping, and a mug of water. After we had finished eating, I got up and went into mam's bedroom. I told Martin I was going to change the water in the jam jars on my little altar. I carried the jars into the kitchen and filled them with water; Martin followed me and helped carried them back. The bedroom window was wide open and we could see mam hanging some washing on the line. She shouted into us, "What are you doing in there?" I told her I was just seeing to my altar and she told us to get out and play. As we were going out of the bedroom, Martin looked on top of the cupboard; he pulled down a packet, and looked in it. He said oh look, there's two doctor's masks. We can play doctors and nurses. We put the loops on our ears, but they were too big, and kept falling under our chins. Martin said, "If we bite it in the middle of them they will stay on", so that's what we did, and off we went out onto the road.

We were pretending we were in an ambulance, Martin was driving it and I was the nurse at his side. We went from one end of the road to the other. As we were coming back up the road, we noticed that all the women standing at their doors had stopped talking, they were all making the sign of the cross, and then they started saying, "Jesus, Mary and Joseph", Martin pulled the mask out of his mouth and said, "What's up with them?". I took my mask out of my mouth and said, "They must have seen something". Off we went to the top of the road again and then back down. As we started to go up the road again, Ray was stood at our gate. When we got to him he said, "In! Mam wants you!" We could see mam stood at the bottom of the hall, she had her hands up to her face, as if she was going to cry. She grabbed the masks off our faces, nearly taking our ears with them, she kept slapping and pushing us and saying, "Oh the shame of it, how am I going to show my face outside this door again".

She stopped hitting us, and burst into tears. When she stopped crying, she told us to get to bed. When we got in the bedroom, Martin looked at me and said, "What have we done?" "I don't know" I replied. Martin said, "All because of a couple of doctor's masks". I didn't find out until years later that our masks were sanitary towels!

I wasn't feeling very well the next day. Martin asked me if I was coming out, but I told him I wasn't well. He said, "All right then biddy." "Don't call me that", I said. "Right then, I will see you later Biddy!" My name was Mary; my second name was Muriel. I got called Muriel at home and Mary at school; and if I had to see the doctor or go to hospital it was Mary. It was all very confusing, and now Martin was making it worse, with calling me Biddy. Mam came into the kitchen. She pulled out a chair and sat to the table. She had a piece of felt and she was turning it this way and that way. She was making a hat and I watched her for a while, and then she said, "Why don't you go down and see your nana for a while?" I told her I didn't feel well and she said, "A little walk in the fresh air would do you good!"

As I was setting off for nana's, she shouted after me, "On your way back, call at your aunt Fanny's, and ask her if she has got some braid for me". When I got to nana's house, I walked up the path and my granda was sitting on the garden bench as usual and nodded to me, but didn't speak. Nana was pleased to see me, she said, "What's the matter? You don't look very happy today." I told her I didn't feel well, and that my head was hurting. She put her hand on my forehead and then my face, "I think you have had a bit too much sun. You are very fair skinned and you should have something on your head when you go out in the sun for a long time." She took me in the kitchen and gave me a cup of milk and a slice of currant cake. I was glad I had come now.

I left my nana's and she called after me, "Your cousins from Limerick are coming in a few days. You will have to come and play with them." I told her I would. I called in to my aunt Fanny's on the way home. I think my aunt had six children or it could be seven, but they were all grown up and working apart from Joan who was about twelve. They were mostly girls and they worked at the Braid Factory. The girls would bring bits of braid that were going to get thrown out and give them to my mam. I asked Aunt Fanny if she had some braid and she asked if mam was making her hat. I said she was making a hat but she never said who it was for. My aunt loved the hats that mam made; she said they had a bit of class about them. She gave me some braid and I went out into the little hall. There was a doll on the stairs and it was upside down. I picked it up and put it the right way round. My aunt called up the stairs for Joan to come down and when she did my aunt said to her, "Have you finished with this doll?", Joan said she had just thrown it down the stairs and she was going to put it in the bin. My aunt said, "Well you might as well let young Muriel have it then", Joan picked up the doll and handed it to me, saying, "Mind you look after it." I told her I would treasure it and ran all the way home. I couldn't believe I had a doll.

I gave mam the braid and showed her the doll. She said, "I think it has seen better days." she smiled and said. "We will wash the doll's clothes and it will look better." I couldn't get the dolls clothes off quickly enough, it had a little matinee coat on and a little nightdress and a shawl. Mam washed the clothes and told me I would have to wait until tomorrow for them to dry. She gave me a towel and an old rag and a bit of washing soap. I washed the doll. It had hundreds of little cracks all over it, all the fingers and toes were worn away and one of its eyes was closed all the time, but it was alright when you laid it down and the other eye would shut and it looked as though it was asleep. I took the doll to bed with me that night. I wrapped an old jumper round it to keep it warm.

When I got up the next morning, Mam had the doll's clothes ready. She had ironed them and they looked nice and clean and felt lovely and soft. I must have had the clothes on and off that doll six times that day, I was so proud of it. I went out in the back lane and sat on the rock nursing the doll. I called Touser Malone over, "Come and see my new doll." He came over and sat in front of me, he put his paw on my knee, and I patted his head. Then he got up and slowly walked away. He didn't seem interested in my doll.

Next day Martin asked me if I was coming down the crags with the gang. I asked him if I could take my doll, he said, "No". I couldn't take a doll when I was in a boys gang, I told him I didn't want to go then. "You will be wanting us when you get fed up with that doll," he said. I told him I would never get fed up with it.

The day after that, I got my doll ready to go to my nana's to see my cousins. I passed aunt Fanny's house, Joan came out. "And where are you off to" she said, I told her I was going to nana's because they were all over from Limerick. "Nobody told me they were coming", she said. I turned to go on my way and she called me back. She took the doll out of my arms and said, "You haven't been looking after it, and its eye won't open!" I told her it was like that when I got it, she said, "No it wasn't, so I am taking it back!" She went off towards nana's with the doll. I thought my heart was going to break. I sat on the pavement outside my Aunts house and cried and cried. Martin came up the road he came over to me. "Have you fallen?" he asked. I said, "No." I told him the story in between sobs. "The bitch," he said. He put his arm round me and we started to walk back to our house. Martin said, "It was a rotten old doll anyway it was full of cracks and half of its fingers and toes were worn away." The more he talked about the doll the more I cried. Mam was raging when I told her, but she said it was best to leave it as she didn't want any trouble.

Next day there was a knock at the door and Mam went to answer it and I followed. It was my cousin from Limerick and she asked, "Is Muriel coming out to play?" My cousin looked at me and said "Do you like my new doll? Joan gave it to me.", and with that I burst into tears. Mam put her arm around me and said to my cousin, "She won't be going out today as she's not well." She closed the door and told me to stop crying or I would make myself ill.

When Aunt Fanny found out about it a few days later, she told Joan off and made her come and apologise. I think Joan was sorry, because she said there was nothing she could do about the doll now as it was gone to Limerick. Mam said that was to be the end of it now and told me to forget about the doll, which was easier said than done. So Martin was right with what he said, that I would want the gang when the doll was gone, and I did! Martin left me alone for a couple of days to let me get over the doll, and then he asked me very nicely if I wanted to go down the crags with the gang. I said I would go with them.

We were all playing games when it started to rain we were looking for somewhere to shelter. We found an old piece of rusty corrugated tin, put it on top of two big rocks and we all got under it. Martin said, "What will we do now?" I said, "We can tell stories!", but they said they didn't know any stories. I said, "But I do!" My granddad told me lots of stories. He would tell me one about Billy the blower. There wasn't anything Billy the blower couldn't do as he was magic. I started to tell them a story about this little girl. She set off one day on her tricycle and when she came to a big hill she couldn't pedal hard enough to get up it. Along came Billy the blower and he blew the little girl and her tricycle up to the top of the hill, then he blew her into a beautiful forest. The forest was full of fairies and they were flying all round the little girl. Then they flew down to the ground and they said, "Hello." and they asked her if she would like to stay for tea. The little girl said "Oh, yes please!" They all sat down and had biscuits with icing on top of them and a cup of tea. After tea they all danced and sang songs. Billy the blower came back and said there would be danger about soon, and it would be getting dark. We should go home where it was safe. He blew the little girl back to the top of the hill and she got on the tricycle and soon she was home.

When I finished telling them the story there was silence. All you could hear was the patter of rain on the corrugated roof. Then they all started talking at once. "That's not a true story", one of them said. "Was Billy the blower a man or what?" asked another. "There is no such thing as fairies!" they went on. "Well," I said, "It was a story wasn't it? And you all sat quiet and listened to it didn't you? And Billy the blower is the wind, so that's true isn't it? They all agreed it was. When my granddad told me this story I would imagine I was the little girl on tricycle and I was having tea with the fairies. It gave me a lovely warm feeling inside. The rain eased off and turned into that fine rain. I said I was going home. Martin got up to follow me and told the others to put the tin roof back where we found it in case we needed it again. They said they would.

When we got home, I asked mam where my granddad was. She said he was at work, that he had got a couple of days here and there. Mam said he was too old for a full time job; nobody would take him on at his age. Granddad came home about an hour later. Mam was dishing the dinner out while he was having a wash. We were having boiled bacon, cabbage and mashed potatoes, which was my favourite. When we had finished our dinner, granddad put his hand in his pocket and pulled out some money. He gave mam some and he gave Martin and me a penny each. Mam and granddad were talking, Mam was telling him when my dad got his wages today she would have enough money to get three pairs of shoes for us starting back to school, which would be in two weeks. But she said she would wait until a few days before we started back in case our feet grew any more. Dad came in from work, had a wash and mam gave him his dinner and then dad gave her some money. She told dad she had enough for our shoes and she was going to put it away until nearer the time.

Mam got ready to go into town to do the shopping for the rest of the week, as dad finished early on a Friday and the shops were still open. She took Martin and me with her to help carry the shopping. I didn't know where Ray was but she told granddad if he came in his dinner was in the oven. We went down O'Connell Street and had a look in the shops and when we got to Jack Duggan's shoe shop I would gaze in the window. There was a little man with a shoe last and his head moved and his arm would go up and down with a hammer in his hand as though he was mending the shoes. I thought it was magic how it worked. Mam dragged me away, "We haven't got all day you know." We made our way back down O'Connell Street until we reached Maloney's grocer shop which was on the corner of the Clare Road. We walked down this road and about half way down there was a big gate that led to the top of our garden and was a short cut home.

When we got back in the house granddad was still sitting at the table reading his newspaper and Mam asked if Ray had been in. He said, "No", and then she asked him where my dad was. "Out," he said. "He wouldn't be telling me where he was going would he?" Mam looked at us and said, "He must have gone down to see your Nana."

A couple of hour's later dad still hadn't come home. Ray came in, "Where have you been?" she said. Ray said he had been to Claire Castle and he didn't know the time. Mam told him his dinner was in the oven and it will be all dried up. He said it didn't matter as he would eat it. "You better do. You can't waste food!" She asked him if he had seen his dad. He said, "No."

Mam was getting very agitated. She would be sitting on the chair one minute; then she would go and look out of the window the next. She came back and sat down again, putting her elbows on the table. She put her face in her hands and all of a sudden said "Oh no!" She got up from the table that fast she gave us all a fright. She ran across the kitchen and into her bedroom and all we could hear was, "Oh no! Oh no! God no!" We all ran to her bedroom to see what was wrong with her. She looked at us and said, "Your dad's gone off with the shoe money!"

Dad didn't come home that night or the next day, but he came home late on Saturday night and he was very drunk. Mam said to him, "How could you drink the money for the children's shoes?" Then he started punching and kicking mam. We were all trying to help her, but we were getting pushed from one end of the kitchen to the other. Mam shouted for us to keep out of the way. We went over to the back door and picked granddad up of the floor where dad had pushed him. Dad went to bed after he had upset the whole family. We were all hoping he would go straight to sleep, which he did. We knew as long as he was asleep we were safe.

Mam didn't go to mass next morning, because she was covered in bruises again, but she made us go. We didn't want to leave her because dad was still in bed, but she said she was all right. "Your granddad is here," she added. When I was in church, I though back to the lovely spring and summer we had. Apart from a few good hidings, which we probably deserved, it had been like living in a normal family. My dad had broken the pledge and committed a big sin; and he also lost his job.

The following week dad was out drinking every day. Mam said, "He must have won money on the horses." She was glad she had got shopping in for the week, but she didn't know what she was going to do when the food was all gone. All that week we went to bed early. We were told it would be better if there was no one up when dad came home. But we couldn't get to sleep until we heard him come in. Then we could hear him giving mam a load of verbal abuse. It would go on for ten minutes, sometimes longer, and then it would all go quiet and we could all go to sleep. One night he came home early, Mam had just picked up the clock from the sideboard to take into the bedroom. He was shouting at her, "Where's my dinner?" She said, "It is in the oven, but will be dried up by now". She opened the oven door and bent down to get his dinner out. He picked up the clock and threw it at her. It missed her, but it hit the range and smashed into pieces. Mam told us to go to bed.

When we got into our room, we could hear him cursing and swearing at her. Then we heard the plate get smashed on the floor, we didn't know if he threw it at her or not. There was a week left before we started school. Mam and granddad were trying to sort out shoes for us. Granddad got the boy's old boots out, or what was left of them. He polished them until you could see your face in them. He told mam they might get a couple of months out of them. The boys tried the boots on, but they were too small. Granddad thought about cutting the toes out, but mam said you couldn't send them to school like that. Martin was the most desperate, because his sandals had been stolen from the wall. Mam told Martin to try Ray's Boots on and they fitted him. Then I tried Martin's shoes on, but they were miles too big. Ray still had his shoes that mam got him for Easter, but they were worn thin, and the stitching had come out at the back of his heels. Granddad told him to take them off and he stitched the backs up the best he could, and then he gave them a good polishing and they didn't look to bad. I had my sandals from my first communion, so I could wear those for a while. Mam told us we would have to make-do with what we had until she could sort something out. She said, "The most important thing now is a clock.", as we had to keep asking people what the time was.

Granddad got three days work that week. He came home on Friday with a clock and a few groceries. Dad came home early on that day also. He looked in a very bad mood. He had no money left and he was asking mam if she had any, she told him she hadn't. He kept on at her, "Just a shilling will do." She turned on him, "Where the hell do you think I'd get money? You stole all the money I had for the children's shoes and drank it, you broke the clock, and we have to go around asking people what the time is. It's me that need's money to feed the children. You should be ashamed of yourself letting them go without". Dad was fuming and I though he was going to hit her. My granddad stood up and moved near mam. Dad turned and went in the bedroom. We could hear things, being thrown about. Mam said, "He is looking for money but he won't find any because there is none!"

Dad came out of the bedroom, opened the hall door and he went into granddad's room. When he came out, he had granddad's jacket under his arm and then he went out the front door. I ran in to tell granddad, that dad had gone off with his jacket. "Which way did he go?" With that Martin ran in and said; "He's gone up towards the Clare Road." Granddad was out the back door like a shot and up the path until he reached the big gate that led on to the Clare Road, he told Martin and I to keep back. When dad got to the back gate, granddad jumped on him and took his jacket back.

Dad lost his temper and started hitting him and got the jacket back off him. Dad started to cross the road and granddad grabbed him. They were in the middle of the road now. People that were walking up and down the Clare Road stopped to see what was going on. Dad hit granddad in the face and his nose was bleeding. Martin and I were going to help granddad when this man pulled us back. He told us to keep out of it. I told the man that dad had stolen granddad's jacket and he was going to sell it, with that the man went over to another two men and said something to them, and then all three men went on to the road. They tried to talk to dad, "Come on now," they were saying, "give the old man back his jacket." Dad was hitting out at the men now; it took the three of them to hold him off granddad. They told him again to give the old man it back. While the men had hold of dad, granddad grabbed his jacket. Dad went up the Clare road towards town, and we made our way back home.

When we got home and told mam all about it, she said there would be trouble tonight. She said we had to have our coats together and be ready to run. Granddad went in his room with his jacket and I followed. He didn't know I was there. And I watched him get down on his knees in front of the fireplace and at first I thought he was praying. But then he put his hand up the chimney and he was feeling around it. I said, "What are you doing"? He jumped. I had given him a fright. He picked up his best boots and he put them up the chimney; then he said, "Don't tell your dad where they are, because he would sell his soul to the devil. It's our secret."

We hadn't been in bed long when mam came rushing in our room. "Up!" she said. "Coats on, out the front door, go over the wall and into the field." We did as she said and she followed with granddad. He was carrying a couple of blankets and she had the clock. We all went into the cowshed and settled ourselves down. Mam said he must have got money from somewhere. She told us to try and get some sleep. She would go over in an hour or so and see if it was safe. Granddad fell asleep first. I was snuggled into him. The next thing I knew it was morning, and we had all gone to sleep. Mam opened the shed door and looked at the clock. It was five o'clock. She woke Ray and Martin. Granddad was trying to get up, but he was very stiff. I got hold of his hand and helped to pull him up. We climbed over the wall and went into the house. Our room was just inside the front door and granddad's was just opposite. Mam got into our bed with us and we all fell asleep again.

We all started back to school and I was going into a new class. I was very nervous, and the nun that was teaching us was very tall and she looked very strict. She told us we would have to work hard in this class and she wouldn't stand for any nonsense. She started asking questions about different things, we had to put our hand up if we knew the answer. I knew the answers to lot of the questions, but I didn't put my hand up as I had no confidence in myself at all. I was glad when the first day was over but it was nice getting the free lunches again.

After school we all went down the crags picking blackberries, as we were supposed to go after mass yesterday, but it rained all day. Mam gave us two billycans, she told us to try and fill them as she was going to make jam and blackberry pies, which she said would keep the hunger from us. We started picking the blackberries, and it was one for the billycan and one in my mouth and so it went on. The best ones were always at the top of the bush, so our arms were full of scratches trying to get them down. We filled the two cans and made our way home. I was still eating the blackberries out of the billycan. Ray told me to stop it or I would be sick.

When we got in the house mam looked at me. "Look at the state of you!" She lifted down the mirror or what was left of it, Dad had broken it when he was throwing things about, but you could still see in the bottom half of it. My face was red from ear to ear and it was all up my nose. Mam told me to get washed with plenty of soap, and then she said to the boys, "I have got a sheep's head broth cooking and we have to make it last two days." The boys said they weren't that hungry as they had eaten lots of blackberries. She told the boys to get washed. When they were finished, she got a bowl and tipped the blackberries in, and as she was washing them she said to me, "You should never eat blackberries until they have been washed." I asked her why, "She said there were a lot of little maggots in them, so they had to be washed first." That did it; I rushed out the back door to the lavatory and oh was I sick. When I got back in the kitchen the boys were doubled over laughing. They said a few maggots wouldn't hurt you that made me worse. I kept imagining all the maggots were crawling around inside me. Mam started to dish up the dinner and the boys said they only wanted a little bit. I said, "I don't want any." The thought of eating sheep's head broth on top of the blackberries with maggots in, was making me feel sick again.

Granddad only got one day's work that week, but it was his pension week, so he got ten shillings and one days pay. He told me he couldn't buy me any biscuits with icing on this month as there were more important things we needed. Friday came we had got the first week over with at school. Mam asked us to go and pick some blackberries on Saturday before they were over. We picked a load, but I didn't eat any. She made a couple of pies and the rest she made into jam. We had some pie for our tea. I was eating it very slowly, and I was looking out for maggots. Mam told me not to be so silly, she had washed the blackberries and they were fine.

After tea, I was sat on the step outside our front door. Martin was talking to his friend Paddy Ryan who lived across the road. I herd a bang in the kitchen, and I could hear mam saying, "Oh god in heaven, and no!" I shouted Martin to come; we ran in to see what was going on. She was thumping her hands on the table and kept saying, "Oh no". We asked her what was wrong. She told us that dad had gone off with the clock and he had even taken the box that it came in, which mam was keeping for a few weeks in case the clock went wrong. She said it would be easier to sell with the box. She sat down on the chair and we were trying to comfort her. She said she wanted to be on her own.

We got up for school on Monday morning but we didn't know what time it was. Mam sent Martin over to Mrs Ryan's across the road to ask her what the time was. This went on for the rest of the week. On Monday morning, of the next week, she sent me over to ask what the time was. As Mrs Ryan opened the door, her dog got out, and went for me, it bit me on the back of my leg. I was terrified and blood was running down my leg. It was in a bad state and ran over to our house. Mam took me to the doctors. He put something on the bite, bandaged me up, and told mam it would more than likely leave a scar. I still have that scar today. After that day, we didn't go across to Mrs Ryan's for the time.

Mam would get us up and ready for school. Then we would watch out the window and wait for the other children leaving for school. One morning mam overslept and came rushing into our room shouting, "Quick get up! The other children are leaving for school". We were all trying to get washed at the same time. It wasn't much of a wash; it was a matter of a few handfuls of water splashed on our faces. Then we were pulling and dragging the towel from each other and there wasn't time for anything to eat.

When I got to school, the gates were locked, so I had to ring the bell to get in. I saw this very old nun walking across the playground; she seemed to take forever to get to the gate. She opened the gate and I started to run across the playground, she called me back and said, "Young ladies don't run! They walk." I started to walk as quickly as I could. When I opened the door to the classroom everyone stopped what they were doing and looked at me. I went up to the teacher and told her we had overslept. She asked me, did I have a note and I told her my mam didn't have time to write one. She told me to hold my hand out, and she brought the cane down on it four or five times, then she told me to go and sit down. The pain in my hand was awful, I was crying and she told me to stop snivelling. I was trying to stop, but the more I tried the harder it got.

By lunchtime my hand was that swollen; I couldn't move my fingers. All the girls that went home for lunch had to have permission. I got in between them; and got out the gate. I went down O' Connell Street and bumped into my dad, who was half drunk. He asked me why I was out of school; I showed him my hand, I said I was going home to see if mam had anything to take the pain away. He asked me if I had my lunch before I came out and I told him I hadn't. I thought he was going to buy me something to eat. He looked at me and said, "You should have had your lunch before you left," and away he went to the next pub, I supposed.

When I got in the house, Mam asked me what was wrong; I burst into tears and showed her my hand; "Good god", she said, "What's happened to that"? I told her the story and added; that I came out of school without permission. Mam took me over to the sink and put my hand in o bowl of cold water, she was feeling my fingers one at a time. My fingers were throbbing; my thumb was up like a balloon. Mam said she didn't think anything was broken. She cut up some rags into strips and put them in the cold water, she squeezed as much water as she could out of them, and wrapped them around my hand. She fastened the end of the rag with a safety pin and said it would help to bring the swelling down. She gave me some bread and jam, and a cup of tea, and when I had finished she said, "Right! Let's go up to the school."

When we got to the school the bell had just gone. I was going to go with the other children, but mam held me back. She said, "We will just wait until they all get settled down." I looked up at my mam. She was a very beautiful woman and had a lovely figure. The boys at Ray and Martin's school couldn't believe she was their mother. In fact she was known as the Lady, and she was a very cool and calm person. She was very calm now as she knocked at the classroom door. Mam said, "I wonder if I could have a word with you outside." the teacher stepped out. Mam said to her, "Well first of all it was my fault she was late for school this morning, I overslept. I have three children and they were all late for school, and by the time I would have found pen and paper they would have been later still. As it was, they didn't have any breakfast, I said I would send a note later and here it is!" She handed the note to the teacher. The teacher said, "Well, she left school without permission." Mam said, "Yes she did, but you didn't do anything with her hand and she was in awful pain". Mam took the wet rag off my hand. "Now you look at that hand. She can't move her fingers. I have checked them. I don't think there is anything broken, but we won't know until the swelling goes down and I am afraid if anything like this happens again I will have to report it to the guards." The teacher said she was sorry, she didn't realise she had hit me that hard. Mam said that would be the end of it now; she wanted things to go back to normal. The teacher asked if I wanted to stay at school. I couldn't very well say no. Mam said to her, "Don't forget, she can't move her fingers. She won't be able to hold a pen". The teacher said that was fine, she would give me a book to read. Mam said, "Good afternoon" to her, and that she had to go to the boy's school with their notes, and she calmly walked away.

I went to my desk and the teacher gave me a book to read, all went well until about half past two. Then the classroom door burst open and my dad, half fell in. He was drunk. He took a minute to look around and then he went for the teacher. He was swearing at her and pushing her around, and he pinned her up against the black board. He was trying to pull her headdress off; he half succeeded, she told him she was going to get the guards. He replied, "It's me who will be getting the guards for what you did to my child's hand!" With that two men rushed in the classroom and got hold of him and dragged him out. The nun that had opened the gate to him, rushed across the room to my teacher, she was asking her if she was alright, she said when she opened the gate he pushed past her, and she had to get help. I think it was the gardeners she had brought. I was wishing the ground would open up and swallow me, I knew at that moment that I didn't like my dad; he was a horrible man.

When I got home from school, I told mam all that had gone on. The boys stood there with their mouths open, they couldn't believe that dad had attacked a nun. Then there was a knock at the door; it was the guards and they said they wanted a word with my dad. Mam told them he wasn't in. They said your daughter would have told you what has happened, and the nun wasn't going to press charges this time, but he was never to go near the school again. Mam told them that they would have to come back and see him, as he never listened to a word she said. They told her they would come back tomorrow, she said; they'd better make it morning while he's sober.

Granddad came in from his day's work, and the story had to be told all over again. He said, "That man is a lunatic; he wants putting away." Then he opened his bag and brought out an old clock; it was covered in spots of rust. He said he had found it in a bin where he was work. It didn't go, but he had fiddled around with it, and put some oil on it, and he had got it going. Then he said, "Well we should be safe with this old clock", because it is in such a state; no one will buy it.

I went to school next day feeling awful, I was so ashamed of what dad had done to the teacher, but she was fine with me. She asked if I could move my fingers, I said I couldn't, and showed her my hand. It had gone purple in colour, and it was still swollen, she gave me a book and told me to go to my desk and read, I sat down and let out a sigh of relief.

Lunchtime came and we all went over to the big hut. Some of the girls were fussing over me. One of them got my mug of cocoa and another got my bread bun. They were trying to find somewhere to put my cocoa down; they found a bit of a shelf, the other girl then gave me my bread bun and said, "Now you will be able to eat your bun first, and then you will be able to drink your cocoa." I was very grateful to them. We all had to stand at the end of the hut and stay there. The other end of the hut was for children who brought packed lunches. They had a table and benches at each side, so theirs was called the rich end; and ours was the poor end, and we weren't allowed to mix.

All the girls were talking about what happened yesterday, I didn't want to talk about it, and I just wanted to forget all about it. I was glad when lunchtime was over. All this had happened because my dad had sold our clock. Next day when I came home from school, Mam told me that the guards and the priest had been to see dad. He told them it was the drink that made him do what he did, and he was never going to let a drop past his lips again. The guards told him, he was very lucky that the nun wasn't going to charge him, but he was warned he was never to go near the school again, which was a big relief to me. Mam was very depressed for the next couple of days; she was worried where the next lot of food was to come from.

Dad was getting up early. He was going out before we went to school and coming back about five o'clock. Mam and granddad were wondering what he was up to. Dad came in the kitchen about four-o clock on Saturday. I was there on my own, and mam had gone to lie down as she had a bad headache. I got a bit nervous, I looked up at him but he didn't look in a bad temper. When he was in a bad temper, a tuft of hair always came down on his forehead, but his hair was combed back. He came up to me and asked where mam was. I told him where she was, and then he pulled a ten-shilling note out of his pocket. He held it in front of me and said, "Look what I have got for your mam. I bet that will make her headache better". He went into mam and I shot out the back door to play. About ten minutes later I watched mam go up the path with a shopping basket.

Dad went off again on Monday, before we went to school. We were getting our free boots today after school. Well mine were shoes, but they were proper shoes, big thick black ones with little dents in them like orange peel and I was very proud of them. Dad went off again on Tuesday morning, and Mam asked him where he was going. He just said he had things to do, she turned to him and said; "Well I wish you would do something to make some money", he told her he would have some money tomorrow.

We all got home from school next day. Ray was at the front door talking to someone and Martin and I were in the kitchen. We were asking mam if we could have a penny each, she said she had no money, but if we waited until dad came home, he might give us a penny. I took my coat off; I knew it would be like getting blood out of a stone. I walked down the hall to granddad's room, but he wasn't in there, I asked mam where he was; she said he had gone for a walk.

Then the back door burst open and dad came in, and I was just going to ask him for a penny, but his face was like thunder, and that bit of hair was on his forehead. I backed away behind the table. Martin and mam were standing by the sink. He went over to mam and started hitting her, he was shouting at her, who did she think she was telling him to go and get some money; he went at her again, and Martin wrapped his arms around her to protect her. Mam told him to let go of her, because he would get hurt, but he clung on to her and he was taking some of the blows. Dad really got mad then, and he got Martin by the scruff of the neck and dragged him across the kitchen floor. Martin got away and started down the hall to get to the front door, but dad caught him and dragged him into granddad's room and flung him on the bed. He took his belt off. Mam was crying, I was crying. Mam was pleading with him not to hit him, but it was no good. He put the belt around Martin's neck. By this time I was screaming my head off. Ray came rushing in the front door, saying, "What's going on?" When he saw what was happening, he got at one side of dad and mam was at the other side trying to pull him off.

The window in the room was half-open. I stood there and screamed for help. There were a few people outside wondering what was going on, and I went back to the bed and looked at Martin, his face was going a blue colour and there was a rasping sound coming from his throat. Mam called to me to go for the guards. I was just going into the hall when some men came in, and all I could do was point to where they were. The men had to be careful because dad had hold of the belt, and if they dragged him away, the belt would tighten on Martin's neck. So they were talking to him, telling him he would end up in jail if he didn't let go of the belt. In the end, he did let go, the men dragged him outside. Mam and Ray were trying to take the belt of Martin's neck as gently as they could so as not to pull it any tighter, Martin eyes were shut, and I was screaming, "Is he dead?"

They got the belt off and they got him in a sitting up position. He started spluttering a bit, and his face didn't look so blue now. He had a terrible mark round his neck where the belt had been, but I was just glad he was alive. Mam had her arms around Martin and she was rocking him like a baby. His eyes seemed to be rolling about. I think he wanted to go to sleep, and I couldn't understand why mam wouldn't let him. Every time his eyes closed, she would say something to him so he would open them again. She was saying, "Now will we go and write a letter to Sue and Willie, you would like to go and see Sue and Willie wouldn't you?" Martin gave a little nod, and mam said, "Oh, thank you god he understands what I am saying." I couldn't make head or tail of this, why wouldn't Martin be able to understand her, but I thought, I'll keep my mouth shut.

After a while mam and Ray took Martin into the kitchen and sat him on a chair. Mam got pen and paper and sat down next to Martin. She started to write a letter to Sue and Willie. When she had finished it, she told Martin she would post it first thing in the morning. Granddad came in, and Mam was telling him all that had gone on. He said, "I told you he was a lunatic and wants putting away." He had a look at Martin's neck, and said, "I think it will heal; but it will take time." He asked mam why she hadn't sent for the guards, she told him it all happened so quickly. She told him she was sending me when some men came in and got him away from Martin.

Mam told granddad she was taking us to Westport on Saturday, as Sue and Willie will have got the letter by then and they would meet us at the station. He asked her where she was going to get the money. She said she would get it one-way or the other. Granddad told her he'd got Two Day's Work, but it wouldn't be enough to pay all the fares. Mam told him he would need his money to feed himself, and she told him not to give dad anything. If he wanted to eat he could go and work for it. Granddad told us to get away and not to worry about him. What dad did to Martin was the last straw, and now we all hated him.

Dad didn't come home for the next two days and nights, and we were all pleased about that. We got up for school on Thursday morning, and though there was only Ray and I going, but mam got Martin ready. She put a scarf round his neck to hide his scars, and we all set off together towards town. I left Ray at the top of the Clare Road, and went on to my school. Mam said she was going to post the letter and Martin went with her.

When we got home from school they were there. Mam was cooking Pigs Cheeks, roasted, and we were having cabbage and potatoes. Granddad would be pleased when he got home from work. The next day she made us sausage, mashed potatoes and turnip, Ray was wondering where the money was coming from; he asked Martin where mam got the money from. Martin said they went to this place and the man in there asked her a lot of questions. Mam signed some papers and he gave her the money. Ray said, "She must have been to a moneylender." Saturday morning we were all ready to go. Granddad came with us to the station, and put our bags on the train. A couple of minutes later the train set off. I was looking out of the window waving to him. I felt very sorry for granddad, as he would have to stay there with dad for a week, and the poor man had to hide his boots up the chimney and his one and only suit under the mattress in between the sheets of brown paper. I hoped dad didn't find them!

My granddad was a quietly spoken man and he kept himself to himself. When he went out for his walks, if he met anyone; he would lift his cap, and pass the time of day with them, but that was as far as it got. But if anyone needed his help he would help them, like when their tin baths and billycans and pans got holes in them, he would mend them. He would put a big washer with a hole in the middle of it over the hole that had to be mended, then he would put a screw in the washer; and then they would stop leaking.

I don't think he ever met any of the people that brought things to be mended. People just knocked on the back door and asked if granddad could mend whatever it was. He would say to tell them to leave it in the yard, and I will have a look at it. When it was done he would send one of us to take it back. I think granddad was just a very shy man, but I was going to miss him for a week.

Chapter 6:
Potato Picking in Ballyglass

We arrived at Westport and Willie met us. They had received the letter that morning and Willie looked worried. He put his arm around mam's shoulder and asked her if she was alright. Mam said she would tell him all about it when we got to Ballyglass. Willie turned to us and said, "Well it's nice to see you all again, and how are you all getting on?" He took hold of my hand and said, "How is my Lovely Legs doing? You have got that big since I last seen you!" Oh, I was so happy to see him!

Sue had our dinner ready and we ate every bit of it as we were all hungry. After Sue and mam washed up and put the dishes away, Sue told mam to go and sit down and she came and sat next to her. "Now tell me the whole story." Mam told her the whole story, and then she started crying. Sue put her arm around mam but she couldn't stop crying. I think she had just had enough, and couldn't take any more. Martin went over and put his arms around mam, and he started crying. Martin had red hair and lots of freckles, with his face being so white at that moment, his freckles stood out as though some one had got a pen and drawn them all over his face. He had hardly said a word in the last three days, and it wasn't like him. Usually you couldn't shut him up, and he was always laughing, He would start with a very slow smile, and then his whole face would light up, and he would laugh. But in the last three days we couldn't even get a little smile out of him.

Mam told Martin to stop crying. She said she felt a lot better now that she had a good cry. She wiped Martin's tears away and he went back and sat down. Willie went over to Martin, and said, "Now young fellow let me have a look at your neck." Martin stood up in front of him and Willie had a good look at his neck, He told mam that the bruising round his neck would go in a week or so, but the place where the buckle of the belt had been would take a bit longer to heal. He looked at Martin and said, "What you need young fellow is plenty of country air and you will be better in no time at all."

Sue said she had put the stone bottle in the bed, when she got mam's letter, so the bed would be well aired. She said she was going to fill it up again, and we would be nice and warm. Martin looked very tired. I don't think he had slept the last two nights at home. He was frightened Dad would come home and start again, but he was first to go to sleep that night.

We all got up on Sunday morning and had our breakfast; we were back to boiled eggs again and fresh Homemade bread. Sue and Willie went off to their church and we went to mass. I prayed to god to send my dad away and never to come back. When we got back to the cottage, the big black pot of potatoes was put on the hook over the fire, and I knew this time we didn't have to eat them all, that we shared them with the pigs. After dinner we squashed all the potatoes and Willie put some pig meal in and he went off to feed the pigs. We played the gramophone and the two records until everyone was fed up of hearing them. Martin's face was a better colour today, but he still wasn't saying much. However, he was sort of half smiling when someone said something funny. Willie said it was early to bed tonight because the second crop of potatoes had to be picked this week and put away for winter.

After breakfast next morning mam, Ray and I set off to the Top Field, Martin stayed with Sue, she had jobs to do on the farm, and said Martin could help her by feeding the hens and collecting the eggs. Willie was already in the field when we got there; he had put the plough on the horse. We followed Willie with our sacks, It was a cold morning and very misty, and every now and then I would look at Ray, and his nose kept running. He had to keep stopping to get a rag out of his pocket to wipe it, so I got in front of him and thought this was great until my sack was nearly half full and I couldn't drag it. I had to keep getting handfuls of potatoes and running back to the sack with them, and I could see a big smile on Ray's face as he went on way ahead of me.

The mist lifted and the sun came out. Now it was too warm and we were taking our coats off. Willie said we would take a lunch break, we started to walk back up the field and I saw Martin's red hair in the distance. I shouted to the others that Martin was here and I ran to meet him and Sue. Martin started to smile and then his whole face lit up, and I was so happy. Sue had brought our lunch, a big billycan of tea and some sandwiches. Sue said she had done her jobs on the farm and she was going to stay and help and Martin said he wanted to help as well. We all started work again. It was a lot easier now that Martin was pulling the sack with me, I was tired out running backwards and forwards. It was about three O'clock and Willie said, "Time to go home. That's enough for today."

When we got home we all had a good wash. We didn't know where we ached most and we were all going about the kitchen holding our backs. Willie was laughing at us, he said, "It will take you a couple of days to get used to it and then you will be fine." Then he said he had a couple of jobs to do on the farm, before he did the milking. He asked us to go to the well to get some water, and said when we came back Ray would go and get the cows in for milking. We moaned all the way to the well about our aches and pains. Ray said, "Well at least we are standing up. It's the bending down that's the worst."

After dinner, Willie put the wireless on to listen to the news. He sat on his chair by the fire and he lifted me on his knee. I was having a problem trying to keep my eyes open. When the news was finished I asked mam if I could go to bed. Mam looked at me and said, "Now there's one for the book", she said to Sue, "We call her biddy last, she's always the last one to go to bed, and we call her biddy early in the mornings, because she's always first up." Martin said he wanted to go to bed as well. I couldn't remember my head touching the pillow I was out like a light. When I woke up next morning there was no one in the bed. I got dressed and went out to the kitchen and Sue was pottering about. She said, "We thought we would let you have a good sleep this morning. You can help me for a while and we will go down at lunchtime to give the others a hand."

Sue made me my breakfast and after that I went to feed the hens. I shouted "Here chucky, chucky, chucky!" and all the hens came running down to me. I scattered their feed like Sue told me to, and then about eight geese came running towards me. They were all hissing at me and I dropped the rest of the feed and ran. When I got in the house; Sue asked me what was wrong. I told her the geese were going to attack me and they were hissing at me. She told me that they wouldn't hurt me, and that they usually stayed in the orchard. She said they were fattening them up for Christmas. Then she said, "Come on, and we will collect the eggs together." I stayed as close as I could to her. She went into the orchard to see if there was any in there. The geese didn't hiss at her, so it was me they really didn't like. We went down to the top field with lunch for everyone and sat down together and enjoyed it. Sue was telling them about the geese and me, Willie and mam were laughing, but Ray and Martin weren't laughing as they didn't like the geese either and had both been chased by them yesterday. Willie said they were good guard dogs. I told him I would rather have their dog Spot to guard us. We started the potato picking again. We had a good laugh at all the different shapes and sizes of potatoes. Willie was right. After the first couple of days you didn't feel the aches and pains as much. The rest of the week flew by.

Chapter 6: Potato Picking in Ballyglass

It came to Friday and we had finished by midday. We all went back to the cottage. Sue had the big black kettle and a big pot on the fire to get hot water. She brought the tin bath in, but it was a lot smaller than ours was at home. Mam went and got some rainwater from the barrel outside. When the kettle had boiled Sue poured it in on top of the rainwater. There were a few leaf's floating about, and I was first to get into the bath. I was trying to get the leaves out of the water and Mam said, "Will you get in; a few leaves aren't going to hurt you." I could just fit in if I bent my legs and Mam gave me a good scrub then it was Martins turn. He had to stand up. It came to Ray's turn and he wouldn't get in. The only way mam could get him in was to ask us all to leave the kitchen for five minutes. We all went in the bedroom and it must have been the quickest bath Ray has ever had. He was all done and dressed in about two minutes. So that was one week finished and we had to go home tomorrow.

We got up early on Saturday morning as we were going to catch the early train. Willie was taking us to the station after he had finished the milking. Sue got a canvas bag and she put cheese, butter, a lump of bacon and eggs in it. Then Willie came in. He had killed a chicken for her, and said you could let the children pluck it when you get home. Mam gave Sue and Willie a big hug and said she didn't know what she would do with out them. Martin asked if he could take some of the potatoes that he had picked, Willie went to the barn with him and found an old piece of sacking, which Martin put some potatoes in and Willie tied up with string. When they came back to the kitchen, Willie told mam that Martin had picked all the biggest potatoes to show his friends when he got home. We said our goodbyes and set off for the station. Willie saw us to the train and shook hands with the boys. He picked me up and gave me a big hug. He gave mam a hug and he put some money in her hand. Mam was trying to give it back to him but he wouldn't take it, he said he would have had to get someone in to help him with the potatoes and that would have cost him more. She had earned it.

Chapter 7: The Woods

We were nearly home and we didn't know who we had to face there. When we got off the train in Ennis, Ray carried the suitcase mam carried the canvas bag and Martin his potatoes. He was struggling to carry them and I asked if he wanted me to help him but he said that he could manage.

When he got to the house there was only granddad there. I ran up to him and he sat me on his knee and said, "How is my wee ducksey? I have been missing you, so what have you been up to?" I told him we had worked hard all week potato picking and I told him about the geese hissing at me and that I didn't like geese. Mam asked granddad if dad had been back. He said, "He came back on Monday. He asked where you all were and I told him you had gone away for the week. He has been moping around the house all week; he even had the cheek to ask me for a couple of bob. I stayed in my room most of the time to keep out of his way. I didn't get any work at all this week."

Mam unpacked the suitcase and the canvas bag. She unwrapped the eggs and straightened the newspapers out, told me to cut them up into squares and put them in the lavatory, and then she sent me for a loaf of bread. She said she would get the rest in town because they were cheaper. Then she got the billycan and asked granddad if he would go and get it filled with milk, we went out the door together. Granddad said, "Why don't you go to the shop on the Clare Road?" We walked up together, I got the bread and granddad had to walk a bit further to get the milk. He asked if I would walk down with him and I did and when we got to the gate of the house he handed me the billycan and asked if I would go in for the milk. He was a funny man, he was so shy he didn't like knocking at the door of the house; he said it would be different if it was a shop. When I got back out of the gate he took the billycan off me and carried it home.

We weren't long in the house when dad came in. He was going on at mam that she had no right to take his children out of school for a week. Mam turned to look at him. "I didn't take the children out of school. They were on holiday for a week, but I had to keep Martin off for a couple of days the previous week, because you nearly killed him. And if you want to go to the brothers and explain why Martin wasn't at school you can. He was saying it was the drink that made him do it, and he hadn't had a drink all week. Now he was saying there was no food in the house for him to eat. "Well why don't you go out and work and buy some food," mam said. "That's what I have been doing; working to feed my children. Dad went into the bedroom and banged the door. He didn't ask how Martin was or say sorry for what he had done. After tea Martin asked mam if he could go out for a while, she said he could. I asked him to wait for me and he said he would be outside on the road. When I finished my tea I went outside, the streetlights were on and I could see Martin half way up the road with some children, they were all under the streetlight.

Martin came running towards me, he was saying if you want to see something special you will have to go home and get a halfpenny. I ran back to the house and asked granddad for a halfpenny to see something special. He gave me the money and I ran back up the road, I told Martin I had the money. But I said, "You haven't any money." He replied he was getting a free go because he was doing the collecting. There was a girl of about fourteen standing under the streetlight, and the other children were in a line in front of her. I got in the line and Martin stood behind me. "What do you think we are going to see? I asked. He said, "Tits!" "What kind of tits?" I asked. "She has started growing tits. That's why she is charging a halfpenny to see them!" he replied. When it came to my turn, she opened her blouse at one side and I was looking at this little bud that looked like a small conker. I asked her if she only had one. She said no and she pulled the other side of her blouse back, I thought it was a waste of a halfpenny. Then it was Martin's turn, she held her hand out for the money he had collected. Then she let Martin have a look, all the other children were giggling. Martin got hold of my arm and said, "Come on."

I went with him and asked him why he was cross. He said because it was a Swizzle, charging people money to see two little buds, my own are nearly as big as hers and she made two and a halfpence for nothing. I asked Martin if that was where babies came from; with her having two was it where twins come out off. He said, "How do I know where babies come from!" Then I asked him was it a sin what we had just seen, and did I have to tell the priest when I went to confession? He sounded even crosser now. "No you don't tell the priest anything, do you hear me? And it's not a sin," he said, I said all right then I just wanted to know. We went in the house and granddad asked me what special treasures I had seen for my halfpenny. I was just about to tell him when Martin butted in. He said it was a Swizzle and they showed us some newborn kittens and that he got a free go because he was taking the money. Martin got me to one side and said, "You were going to tell him weren't you?" I replied, "You told me not to tell the priest, so I thought it was all right to tell granddad." He said, "You are not to tell anyone or we will be in trouble, do you understand?" I told him I did.

Mam came in the back door with the chicken and we all stared plucking it. As we were plucking it mam was talking to herself all the time, about how many meals she could get out of the chicken, and how many she could get out of the bacon. We all went to mass on Sunday morning and when we got home we asked mam if we could go picking hazelnuts. She said she thought they would be over by now but we could go and try as long as Ray went with us. He didn't want to go as he wanted to go out with his friends. Mam asked him would he take us just for an hour, he gave in and said one hour and that's it.

We went down the Clare Road to St Flannon's College; we turned right up a lane at the side of the college, climbed over a wall and went across a field until we came to the nut trees. There were still some nuts on the trees and we started picking. They were so ripe and a lot of them had fallen on the ground. Usually we had to get them out of the green pod with our thump nail and it made your nails very sore. We had picked a good few when Ray said time to go. We were begging him; please just a little while longer. He said, "No. There are some Leprechauns watching us in the bushes over there. If you watch you will see the bushes moving. We watched and one of the bushes started rustling and then another started. Ray said, "Run as fast as your legs will carry you and don't look back", and we ran as fast as we could, we reached the wall and climbed over. We sat down on the ground and my heart was thumping, I was so frightened. Martin said, "They must have got Ray," and we looked through a slit in the wall and saw Ray walking towards us, he climbed over the wall and he was laughing. "That was one way of getting you home quickly," he said. We said, "But the bushes were moving." "Yes" he said, "Because I was throwing stones at them, and don't tell mam."

We got back home and sat on our front step and started cracking the nuts open with stones. About an hour after that, mam called us in for our dinner. We were looking forward to the chicken dinner; the grownups had already had theirs. My granddad had gone to his room and dad went for a lie down. Mam put our dinners on the table and went back to the sink where she was washing up, we only had two chairs Ray sat on one and Martin on the other, I stood up because I could reach the table better. I was just about to start eating when I caught Ray starring at me. He had a grin on his face, and I asked him what he was grinning at. The next thing I saw was two claws gripping on to the edge of the table next to Ray. The claws were moving along the edge of the table, I let out such a scream out that mam dropped one of the pans, ran over to me at the table. "What's wrong?" she asked. I told her there was a claw moving along the table next to Ray. Mam went over to Ray at the other side of the table, "Right" she said, "Hand them over." Ray put his hand in his pocket and pulled out two chicken's feet and she gave him a slap and told him to behave. Then Ray and Martin got a fit of the giggles. Mam threatened to take their dinners from them if they didn't stop it. They didn't want to lose their dinner so they shut up, but that was Ray always playing tricks on us.

We all went back to school next day. Mam went with Martin as she would have to explain what happened to him. His neck was a yellow colour now but his shirt covered that, but the bit where the buckle had been was scabbed over. I don't know what she told the teacher. Mam said she had done her best to make the money stretch as far as she could in the two weeks that we had been back from Westport. Now she was saying there were only about ten sods of turf left in the shed for the fire. My dad had been drunk three or four times since we came home, so he was getting money from somewhere. Mam asked him for some money but he said he didn't have any. Mam told him she couldn't keep us on fresh air and that the turf was nearly all gone. He said there was nothing he could do about it but he had a job tomorrow. Mam told him we would all have to go to the woods on Saturday and saw down some trees, he said that was fair enough.

When he came home the next day he gave mam five shillings. He told her he wouldn't be able to go with us tomorrow because he had a job to do and he had to take the work while it was there. Mam agreed, but she told him to go and ask his father if he could borrow the horse and cart to collect the logs that we would have ready. He said that was fine and he would go and make sure it was all right. My Granda was a carrier and he would go and meet the trains and deliver the goods wherever they had to go. He went and asked my Granda and he said, yes, he could.

We set off early next morning it was a cold dark and damp. Granddad was carrying the big axe, that he had spent hours sharpening. Ray carried the big saw and Martin had a small saw and rope. Mam had a bag with bottles of cold tea and a little pan to heat the tea up, a couple of mugs and some sandwiches. We walked towards Doura, We seemed to be walking forever, but we got there eventually. We went into the woods and it was dark and dismal in there, Granddad and mam went to look at the trees to see which one they would saw down first. They picked one and started sawing; Granddad at one side and mam at the other, then Ray would take over from mam. When the first tree was about to fall, Granddad put a rope around it and they all pulled until it came down. Ray was cutting all the small branches off and they came off easy because they were rotten. Martin and I were putting the branches across our knee and snapping them. Ray got the smaller saw out and started sawing the tree into logs, Martin was trying to chop the logs in half, but the axe was nearly as big as him. Mam and granddad were working on the second tree, my job was to take the logs when they had been chopped over to a clearing and stack them up ready for the horse and cart to collect. I was very cold standing around waiting for the logs. The second tree was down and mam told the boys to go over and get the branches off it. Now granddad had the axe and he just seemed to hit them once and they split, so I was kept busy and started to warm up.

Lunchtime came and mam had lit a little fire. She put the cold tea in the pan and warmed it. We took it in turns to have a drink, as there were only two mugs. We had bread and butter with sugar on. I don't know what mam and granddad had. After we had finished we started work again. Mam kept praising us for all the hard work. The more she praised the harder we worked. Instead of carrying three logs over to the clearing I was carrying four. We were glad when mam said we had done enough work for today, but I wasn't looking forward to the long walk home. Granddad had tied about seven logs up with the rope and put them on his back. Mam said there was no need, but he said never go home empty handed, he told us all to carry a couple, Mam put three in her bag and we started for home.

We had no idea what time it was but it still seemed to be dark, I was so glad to see our house. We had some sheep's head broth for dinner and even that tasted nice I was so hungry. My dad came in and had his dinner and then he went to get the horse and cart. He said he would see us in a couple of hours and it was just past five when he left. We could have gone out to play for a couple of hours if we wanted to, but we were all too tired. Mam said it's not over yet, you couldn't get a horse and cart down the back lane so dad would have to bring it to the front, so that meant we would have to go through the front door and carry the logs through to the shed at the back of the house. Mam said, "Don't look so fed up. We will have it done in no time at all with six of us doing it" So we all sat around waiting for the horse and cart to come. He said he would be a couple of hours, but he had been gone for three and half-hours now. Mam put her coat on and said she would be back in ten minutes. When she came back she had a shocked look on her face. We asked what was wrong. She said she had been to his fathers' house and asked him if your dad was there, he said he had been, but left a couple of hours ago. She asked did he bring the horse and cart back and he said he had, and that the logs had been delivered. She told him that they were our logs, we

Chapter 7: The Woods

had been out all day cutting them and he hadn't been back with any. Mam started to cry and she said he must have gone and sold them.

Granddad was trying to comfort her. "Maybe we could go and cut a tree down tomorrow and we could carry a few logs at a time," he said. Mam said she had to take the big saw back, she had borrowed it from her friend and it was needed. "Anyway," she said, "the children are tired out and so am I and you don't look too good yourself."

We were all worn out. I couldn't believe my dad had done that after all the hard work we had done. It was a good job granddad had strapped those logs to his back and told us to carry a couple under our arms. My dad didn't come home that night.

We all went to mass next morning then we had to take the big saw back. We took it to a little white cottage. When the man came out I knew him. His name was John Joe, and he had been to our house a few times to see mam and dad. His mother came to the door. Mam was telling them what had happened. His mother said we could cut down one of her trees. There were lots of them growing at the back of the cottage. John Joe and mam started sawing one down, then they were sawing it into logs and Ray was splitting them with an axe. Martin and I were told to put them into this handcart. It looked like a very big box with a wheel at each side and two handles at the front to push it with. When it was full, mam thanked them for all the help. We set off for home, Mam was pushing it at first but it was very heavy, then Ray and Martin took a turn each holding a handle. It took us a while to get home. We emptied the logs into the shed, and then mam told the boys to take the handcart back. They were going to take it in turns to have a ride in it. Granddad came out and asked where the logs had come from. Mam told him the story. Mam was putting some potatoes on to boil in their jackets; we were having them with broth that was left from yesterday. I would be glad to go to school tomorrow to get my bread bun and my mug of cocoa.

We all went to school next morning and there was still no sign of dad, we all thought our prayers had been answered, that he was gone and he would never come back. When we got home from school, we asked mam had he been back, she said no she hadn't seen or heard from him. We were all very happy about that. But then we heard the back door open and we all looked towards it, we let out a sigh of relief when my two cousins walked in. They lived on the Clare Road with my Uncle Miko. He was dad's brother, they were well off, and I think the boys went to college. My Uncle Miko was the manager of the brewery in Ennis. The two boys would leave their house by the back door cut across all the gardens, in our back door and out the front door. It cut a big chunk off their journey, they were always very polite and passed the time of day with whoever was in, but today they stopped in the middle of the kitchen because we were all staring at them. They asked mam if everything was all right, she said "yes" "yes" everything's fine, and then she asked them if their mam and dad were all right. They said, "Yes fine", and off they went out the front door.

Mam got on with the dinner, she said she had got a bacon shank cheap, but she could only afford the one, and we weren't to moan when we only got a little bit. It was the best she could do. We all asked her at the same time if we could pick the bone, she said there would be nothing left on it by the time she had finished with it. We played out for a while after dinner but we were all still tired. Mam said we should have an early night as we all needed it. She picked up the old clock and we all went to bed and we were soon asleep. We were all woken up with piercing screams. We all jumped out of bed, and as we opened the bedroom door, granddad's door opened. He was trying to fasten his trousers and he was in his bare feet. He told the boys to put their trousers on. We were asking him what was going on when we heard another scream. We all ran to the kitchen and there was dad, thumping hell out of mam, all her face was covered in blood and so were her hands. He was shouting at her, "What right did you have to go looking for me at my fathers, telling him you didn't get your logs?" Then he gave her another thump.

Granddad started shouting at him, "Take your hands off her; you big lazy lump of shit; you're not fit to call yourself a man. She was out there all day sawing logs and so were your children. You sold the logs that were to keep your children warm. What sort of a man would do that to his children?" Dad let go of mam. She made for the back door, and the boys were with her. Dad was shouting at granddad now, "Who do you think you are talking to you Protestant Bastard?" Dad was making for the back door, Mam and the boys ran out, but he didn't go after them, he just put his hand outside the back door and picked up the big axe. Granddad said to me, "Come on run", we ran down the hall and out the front door. When we got on the road granddad took my hand, he told me I had to run as fast as I could. We ran down past Aunt Fanny's until we got to the turning for Ard Na Greine, and ran behind Mrs White's hedge, who was the dancing teacher. We went right up to the corner of her window, so that the hedge hid us. Granddad told me to be very quiet. There was a street light just outside and my dad was standing under it. We couldn't see him but we could see the head of the axe shining under the light. He must have been walking backwards and forwards because you could see the head of the axe moving up and down.

He started shouting again, "I'm going to get you, and when I do, I'm going to split you down the middle, and that little bitch that's with you." When I heard this, I wet myself; I was just about to scream when granddad put his hand over my mouth. Dad stood there for a good while and to me it seemed like hours. He started to move back up the road. We could tell with the top of the axe moving away. Granddad took his hand away from my mouth and told me to be quiet. I whispered to him that I had wet myself. "Is it any wonder?" he said and told me I wasn't to worry about it. I asked him if we could go; I was all wet and cold I only had my pants and vest on, and granddad only had his vest and trousers on. He said we would have to wait a while because we could still hear him shouting. We seemed to be waiting for ever and I was getting colder. The mist was coming off the hedge and we were both soaked. Granddad was rolling up the legs of his trousers because they were so wet.

Everything went quiet and Granddad said, "Right; I can't hear anything. We can go now". He told me we had to keep in the shadows as much as we could, as we got near our house we could see one of the boys on top of the cowshed beckoning to us, I didn't know which one it was. We crept past our house and made for the cowshed, I couldn't stop shivering. Mam took my pants and vest off and wrapped a blanket round me. Martin came over to me and put his arm around me, he was saying he had kept watch over the gate when dad was chasing us. I told mam he wouldn't catch you because he kept stumbling all over the place. They went in the house and got all the clothes and blankets out, Mam had lit a little bit of a candle. She said she couldn't light a fire, as someone would see the smoke. I told mam that I had wet myself. It seemed to be bothering me, but she told me not to worry about it. Granddad had put some clothes on but he was still shivering, he wrapped his blanket around himself, I got into it with him and snuggled in to him. He asked mam what time it was, and she replied it was half past two, and then he said well so much for the early night.

We all trailed across the road about six o'clock that morning carrying our blankets. Mam lit the fire, and when it got going she put the kettle on. When it boiled she made us all a mug of tea. The hot water that was left in the kettle, she poured into a bowl in the sink, then she put the kettle back on again, she said one of us could be getting washed. Granddad told her to see to herself first. All the blood on her hands and face had dried; she said it wasn't as bad as it looked. Her nose had been bleeding and it was a bit swollen. She had a cut at the side of her ear, and one on her lip. She said she had put her hands up to her face, to protect herself and that's why her hands were all blood, but her arms were covered in bruises. She looked a lot better when she got herself cleaned up. We all got washed and felt a bit better, Mam was going to keep me off school that day but I begged her to let me go, I didn't want to be in the same house as my dad as I couldn't bear to look at him.

All our friends in the street and surrounding area with Cousin Joan (first left) me (second left) and Martin in the middle at the back!

Uncle Miko (my dads brother) and Aunt Chrissie.

Chapter 8:
Where is my doll?

I went to school Tuesday and Wednesday. Thursday morning I wasn't feeling well but I went, and was sent home from school that morning. I was shivering one minute and burning up the next and Mam took me to see Doctor Bugler. He said I had a high temperature and needed to be kept warm and drink plenty of liquids. Mam told him I was having bad nightmare and about all that had gone on Monday night. He said it was no wonder I was having nightmares. "Can't the guard's do anything about it?" he asked. "They just say it's a domestic row," she replied. Doctor Bugler told mam to take me home and put me to bed.

We got home and she put me to bed. I was asking for my granddad but she told me granddad was in bed because he was sick as well, but he wouldn't see a Doctor. I had another nightmare that night. My dad was standing over me with the axe and he was going to split me down the middle. Then I woke up and started to scream. I remember feeling myself to see if I was in one piece or two halves. Next thing I remember was mam lifting me back in the bed. She said I was halfway out the window and I was shouting, I had to run, but I couldn't remember going to the window. I was very frightened and I wanted to go to my granddad. Mam knocked at his door and went in. "What's up with the wee lassie?" he asked. Mam told him and he said, "Bring her in to me". As I lay there beside him I felt safe.

Mam came in next morning and said Doctor Bugler was doing his rounds. She had seen his bike half way up the road. Granddad got out of bed; in no way was he going to see a Doctor! The doctor was examining me and my temperature had gone down a bit, and then he was giving me some horrible medicine. Mam was telling him about last night, me trying to climb out the window. He said there was nothing he could do about my nightmares and that I would always have a problem. He told mam she would have to try and get me in somewhere when dad started again. "She isn't very strong you know. You nearly lost her a few years ago." He told mam he would be back on Monday. When he had gone granddad got back into bed and we both fell asleep.

Chapter 8: Where is my doll?

When I got better mam took me down to my aunt Fannies and she told her what the doctor had said. She asked my aunt if she would take me in if he started again. Mam told her she wouldn't wake them up in the middle of the night, but if it was around eleven, would that be all right. My aunt said of course she would. She said, "I didn't know things were as bad as that". So that was me, sorted out for a while. I went home and picked some Michaelmas daisies out of our little front garden and put them on my altar and prayed for help. My dad behaved himself for about three weeks. His father had a long talk with him and told him he had to look after his family. When he got his dole money he was giving it to mam instead of going to the pub. The forth week he didn't come home when he got his money. Mam was pacing up and down the kitchen. The boys were out and granddad had gone for his walk. Mam was looking at the clock every five minutes and it was nearly half past eight now. Just after that we heard a noise in the back yard and then the door burst open, he stumbled in cursing and swearing and he started throwing things about. Mam told me to run, "Go to aunt Fannies; tell her I need help." I ran as fast as I could.

When I got to my aunts I was shaking, I shouted to her; "Mam needs help!" My aunt told me to sit down and said she wouldn't be a minute. I could hear shouting up the stairs to her son Flanchie. She was saying, "Could you go up to Muriel's and give her a hand? He is at it again, and she's by herself." I heard Flanchie run down the stairs and out the front door. Flanchie was my cousin but he was a grown man. He had been to our house lots of times to help my mam, He would even go up and talk to dad when he was sober, and try and make him see sense, but it didn't do any good. My aunt came back in the room and I asked her if I was to go home now. She said, "No, you will be staying with me tonight. Look at the state of you shaking like a jelly." She went into the kitchen and made me a cup of tea and a biscuit. She was trying to make me feel at ease. She opened a packet of five woodbines and took one out and said, "I like a smoke every now and then". She got up and opened up the airing cupboard and lifted some of the linen up and put the remainder of the woodbines in between them. She was smiling at me and said, "If you have anything to hide from the men, then that's the best place to hide it. They would never think of looking there so that's our little secret. You won't tell anyone, will you?" I smiled and said, "No! I won't". I was honoured she was sharing her secret with me, but I told her we didn't have an airing cupboard. Then she said, "It's only a few weeks to Christmas. What do you think Santa will bring you?" I told her I didn't believe in Santa, "My brothers told me there wasn't a Santa when I was six, and I was glad they did because when we didn't get any presents I couldn't understand why Santa was leaving us out. But now I know why." My aunt said, "Oh you poor little thing".

My cousin Joan came in and my aunt told her I would be sleeping with her tonight. Joan asked what was wrong, my aunt told her, and Joan went up to bed. My aunt said she would bring me up in a minute. I asked my aunt if I could sleep on the chair, she said, "What for, there's a nice warm bed up stairs". I told her that I was frightened to go up stairs because if my dad came after me I wouldn't be able to run. He would be able to catch me on the stairs. She said, "Listen to me child, if Massy Burns comes here he won't get a foot inside this door. I promise you, so come on; up to bed!" I followed her upstairs and got into bed with Joan.

I woke Joan up in the middle of the night screaming my head off. I was having another nightmare. I could hear Joan shouting for her mam, but it sounded far away. The next thing I knew my aunt was putting me back in bed. Apparently I was on my way out of the window. My aunt locked the window, Joan cuddled me and I went off to sleep again. My mam came for me next morning. My aunt was telling her what had happened. "God in heaven if she had gone another few inches she would have hit that concrete down below. It's a good job I got to her on time". Mam said she was sorry for all the upset. My aunt said next time she comes I will make sure the windows are locked. I stayed at my aunts a couple more times before Christmas and the nightmares continued.

On Christmas Eve morning Martin and I were in the kitchen. Mam had gone up to town shopping. Martin said he had something to show me. He said, it was a secret but before he showed me I had to cross my heart and hope to die if I told anyone. I did as he told me. I asked him what he was going to show me. He opened the doors of the sideboard and on the top shelf there was a big rag doll it was nearly as big as me. I stood there with my mouth open I couldn't believe it. Martin said it had come in the post from England. "Look down there," he said. I looked at the bottom of the cupboard and there were games and packs of cards. Martin said, "They must be for Ray and me." He was talking that fast I had a job keeping up with what he was saying. He said, "And do you know something else? Uncle Bert sent mam a postal-order for a pound and one for granddad for ten-shillings. That's why mam had gone up the town to buy some food. And mam told granddad that the money was a blessing."

I got my doll next morning and I had to pretend it was a big surprise. It wasn't as big when it was out of the cupboard, but it was big enough. I was thinking of a name for the doll, but I kept changing it every five minutes. After dinner dad kept asking mam for a couple of bob, but she kept telling him she didn't have any money. He was saying, "Well where did you get the money for the shopping yesterday?" She said, "My brother sent me a pound for Christmas and I spent every penny of it on food". In the end he gave up and went in the bedroom sulking. Mam said she was going for a little walk to get some fresh air. And the boys were out somewhere. There was only granddad and I left in the house. I was sitting on his knee and the doll was sitting on mine and I asked him would he sing me a song. Granddad knew lots of songs but he would only sing when there was just the two of us. He said, "I will sing you one song and then I am going for a lay down", he started singing daisy give me your answer do, In the middle of the song I said, "That's it", Granddad stopped singing, I said, "That's what I am going to call my doll. Daisy!" I said, "Look at her skirt and bonnet; they have daisy's on". Granddad said, "Could I go and lay down now?" I asked him if he would sing it once more, for daisy and me, and he did.

The next day was St Stephens's day, which is known as Boxing Day. All the children got dressed up and went round all the doors singing this song called the wren the wren the king of the birds St Stevens day we are up with the birds and so on. I had learnt all the words of the song off by heart. The boys were just about ready to go out. I asked mam if I could go with them, but she said no as it was begging. I said but Ray and Martin are going out. She said that was different as they were boys. She said we could go in our bedroom and watch them out of the window, but we would have to hide behind the curtain and it would have to be not moving or they would know there was someone in and we didn't have any pennies to give them. She told me to take my doll in the kitchen because she didn't want the dolls head to be bobbing up and down. I sat the doll on a chair and I went back to the bedroom, there was lots of children coming to our door singing the wren the wren the king of the birds, but they got no answer then they would curse a bit and went off to the next door.

My dad came in the room and asked what we were doing. Mam told him we were watching the wren boys. Then he was asking her again have you got a couple of bob, I know you have something stashed away somewhere. She said, "I told you yesterday I have no money. I can't even open the door to the wren boys because I have nothing to give them." With that Ray and Martin came in the front door, they both started counting their money that they had made. Martin had made one and three pence and he gave mam a shilling and kept the rest, Ray had just finished counting his, he had one and sixpence. Dad took the money out of Rays hand and said, "That will do me nicely" and left the room and up the hall, we heard the back door bang and he was gone. We all looked at each other; Martin looked at the three pence in his hand and said, "We will share it. We can have a penny each." I asked Martin if he would take me out to see the wren boys just for a little while. We went up our road to Captain Mack's Corner but there was none around. We went up the Clare Road but we didn't see many wren boys. They were all going home.

We turned into the gateway to the backs of the houses, Martin and I were singing the wren boys song, so I was happy I hadn't learnt it for nothing. We met mam on the back lane. She had been visiting a friend. When we got to our back gate, it was open and so was the back door. Mam followed us in. she said "Did you leave the back door open? The kitchen will be freezing even though I was only gone for a couple of minutes." We went in and took our coats off. I went to get my doll and it was missing. I asked mam where she had put it, but she hadn't touched it. "It was sitting on this chair," I said. Mam said. "Well, if it was it would be their now. You must have taken it with you when you went out and left it somewhere." "I didn't take it out, did I Martin?" He said I hadn't. I asked granddad and Ray if they had seen it, they said no. Mam said, "You will have put it down somewhere, it will turn up", but it didn't turn up.

Next day I kept on at mam about the doll, but Mam had had enough, she snapped at me and said, "Touser Malone has eaten it!" I burst into tears. I couldn't believe that Touser Malone would do that to me. I would never be his friend again. I went out the back lane and sat on the rock, and Touser Malone was sitting outside his gate. He was eating something and I saw him swallow it, and then he came across to me. I told him I didn't want to talk to him because he had eaten my doll. He was looking up at me with those big sad eyes, but I told him to go away. I got down off the rock and he came back to me, I made him open his mouth and I looked in to see if I could see any bits of the doll, but there was nothing there. Then I felt his tummy, but it didn't feel hard. I couldn't understand how he could eat a big doll like that! I told him to go as I didn't want to be friends any more. He went slowly to his gate and flopped down.

A few days later I was out in the back lane and Touser Malone didn't even bother to come near me. I felt sad then because I missed talking to him as I used to tell him all my secrets. I went into the back yard. When I got near the back door it was open a little bit, I could hear mam and dad arguing. Mam was saying to him, "Don't lie to me, the woman told me her husband had bought a rag doll cheap in the pub on Boxing Day and you must have picked it up on your way out after you took the money off Ray. How could you do that to your own little girl?" The back door opened and he must have had his hand on the latch all the time. He dashed past me and up the garden path. I went back to the lane to see Touser Malone and I told him I was sorry for blaming him and could we be friends again. Mam told me a couple of years later about the doll, and I told her I already knew. I don't think I was meant to have a doll.

Chapter 9: Granddad Goes to Cork

New Years Eve came along and we all liked that night as we were allowed to stay up late. My Granda Burns would go around all his children's houses after the bells to drink to their health and wish them a Happy New Year. I remember mam being in a bad state because she didn't have the money to get the bottle of stout for him coming. In the end it was granddad that went out and bought one. He put it on the kitchen table and told mam that was for Granda Burns. She was very grateful to him.

When my Granda Burns came we were all standing behind the kitchen table, while this little bottle of stout looked lost on the big table. He drank the stout and wished us all a Happy New Year then he went. Dad saw him to the front gate, then he came back in the house and he went out the back door. We knew we wouldn't see him again until tomorrow after noon. That's why New Years Eve was so special, as there would be no arguing or fighting that night, and we could all relax. I asked granddad if he would sing a song. He didn't like singing in front of the others, but that night he did it for me. He sang Sweet Rosy O' Grady and we all joined in, followed by Silver Threads among the Gold. Then he would put his fists, one in front of the other and blow into them and it sounded like he was playing a bugle. Ray and Martin had combs with paper over them and they played along with him. This went on for hours and I will never forget that New Year's Eve.

A few weeks after the New Year, when I got home from school, there in the kitchen sat a beautiful new sewing machine. It was one you worked with your feet so you could have both hands free to do the sewing. It had a smell of oil and the wood was all shinny and new. Mam looked very pleased with herself, I asked her where it had come from, She said she had seen an advert in the newspaper and it said you could have a sewing machine on trial for two weeks, and if you didn't want it after that, you could return it and not have to pay as it was only on trial. She said she was going to town tomorrow to see if she could get some material on credit and make clothes up in different sizes and sell them. She could make a lot of things in two weeks. She got a couple of pieces of old cloth and said I could make some hankies. It took me a while to get used to the treadle on the machine, but I managed it with mam's help and made my first hankies. I was very proud of them. I asked if I could make some more but she said she had to make our dinner now but we could have another go later on. Mam gave us our dinner, but Dad hadn't come home for his, and so she put it in the oven.

The boys went out to play, and granddad went for his walk about seven O' Clock. Mam went over to the machine. It had singer wrote on it in gold letters, I asked her what it meant. She told me it was the make of the machine and it was one of the best ones you could get. Mam tried so hard to make some money to keep us. I wished I had the money to buy the sewing machine for her so she wouldn't have to send it back. She sat down and started mending holes in the boy's trouser pockets. The boys always had holes in their pockets it was all the rubbish they would stuff in them. The back door opened and dad came in. Mam didn't hear him because she had her back to the door and with the noise of the sewing machine. I looked at him. His tuft of hair was down but he wasn't swearing or anything. In fact he never said a word. I looked down at what mam was doing. My hands were on the sewing machine. Next thing I knew there was this terrible bang. I could feel the machine vibrate under my hands so I moved them off as quickly as I could. My dad had the big axe, and he had brought it down about an inch from mam's arm. She jumped up off the chair as the axe came down again; if she hadn't moved so quickly I think she would have lost her arm. Now she was trying to get him away from the machine but it was too late all the beautiful wood was broken and the machine itself had all big dents on it. I was screaming my head off and Mam shouted to me to go and get Mr Riedy. I ran out the front door and banged on the Riedy's door. Mrs Riedy opened the door and took me in; I didn't have to say anything as they had heard all the banging and they were ready to go out the back door to our house.

Mr Riedy went first and his daughter Maude who was as big as him went after him. She was calling dad all the names under the sun, and Mrs Riedy told me to sit down. She was a small frail woman and she got ill a lot. When she was in bed ill I would go into her bedroom and kneel by her bed and pray for her. Her bedroom was like walking into heaven. She had a beautiful altar and lovely big Holy Statues. She would pat me on the head and tell me I was a good girl. Then a few days later I would see her in the back lane and I would think it was me that made her better with my prayers. Mr Riedy and Maude seemed to be gone a long time and I was worried about my mother. Mrs Riedy said she would go and see what was going on, but told me to stay where I was and drink my tea and eat my biscuit. She was gone about ten minutes. When she came back in she told me not to worry about my mother as she was alright. She had my school clothes and my coat in her hands. She told me I was to go to aunt Fannies and I was to go to school from there. I went down the road to my aunts looking behind me all the time in case dad was coming after me with the axe. After school next day I went straight home and into the kitchen, Mam was sitting by the table and her eyes were all swollen from crying. She looked as though she had given up, and I felt so sorry for her. There was no trace of the sewing machine. I don't know to this day what happened to it or if she had to pay for it or not.

It was my Birthday and I was eight years old, I got two satin ribbons wrapped in tissue paper one pink and one blue, and I was over the moon with them as they were my favourite colours. My dad carried on as usual, and we spent a couple of nights over in the cowshed because it was too late to take me to my aunts. I had stayed a couple of nights with my aunt as well. I think my Granda Burns heard all that was going on, as he sent for my dad. When my dad came home he had the money to go to England. I don't think he went to England because someone had told mam they had seen him in some town in Ireland, but I can't remember where. Mam didn't seem to care where he was as long as he didn't come home. Mam and granddad were discussing what they could do to make some money. Granddad came up with the idea to sell tripe and black pudding because he was a Butcher by trade. They would go to the slaughterhouse and get the inner lining of the beasts stomach delivered to the house and it would the whole kitchen table. They would scrub and scrub it for ages, and the sweat would be pouring off them. Then they would rinse the stomach with cold water. I used to go to the slaughterhouse with granddad and Ray for buckets of blood. Granddad would bleed the pig into a bucket and Ray had to keep stirring it all the time because it was still warm and would go lumpy if you didn't. When we got home Ray and Martin had to wash all the guts out and turn them inside out to get all the mucus off them and then wash them again. The boys hated that job. My job was to keep stirring the bucket of blood while mam put in the bits of fat and whatever else she put in it. When it was all ready mam would wrap her orders in greaseproof paper and Martin and I would deliver them and collect the money.

They got to know me quite well at the slaughterhouse, and one day when we were leaving with the blood, one of the men came over to me and gave me a bit of sacking with something in it tied up with string. He said "There you are little girl. That's a present for your mammy". I asked granddad what he thought it was. He said you would have to wait and see. When we stopped on the path at the top of the garden to rest their hands, I couldn't wait any longer. I untied the string and there looking out at me was a sheep's head, I made some sort of sound, and Granddad asked me what was wrong. I told him it was a sheep's head. Granddad and Ray were laughing and he said, "Well it would be a change from tripe!" I went with them a few more times. The weather was getting warmer and the smell in the slaughterhouse was awful, so I thought I would just stick to my deliveries and stir my bucket of blood at home, as it smelt a lot nicer.

The tripe and black pudding business lasted until the end of May, The weather was warmer, and people didn't want it any more, and the ones I delivered too kept saying "Tell your mammy I will pay her next week", so they decided to give it up. Granddad said it was better to break even than get in debt, so that was the end of that. The boys were very pleased. Granddad told mam he had applied for a job in Co Cork, working for a Bishop for three months, as the man that worked for him was ill. He said it wasn't much money but it would be one less for her to feed in the house and he would try to send her a few shillings every now and again. The Bishop wanted whoever got the job to start right away. Mam told him not to be silly, "No one is going to employ you at your age—you are sixty-eight years old!" He said we would wait and see. I didn't worry about it that much because mam had said he was too old.

Sunday came and the Sunday matinee was on at the cinema, I had been last week and it had finished at a very exciting part, but you had to go back the following week to find out what happened. I was desperate to go but I needed four pence. I kept asking mam for the money, but she said she didn't have it and if I asked her once more she was going to slap me. I went over to granddad who said "It's no good asking me, as I have no money." I went out into the back lane, and Touser Malone was sitting outside the gate. I went over to him and I was telling him all about it. The two ladies that dressed in black that Ray said were witches were pottering about in their yard and I was keeping my eye on them. There was a lovely tree nearly opposite their house the ground there was nice and soft with thick grass, so I got on my knees and joined my hands together closed my eyes and I prayed for the four pence. I heard a little thump and then another, I opened my eyes and looked down in front of me there was two pennies. I looked up at the tree and there was another one coming out of the tree and then another one, and there was four pennies. I felt frightened and excited at the same time, and I blessed myself and said thank you! Then I was running up and down the back lane shouting, "There's been a miracle!" I told some of the children what had happened and the news spread like wild fire. Now there were about ten children praying under the tree. I ran into our kitchen and I was telling mam and granddad there had been a miracle and showed them the four pennies. She said, "Were did you get that money from?" I told her it had come from heaven. She told me to stop telling lies. "Show me where you got the money from," she said. I took her into the back lane, and Mam couldn't believe her eyes when she seen all the children praying under the tree. She asked me again where the money had come from, and I told her out off the tree. The two old ladies in black, who were standing inside their gate, said something to mam and went in their back door. I asked mam if I could keep the money because it was me who had prayed for it. She said I could, and went back in our house with a little smile on her face.

My granddad's letter came on Monday morning before I went to school. I took it into his room and I was joking with him as I thought it would soften the blow when he didn't get the job. I said, "Are you, W.J.Hegan?" He looked at me and said, "I am!" I gave him the letter and I stayed there while he read it. He said, "Well that's it. I got the job, and they have sent me a ticket. I leave tomorrow for Cork". My face dropped and I ran into the kitchen and told mam he had got the job. "But you said he would be too old!" "Well, I thought he would be, but it's only for three months." That seemed a lifetime to me without my granddad. He left next day. He told me to be good for mam and he would bring me a present back.

Chapter 10:
Dad Returns

My dad came home the following week and it was Saturday. He was half drunk. He threw his bag in the bedroom and told mam he couldn't get much work in England. Mam said, "From what I heard you didn't go to England! I was told you were in Ireland and not so very far away! So what would your father say if he knew that after he gave you your fare?" Even I knew she had said the wrong thing and now she knew she had. Dad got hold of her hair and he was dragging her into the bedroom backwards. Her feet kept missing the floor and all the weight was on her hair, and she was crying out with pain. He threw her on the bed; tore the top of her dress away and lifted the bottom of her dress over her head. I had followed them in the bedroom, and I was crying and I didn't know what to do. Dad told me to get out and shut the door.

I stood in the kitchen and I could hear her cries. She kept saying, "No-Massy-no!" and then she screamed. I heard the sound of a very hard slap and then there was silence. I didn't know what to do. I thought about going for Mr Riedy but it was so quiet now I thought I better not. I seemed to be in the kitchen for ages, and then I heard dad snoring and the bedroom door opened and mam came out. She looked awful and there was a big red mark down the side of her face, she had a vacant look on her face again. She put a chair against the door leading to the hall and she told me to stand against the back door and not to let anyone in. She put some water in a bowl and got the washing soap and a scrubbing brush. She wet all her body with a cloth, got the scrubbing brush, put some soap on it and started scrubbing herself. It was making all red lines on her skin. She started on the bottom half of her body and was doing the same thing, and making awful noises in her throat but kept shuddering. I got frightened and started to cry. I went over to her and told her, "Stop it! You have red scratches all over you." She told me to go back to the door. She put the brush down and wiped all her body with a cloth; put some more clothes on and told me to go out and play. I stayed at the front of the house.

Ray and Martin came up the road they were carrying wood for the fire from down the crags. Rays friend called him from up the road and asked him if he was coming out. Ray said he would be there in a minute as he was just going to drop the wood off. When they got up to me I told them dad was home. They both said at the same time "Oh no", and went in the house with the wood. Ray came out first and ran up the road to his friend. Then Martin came out; he said mam had told him to get out and play. He asked me was she in a bad mood and then he said she had lots of scratches on her arm as though she had walked through the blackberry bushes. I told Martin the story from dad walking in the house to mam scrubbing her with the scrubbing brush. He said "My god that was rape! That's a very bad thing". I asked him what rape was. He said, "I told you, it's a very very bad thing".

We got ready for mass next morning, Mam was trying to comb her hair and you could see the pain in her face. After mass all the men would go across the road and stand together and they would be talking and laughing. It happened every Sunday and I don't know why they did that, but all the women would make their way home and leave them all standing there. I could see my dad in the middle of them laughing and carrying on with this other man. I thought to myself he should be in church praying for forgiveness for what he had done to mam yesterday. We had our dinner dad hadn't come home for his; Mam put it in the oven.

It was a lovely day so we were all sat on the front step but mam kept her coat on. She was talking to Mrs Riedy's three daughters, Ninie, Maude, and Nan and they were saying that she didn't look herself today asking if there anything wrong. She said she was all right. Ninie & Nan went back in the house, and Maude was still talking to mam. She said "Look, I know there's something wrong with you." Mam said she couldn't talk here. Maude suggested going for a walk up The Rocky Road, "We could take the children and they would love it and we can talk," she suggested. We all set off for The Rocky Road which was a child's paradise. There was a little bridge to cross and a stream with rocks everywhere of all shapes and sizes. You could play all sorts of games. There was a good few people there having picnics and it was where all the courting couples went. Mam and Maude were sat on a big rock and I heard Maude say, "The Bastard I'll kill him". Mam started to cry and Maude was trying to comfort her, Mam said "Please don't say anything because he will take it out of me!" Maude saw me she said, "Get away and play with the others", so I didn't hear any more of the conversation. We all had a lovely afternoon and didn't want to go home.

The next week the ragman came round with his horse and cart. He had all different coloured balloons and would give you a balloon for a few rags; but if you had a big bundle he would give you a whip and top. Next thing, Martin came running out of our gate with a big bundle of rags and gave them to the man. He gave Martin a whip and top. Ray went closer to see what Martin had given him. He saw mam's coat and some of our things as well. Mam came out to see what was going on. Ray told her Martin had given the ragman her coat. "Oh my god," she said, "You can't have that; it's the only one I have". Mam argued with him but it was no good he wouldn't listen to her. Mam sent for Martin and he didn't know what all the fuss was about. "But mam your always saying you will have to get yourself a new coat," he said. "That was just a figure of speech." she said. "I have been saying that for years." Poor mam she couldn't win. Mam told us she would have to try and get a job. She applied for a few but had no luck. I think it was because she was married with three children. Married women didn't go out to work. She said she would give it one more try and she applied to Shannon airport for a job in the linen room. She got a letter back to say she was to go for an interview.

She took me to Limerick the day before her interview where we were to stay with my aunt May overnight. She had gone a day early in case my dad beat her up the night before and she couldn't go for the interview with bruises on her. She set off early next morning to go from Limerick to Shannon. She had borrowed my aunt's short jacket because she hadn't one of her own. She looked very nice and it was a beautiful day; we all wished her well and hoped she got the job. Later my cousin Thomas asked me if I wanted to go and have a look around the shops in Limerick. He was a couple of years older than me. Aunt May told him to look after me because Limerick was very busy; not like Ennis. We only seemed to be walking for a few minutes and we were there. Thomas said he was going to show me one of the biggest shops I have ever seen. We went into this shop and I couldn't believe my eyes. Everything looked shiny and new and it was huge. I could have stayed in there all day. We went to the jewellery counter and all the rings bracelets and necklaces were sparkling. Thomas bought me a bracelet. It had little blue flowers on it and it stretched to fit anyone. It cost him sixpence and I thought I was the luckiest girl in the world. I couldn't wait to tell my friends about this shop. I asked Thomas what the shop was called and he said, "Woolworth's."

Mam came back from her interview; she told us she had got the job on condition she had a smallpox injection. It was something to do with working at the airport. Mam said thank you to aunt May and we would have to go now or we would miss the bus and she hoped to see them again soon. I was told on the bus going home that I wasn't to say anything about the job until it was all settled. I asked her what I had to say to dad if he asked me where we had been. Just tell him we went to see aunt May and she talked us into staying the night. We got off the bus in town and went to Doctor Bugler's surgery to make an appointment for mam to get her injection. They said she could get it done tomorrow. Next we went to Aunt Fanny's to get the boy's. She said they were up at the house and Massy was going mad. I told him you had gone to see his sister in Limerick and you decided to stay overnight. Mam thanked my aunt and we went up the road to our house. There was only the boy's in, and they both started talking at the same time. "Dad is going mad! He is in a terrible temper and has been throwing things everywhere. We have just been cleaning the place up." "You didn't tell him I was going for a job did you?" They said, "No we told him you had gone to see aunt May. He left the house about half an hour ago." She asked them if he was drunk and they said, "No. Just in a very bad mood."

He was drunk by the time he got home that night. It was about eleven o'clock when he came in. He looked at mam and said, "I heard you were back." Then he started punching her and pulling her hair, He kept saying "Who did you spend the night with you whore, you better tell me because I will find out". He grabbed hold of me and he kept asking "Where was your mam?" I kept telling him we were at aunt May's. He dragged me across the kitchen to mam, and said "She's got you telling lies for her now, hasn't she," I told him again we were at aunt May's. Mam got hold of him and said "Take your hands off her now!" He let go of me and turned to mam, "Who do you think you are? Telling me what to do." He grabbed her again. She called to the boys to take me to my aunts, "Run. Go on, run." The boys left me at my aunts and ran back up the road to get help. My aunt said she thought there would be trouble tonight.

She took me upstairs. Joan was asleep but as soon as I got in the bed. She woke up. I was cold, but it wasn't outside. I was sobbing, and Joan said, "Come on. Cuddle in and we will soon have you warm." She asked her mam to make sure the window was locked. Mam went for her injection next day and I went with her, normally she wouldn't have gone out with a black eye and a swollen mouth but she was determined she was going to get a job. Doctor Bugler looked at her and he was shaking his head and he said not again. He had a look at her eye and mouth. He asked her if she was alright to have this injection today. He could leave it a few days until she felt better. She said she would rather it be done today. When we got home dad was in he and asked her where she had been. She told him she had been to see the doctor because she wasn't feeling well. He looked at me, "Did you go with her?", and I told him I did. Mam couldn't go anywhere or talk to anyone, even women because he was so jealous. I don't know how she was going to go out to work with him being like that.

Now she asked him for some money, as she had no food in the house. She had enough flour to make one loaf of bread and that was all. He said, "You should have thought of that before you spent money going to limerick!" She replied, "You must have got your money this week. It's to feed the children," and he just walked out and up the garden path. Mam made the bread and told us we had to use it sparingly, we had bread and dripping for our dinner. About eight o'clock that night mam was burning up and feeling dizzy. I went next door to tell Mrs Riedy. Maude was there; and said she would come and have a look at her. She asked where dad was. I said he was out. Maude had a look at her and said she needed to be in bed. She asked me which room was granddad's. I showed her and she started to strip the bed and then she said she would be back in a minute. She came back in with the whitest sheets and pillowcases I have ever seen and a stone bottle. She made the bed and put the bottle in and said she would wait ten minutes for the bed to air. Mam was saying something to her about the children but she told her not to worry. Maude asked us if she was like this after she was beaten up last night. I told her no it was since she had the injection for smallpox. Maude got her into bed and settled her down. She told us if she was like this in the morning we were to get the doctor in. She had to go to work in the morning but she would call after work. When your dad comes in tell him we had to put her in granddad's room because she has a fever and if he goes near her he might catch it. That would keep him away from her. We told him when he came in and he didn't even bother to go and look at her.

When we got up next morning we went in to see mam. She was shaking her head from side to side and was rambling on about things we couldn't understand. We went into the kitchen and dad was there. We told him we should get the Doctor. He said, "She's alright. I just put my head in the door and she was asleep. That's all she needs, is a good sleep." Ray asked him for some money for food. He said he didn't have any, and told us to go and ask mam. Ray told him she didn't have any. He said, "She will have some stashed away somewhere," and he went out the door. Ray said he was going to get the Doctor no matter what he says. The Doctor came later on that morning when he was doing his rounds. The three of us were standing at the side of her bed. "Now if you stand back, I will take a look at her." He said. After he'd finished he turned to us and asked, "Where's your father?" we all said at the same time, "Out!" The Doctor was talking to Ray, "Now it'll be the injection she had yesterday. Some people get a bad reaction and other people are fine. Your mam is one of the unlucky ones." He told Ray to keep her warm and make sure she drinks plenty of fluids, and by tomorrow you can try her with a bit of solid food. He said if she was no better to call him. We hung on for as long as we could before we had our tea, but by about four o'clock we couldn't wait any loner. Ray told Martin to get the tea ready as he was going to see mam and try to get some water down her. Martin shouted, "Tea's ready!" Ray came back in the kitchen and said mam seemed to have cooled down a bit. He walked over to the table and looked at the bread, "What have you done? Didn't mam tell us to use the bread sparingly and look at all the dripping on it? Scrape some of that off and put it back in the dish." Martin replied, "What for? We have no bread left to put it on!" Ray said "We would have if you hadn't cut a half loaf into three slices!" They carried on arguing so I started eating mine in case they took it off me. Oh how I wished my granddad were here.

Maude came in after work and she went straight in to look at mam. She asked us if we got the Doctor in and we told her we did and what he said. "And have you been giving her drinks of water?" she asked. Ray told her he had. She said she had cooled down a lot and she should be a lot better tomorrow. She asked us if we had our tea and we said we had. As she was leaving she said, "I will call in tomorrow after work." There was nothing more we could do so we all went to bed early.

Dad hadn't come home, but when we got up next morning he was in the kitchen. He was looking for the bread and Ray told him there was none. He said, "I told you yesterday we have no money to buy food." He said he would get some money this afternoon and he would buy some and went out. We went in to see mam and she looked very white. The only colour you could see was the bruising on her eye and mouth. She looked at us and asked if we were all right and asked how long she had been in bed. We told her two days and that Maude had been in to see to her. We asked her how she was feeling. She said she felt very weak and that her arm was sore and asked us if dad had given us some money for food. We said no; but he was going to bring some home this afternoon. She dropped off to sleep again, so we went back in the kitchen.

We waited for hours for dad coming back with something too eat but he never came. We went back to mam and told her we were hungry. In the end she told us to go to uncle Miko's house and see Aunt Chris. She always had lots of bread and other stuff in. She told Ray he was to go and ask. Tell her you're mam's in bed ill and that you are all hungry. We were surprised at mam sending us to ask for food as she was a very proud woman and never asked anyone for anything. We went up through the back gardens and when we got to the house, we stood behind some gooseberry bushes waiting for Ray to go in, but he said he didn't want to go. He said "Martin; you go, you have a gift of the gab!" Martin said he wasn't going and they both looked at me. I said "No! Mam told Ray to ask." Ray said, "It would be better if you went, you are a little girl and you look hungry. She will feel sorry for you." They both pushed me towards the door. I knocked on the door and my aunt opened it, "Oh hello," she said, "Come in." My aunt had visitors, the table was laid with a china tea set and I could smell the tea. There was a plate of sandwiches cut into quarters and a cake stand that had scones on the bottom plate and cakes on the top one, my tummy was rumbling and I was sure everyone could hear it. My aunt said, "Have you just come to see me?" I said "No, my mam sent me. She is in bed ill and my dad was to bring some food home and he hasn't and we are all hungry. We haven't had anything to eat since yesterday." I could tell my aunt was embarrassed and the poor woman didn't know where to put herself. She took me to the back door and she gave me a crust of bread, she said she was sorry but that's all she had at the moment as she didn't get her shopping in until tomorrow. I will never forget that crust of bread as long as I live. It was three or four inches thick at one side and wafer thin at the other.

She had forgotten to put the bread in paper for me. I went back to the boys and they said, "Is that all you got? How is that going to feed us all?" I told them that's all she had as she doesn't get her shopping in until tomorrow. Ray said we would have to eat the gooseberries off the bushes to fill ourselves up, so that's what we did. I don't think they were ripe enough, they were very sour but we filled ourselves up with them and went back home. I put the crust of bread on the table. Ray shouted at me, "Look at the state of that bread! It's all black finger marks and it's covered with hairs off the gooseberries." Martin butted in, "We have no milk. We'll have to go and ask Mrs Riedy." We knocked at her door but there was no one in. Martin said we will have to go and ask Florrie, but she was out too. I said mam would go mad at us for begging at people's houses. Martin thought for a minute; then said, "I know! Come on." And before I knew it we were over the wall and going to the crags. "What are we going down here for?" I asked. Martin said, "We could get milk out of the goat." I said "You can't just take milk from Florrie's goat." "Yes we can, she won't mind". He told me to hold the goat's head; I refused. He said, "Well you come and milk it and I will hold its head." I tried but I only got a few squirts out, he said "Well you pick a load of grass and feed it while I milk it". He started milking it and we finished up with the mug three quarters full. We got back in the house Ray said, "Where have you two been all this time?" We told him we had to go and milk Florrie's goat because no one was in. Ray had cut all the bread into pieces; he said there were still some gooseberry hairs on it but he couldn't help that. He asked Martin if there was any sugar, He said a little bit the size of a thumbnail and Ray said it would have to do. He told Martin to put the milk and sugar in the pan; then he added the bread and boiled it all up together. He put some in a mug and took it in to mam. Ray was feeding her at first but she said she would manage it herself. Ray came back into the kitchen he said; "You better not have eaten the rest of that goodie." We told him we hadn't. "We'll go and get some spoons and we can all have a couple of spoonfuls each." We went back into mam. She said it was the best goodie she had ever tasted.

We didn't see my dad again that night and when we got up in the morning he had gone out. There was no bag of food on the table, so he had forgotten about us again. We went into see mam and she had a bit of colour today, and she asked if she could have a cup of tea. We had to tell her there was no tea, sugar or milk. She said, "I thought your aunt had given you some things? How did you make the Goodie last night?" We had to tell her about the bread, the goat and the gooseberries we had eaten and the pains we had in our stomach this morning. She said she would have to get herself moving, She tried to put her legs over the side of the bed, but she had to lie back down as she was very weak. Our lavatory seat didn't get a chance to cool down that morning; if it wasn't one of us on it, it was the other. Yesterday I was wishing we had a gooseberry bush, today I never wanted to see a gooseberry ever again. My dad came home about two o'clock that afternoon. He was drunk and in a very bad temper shouting, "Where is that lazy bitch?" He came down the hall. Martin and I were in the room with mam. He pushed us to one side he got mam by the hair and pulled her out of bed. He was shouting at her, "You lazy whore. Get up and look after your children. Having them going out begging for food." Martin and I were trying to get him off her hair, but he pushed us back against the wall. Mam's legs gave way and she was in a heap on the floor. He lifted his hand to hit her when uncle Miko walked in with Ray behind him. Uncle Miko said, "If you touch her again I'm going straight down for my father." Dad put his hand down and uncle Miko and Ray lifted mam off the floor and put her back into bed. He turned to my dad, "Now you listen to me, it's your fault your children had to come begging for food. They have been telling you for two days there was no food in the house. Your wife is ill and they have been trying to look after her. What sort of father are you? You make me sick!" Dad walked out of the room.

Uncle Miko turned to mam and said, "I am sorry about this, I met him in the town and I was so mad I had a go at him. It was me that told him about the children begging for food and Chris felt awful about it. But that was all the bread she

Chapter 10: Dad Returns

had left." He said he was going to give dad a full time job at Downes Brewery and his wages would be sent down to her. Mam thanked him for all his help. He gave Ray five shillings and told him to get some food in, then he went in the kitchen and we heard him tell dad about the job "and your wages will be sent home to your wife because I want to make sure your children are fed. Do you understand?"

Maude came in to see mam she asked her if she wanted to try and get up for an hour. She managed to get her to the kitchen and sat her down, and then she said she would be back in ten minutes. We were all happy to see mam sitting at the table. Maude came back in she had a plate with four fried eggs on it and a big plateful of bread and butter. She gave us one each and told us to help ourselves to the bread and butter. God, it tasted like heaven. We finished the lot and said thank you. Ray told Maude he had got some food this afternoon. "That's fine. You can eat that tomorrow," she replied. Maude put mam back in bed before she left. She made sure she was warm enough and gave her a cup of tea. Mam told her she didn't know what she would do without her. Florrie came up to see mam the next day. She had been talking to Maude who told her mam was ill. Florrie said, "Why didn't one of you come to the house and tell me?" Martin said, "We did but you were out, so we had to borrow some milk from your goat." He started telling Florrie the story from one end to the other including the finger marks on the bread and the hairs off the gooseberries, which mam didn't know about. Florrie burst out laughing and her whole body was shaking. She had us all laughing including mam. Martin said, "See, I told you she wouldn't mind."

Dad started work at Downes Brewery on Monday, but he seemed to be drunk all the time. Mam couldn't understand it. "They must be paying him daily," she said. Mam had written a letter to Shannon airport to explain what had happened about the injection and my granddad had sent her a Five-Shilling Postal Order. She said she would go to the Post Office and get it changed and post her letter at the same time. She was back in half an hour and she had just got in and there was a knock at the front door. Martin answered it and a man handed him an envelope and said, "For Mrs Burns." Mam nearly passed out when she opened it. It was dad's wages. She was all excited saying, she was going to pay this and buy that, and get food in for the week, when it's gone it's gone, and that was it, we would live well this week. She had got two bacon shanks while she was in town this morning and she was putting them on to boil. Mr Riedy had given her a cabbage and some potatoes out of his garden; we were going to have a great dinner tonight. She told us to watch the bacon shanks; she was going back to town.

Mam came back with enough shopping to last us all week. She finished making the dinner and served it up; we ate every scrap; then she let us pick the bones.

We had just finished when dad came in the back door and he was sober. Mam put his dinner on the table; He ate it and went in the bedroom. Mam started ironing Mrs Riedy's sheets and pillowcases that she had washed to give back to her. It took a long time with the flat iron. She had to keep putting it on the fire when it went cool to heat it up again, then she would spit on it and wipe it with a rag to make sure it wasn't to hot, When she had finished; there wasn't a crease to be seen and they looked like new. She put them on top of the sideboard and said that's another job done. Dad came out of the bedroom and asked her for same money. She gave him Half a Crown and told him she had spent the rest on food and paying things that were owed. He said "And what am I supposed to do with this?" Ray put his head in the back door and said, "Mam, Florrie wants you." She went out into the back yard. Florrie said; "I didn't know if himself was in or not. That's why I didn't come in." Mam told her he was in the kitchen. Florrie asked mam if she fancied going to Lahinch tomorrow. "With you being ill, the sea air would do you the world of good." Mam said she didn't know she would have to see. Lahinch was about twenty miles from Ennis and you had to go on the train. Florrie kept on at mam, "Come on it'll do us all good, I will pay for her," she said looking at me. "We can take a picnic, so all you have to do is scrape up enough for your fare". Mam said she had the change from the bacon shanks that she had bought out of granddad's money that he had sent. I didn't know how much it cost to go to Lahinch, but it was decided we were going.

With that Martin came dashing in the back gate nearly knocking us all down. He was trying to get something out but he was out of breath. Mam told him to calm down. When he did he said, "I have just seen dad going up the Clare Road and he had Mrs Riedy's sheets under his arm.", Mam dashed in the kitchen with us all behind her. "Oh no! Now what am I going to do?" Florrie put her arm round mam; she was telling her not to get upset and told her she would come with her to explain to Mrs Riedy. Mam thanked her but she said she would rather go on her own. "Well if that's what you want but I don't mind coming with you." Then she said "Jesus, Mary and Joseph, what sort of man is he? He would sell his soul to the devil, and don't let it stop you going tomorrow because there isn't a thing you can do about it now". Florrie left, and mam cried and cried. Later she went in to see Mrs Riedy about the sheets and pillowcases. When she came back in the house she didn't say anything. I never found out what happened or what Mrs Riedy said, but mam looked very sad.

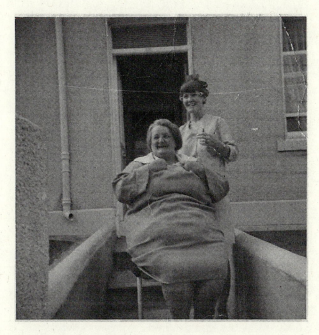

Florrie Marone with her friend Margaret Sheehan doing her hair.

Chapter 11: Florrie and the Low-flying Beachball!

Florrie had one child, a boy. He was about ten years old and was a very quiet boy and I don't think he was a very good mixer. I think he was clever though, because he seemed to study a lot. You would never believe he was Florrie's son as they were as different as chalk and cheese. He knocked at our front door and said "My mam said you have to come now as we have to be early to get a seat on the train". We went down the road to Florrie's house. She was standing outside. By the size of the bag she had you would think she was going for a week!

We all made for the train station. When we got there, the station was packed with people. I think everyone had the same idea, to get there early. When we heard the train coming, Florrie told us to get hold of the back of her coat and push. When the train came in she rushed forward dragging us with her and pushing everyone out of the way until she got to a compartment and climbed in. We all followed her and sat down. When the train pulled into Lahinch station everyone was trying to get off at the same time. Florrie told us to sit where we were as there was no rush to get off, only to get on. She took us away from the town down onto the beach next to the golf course. There were sand dunes all down one side. She started climbing up and I though she was never going to stop. She settled us down in a big hole full of sand. She said to mam, "Its better down this end because the children can't smell the food that was coming from the restaurants and other places; what they can't smell they won't want! Come on then, get your togs on and we'll all go for a dip." Ray and Martin started to laugh and Florrie said "What's wrong? Don't you like my swimsuit?" I looked up at Florrie and I couldn't believe my eyes. She had a man's vest on. The biggest I had ever seen and a big thick pair of green knickers with elastic round the knees. She took it all in good fun and we all went down to the sea laughing.

Florrie was first in the sea and the others followed. I went in up to my knees and that's as far as I would go as I was frightened of the water. I watched them all

Chapter 11: Florrie and the Low-flying Beachball!

splashing each other and then Florrie started jumping up and down. Her vest and knickers filled up with water. She looked like a giant ball with a little head on top. They were all howling with laughter. There were people walking along the beach and they all stopped to watch her and they were all laughing at the things she was doing. They all calmed down a bit and started swimming. I didn't even know mam could swim but there she was now having a race with Florrie. The boys were shouting and cheering but it was Florrie who won. As I watched I wondered why Florrie didn't sink, as she was so fat. They all walked back to where I was stood, "Come on," Florrie said, "we'll go and have our picnic."

Mam gave Ray three-pence to go and get us a pennies-worth of sea grass or periwinkles. We all decided we would have sea grass. Ray went to this woman who had a handcart just down the beach and came back with the sea grass. Mam got our bread out of her bag and we made sandwiches with the sea grass. You had to be careful in case there were shells stuck on to it. Florrie lit a little fire and got a bottle of cold tea and a small pan out of her bag. She heated it up for mam and herself. Then she told us she had a treat for us. She told us to drink some of our water, which we did. She took our bottles and poured some sort of powdered stuff in them, she told us to put the tops back on and shake the bottles. "Now you can have a drink!" she said. We all had a sip and it was lovely; it tasted lemony.

After about half an hour they were all going back in the sea, but I had got dressed. I didn't want to go; but I wasn't going to stay in this big hole on my own. Mam said, "You can come down and watch and make sand castles." They weren't as long in the water this time, as the sun had gone in and it started to get very windy. By the time they got back to the hole they were all shivering. Martin was first to get his clothes on. He was covered in sand but he put his clothes on anyway. Then they were all getting dressed except Florrie. She sat there with a towel round her and said "I'll hang on a bit longer; the sun might come back out".

We started putting our things away in the bag, and Martin was handing me his empty bottle when a ball came out of nowhere and hit him on the head and knocked him out. Mam and Florrie dashed over to him and it was a good five minutes before he came round. They were asking him if he was all right, and he was saying his head was hurting. Mam told him he'd been hit with a ball. Next thing, this man was looking down into the hole and Florrie started at him. She was stood there in her vest and knickers, pointing a finger at him and saying, "What the hell are you doing hitting a ball about where there are children?" Now she pointed at Martin, "You have just knocked him out and you're not having your ball back." The man said he was sorry the ball had hit the child, and that a doctor should check him over, to make sure he's alright. The man said we shouldn't be here and that we could be fined. Florrie butted in, "Fine my arse, it's a free country!" The man replied, "You are on the golf course, you have lit a fire, and if you don't move I'll get the guards." Mam said, "Come on Florrie. Its time we were making for the train anyway." We picked up our things and made our way down to the beach, while the man was looking down the hole in shocked disbelief and watched us go. Before we got to the beach, Florrie stopped and went in the long grass to get dressed. Then we walked slowly to the station.

When we arrived the train was in and she pushed her way through the crowd with us hanging on to her and found an empty carriage. When we got sat down she said, "Now haven't we all had a great day apart from that young fellows bump on the head"? We all burst out laughing and laughed all the way home. Next day mam took Martin to the Doctors to have his head looked at, and they told her he was all right; but she had to keep an eye on him. If he started having headaches or anything she was to bring him back.

Dad went back to work but he was still coming home drunk. Mam couldn't understand it, but when Friday came she understood, when uncle Miko came down to the house with his wages. He sat at the table with mam, and told her he had to sack dad because he was drunk every day, and there had been a lot of complaints. He said he had tried talking to him, but it was like talking to a brick wall. Mam asked him where he was getting the money from to get drunk and he told her he was drinking the profits at the brewery, and he was sorry there was no way he could keep him on. So dad was out of work again. Mam thanked him for trying and said, "I thought it was two good to be true!" She put some of the wages behind the holy picture and said, "I think we are going to be needing that". At the beginning of the following week, Mam received a letter from Shannon airport saying she could start the following week. She was over the moon, but she had to tell dad. After she told him she was going to start work the following week, living in our house was a nightmare. That night they were arguing for hours, and we dare-not go to sleep in case we had to run. Eventually everything went quiet, and only then we could close our eyes.

Next morning dad was away early as he must have got a days work, and he didn't come home for his tea. Later on that evening he still hadn't come home, Mam told us to go and get the blankets ready just in case they were needed. We all heard him coming down the back path to the house. He was cursing, swearing, and shouting the most awful things. Mam told us to pick up the blankets and coats, and run, but to be very quiet. We went over the wall and when we got to the cowshed we could hear noises inside. She pulled us away and back up the field along the wall to the road further up. She said we would have to go down Tobarteascoin, which was a bigger crags than the one we usually went to play, and it had big patches of grass. Ray went they're to practice his Hurley with his friends. We went down and found a grassy bit in-between some rocks and settled in. Mam was worried because she hadn't brought the clock. Ray told her not to worry about the clock as no one would buy that from him. "I know that, but I wanted us to be up early in the morning. We have to walk all the way down St Flannon's Terrace and I didn't want people to see us" she replied Ray said, "Mam, everyone knows what goes on. There is no point in trying to hide it." Next day dad had no money to go to the pub, so he and mam were arguing all the time. He was saying she wasn't going to work, and she was saying she was. Then he said she was trying to shame him and it looked like he couldn't support his family. She said, "Well you can't, can you? And I am fed up with my children going hungry!" Martin popped his head round the back door and called me out. He said, "Do you want to come fishing with us?" "Yes," I replied, "Anything to get away from this arguing."

We got our jam jars and I went to call for my friend Miss. Her name was Ann but she was always called Miss or Missy. I asked her if she wanted to come fishing for Thorny Backs with us, she said, "Yes", and went in the house for a jam jar. Her little sister asked if she could come and Miss said no. You wouldn't think they were sisters; Miss had straight hair like mine even the same mousy colour, but her sister Angela had lovely fair hair with curls, beautiful eyes and a lovely smile. She was giving that smile to Martin now. "Oh let her come; the more the merrier!" We spent an hour putting our hands in the water trying to catch the little Thorny Backs. You had to be quick and close your hands so they didn't get away and then put them in your jar. Sometimes when you opened your hands there was nothing there and you wondered how they got away. We would see who could catch the most. It was great fun! We would carry the jam jars home with the Thorny Backs in them and be very proud of our little pets, but they would only last a few days and then they would die. You would shed a few tears and then bury them and the jar's would be empty again. You would wash the jam jar, and if there were no cracks or chips in it you could take it to the shop and they would give you a halfpenny for it.

By Friday they were still arguing. Dad said in no way was he going to look after us while she went to work, so she would have to stay at home. Later she said to him, "I'm just going down to see Fanny." He said "Well you better not be asking her to look after the children because I will put a stop to that". When we got to my aunts she said, "Sit down and I will make you a cup of tea." My aunt asked if dad had come to terms with her starting work. She said "No. Its worse he is getting, but I have everything sorted out, apart from a coat. You know Martin gave mine to the ragman. I wondered if Margie could lend me one just for the day. They will give me a uniform when I get there and it's a jacket and skirt. But if it rains on Monday I can't turn up soaking wet". My aunt said she would call her. Margie was up stairs getting ready to go out. I think my aunt had six daughters and they were all fashion conscious apart from Margie as she couldn't care less about fashion. She was a very good-humoured person and she laughed a lot, I think she was like my uncle Pappy. He was always good humoured. It's a pity dad didn't take after him. Margie came in the room, and said, "You could borrow this one if you like. I might need it over the weekend, so if you want to call for it on Sunday night you would be welcome." Mam thanked her and we went back home.

When we went in, Martin was in the hall and he said dad was in a very bad mood. He had no money for drink and had no woodbines and that's was making him worse. Mam said, "Its alright I am here now." Martin asked me if I wanted a game of Ludo or snakes and ladders. We played both games for an hour or so, but there was an awful atmosphere in the kitchen. Then Ray came in and mam sent us to bed, and for once were glad to go.

Chapter 12: Shhhh! Mams Got a Job!

Mam got up early next morning telling us to be very quiet. She told us to put on the clothes she had left out for us and to stay in the bedroom until she came for us. We didn't know what was going on. After about five minutes she came to the door of the bedroom, and put her finger to her lips warning us not to make a noise. She beckoned us to follow her to the front door, and we went out and she followed. She closed the front door very quietly and we went out the gate. She had a suitcase in her hand and a brown paper bag and we went towards the train station. We asked her where we were going and she told us to Ballyglass. We were all excited about that. When we got to the station she gave Ray the brown paper bag. It had bread and jam and a bottle of water in it. We were told to eat the bread and jam, as we hadn't had any breakfast. I don't know how long we were waiting at the station but it felt like hours. She turned to Ray and said "When the train comes, I am going to put you on it. I want you to look after those two and no fighting. Willie will meet you at Westport and you are all to help him on the farm and you are all to be good. I can't come with you because I have to start work on Monday; but I will come for you in a couple of weeks." So that's what mam meant when she told my aunt everything was sorted out. She must have been in touch with Sue and Willie. Otherwise Willie wouldn't have known to pick us up at the station. The train came and she put us on it, and she waved us off and then she walked away. Ray said, "Now you heard what mam said. I am in charge."

She was determined she was going to go to work one way or the other and I was worried what dad would do to her. She would be in the house on her own with him. Martin was asking Ray if he knew about this, but he said no he was as surprised as we were but it was great to get away from the house for a couple of weeks as he was fed up with all the arguing. Willie picked us up in Westport. He had got a lovely new car and we went to Ballyglass in style. It was lovely waking up in Ballyglass with the cock crowing and the ducks quacking. Sue came in, "Come on children, time to get ready for mass and your breakfast is ready, so get a quick wash". They went in the new car and dropped us off as usual, and said they would be home sooner today with having the car. We were walking up the hill to the church and Ray kept talking about the car. It was so big, lovely and shiny. The leather seats were so comfortable and he said, "If we walk slowly when we come out of mass we might get a lift back". Martin said, "Willie must have had to pay an awful lot of money to get a car like that. I bet you could get six or seven people in that car. Wait till I get home and tell my friends". I said "If it was my car, I would put some blankets on the seats, because it was warm today and when I sat on my seat it felt very cold." Martin said, "Don't be daft. You don't put blankets in a car. No one would be able to see the seats." "Well," I said, "it's different for you two. You have trousers on and I don't!"

We walked very slowly on the way home from mass. We were almost there when the car pulled up and we nearly killed each other trying to get in it. Willie had a smile on his face as he said "A long service today was it?" We said no, we just walked slowly. Willie said after we have had our dinner and the milking was done, we were going to see the Clinton family. That was Sue's sister Emily and her husband Harry and they lived near Westport. So we all needed to help out after dinner. Sue asked Martin to go and get some turf in, as there was a big stack of it by the side of the house, and Ray and I were asked to do the potatoes for the pigs. Ray got the pig meal from the cupboard. He knew how much to put in and we mixed it all together. Sue asked us if we wanted to have a go at feeding the pigs and although we weren't so sure but we had a go. Martin opened the door to the pigsty, and Ray was emptying the bucket into the pig trough, and the pigs were coming at the food as though they had never had anything to eat before, with the big sow was in the middle. There was one pig that couldn't get near the food and it came up to us. Ray scraped what was stuck to the bucket and gave it to him, and I patted it on the head as it seemed very friendly. Then the big sow let out such an awful roar. We all flew out of the pigsty closing the door as quickly as we could. Ray put the bolt on and we all stood with our backs against the door with our hearts thumping.

We went back in the house, and Sue asked us if we managed all right, we said yes but I think she could tell by our faces, we were terrified. I told Sue one of the pigs couldn't get any food, and she said she had noticed that. She would let it out in the field tomorrow and feed it separately. Ray called the dog and they went to get the cows in, and Martin and I went to the well for water. Sue told us to take a stick with us, as we were at the well we could go out the gate next to it and see if the ducks were at the other side of the road. When we got there we looked over the road and there they were. We guided them through the gate and they went

Chapter 12: Shhhh! Mams Got a Job!

waddling down the boreen to the duck pond. Willie finished the milking and he said he was going to get changed and then we will go.

The boys couldn't wait to get back in the car. It was a very smooth ride and we were there in no time at all. Willie parked near the sheds in the yard and we went through a little gate that led to the front door. There was a little girl standing on the step outside the front door. She had lovely blonde curly hair and she was all tanned with the sun. Sue said "This is Georgie." We said hello to her and she smiled. She was only about four or five. We went into the house and there were another two girls, who we were introduced to. "This is Hild. She is the oldest and this is Olive." We said hello and then we met their parents, Harry and Emily. The grown ups started talking to each other, and stood there like spare parts for a while not knowing what to say. Then the girls asked us if we would like to see the farm. We all went off together, and by the time we got back you would have thought we had known them for years. Emily had made us a lovely tea, and after we had finished, Hilda and Olive took us into the parlour where there was a piano. They lifted the lid and we all had a go at pressing the notes and there was lots of laughter. Willie said it was time we were going as we had to be up early in the morning. We said our goodbyes and the girls said we were welcome anytime. We got in the car all happy and contented as we'd had a lovely time.

Next day Sue let the pig out in the field and it would come over to the stepping-stones in the wall and give little squeals. I went over and patted it. Then I got a bit braver and went in the field. I walked past the pig and it started to follow me. I stopped and the pig stopped; I would say come here and it would come to me; it was like a dog. When the pig feed was ready I went out to the field and fed it. I thought it was going to eat the bucket as well and I had a job getting its head out of the bucket. Sue said it had to go back in the sty for the night and I said I would bring him. I called the pig and it followed me, and when I got to the pig sty it was looking up at me and I felt sorry for it. Sue opened the door and let it in. She said we would let it out again tomorrow. I was telling Willie all about the pig, I said, "I was going to call him Pinkie". Willie said, "Now I don't want you getting too fond of that pig as it will have to go soon." I didn't know what he meant and I didn't ask.

Next day after I had finished my jobs, I was straight into the field with the pig and I played for hours. By the end of the day I was riding round the field on the pigs back. I would keep falling off and the pig would come and nuzzle me until I got up and this went on all week. Now, when I had to go to the well for water; the pig would come with me. If I went into the kitchen for a drink the pig would follow and Sue would shout, "Get that pig out of my kitchen". At the weekend we all went to see the Clintons again, and they were all pleased to see us. We all had our shoes off as we went from one field to another, and Hilda and Olive had a lovely suntan. Even their feet were brown, and they both had lovely hair. Hilda's was brown, very thick and long. Olive's was very dark, long and curly. Last week they had it in plats, this week it just hung loose. I had always longed to have plats, but mam would never let me grow my hair. She said it was too fine to have plats, but how did she know if we didn't try? Later on, Hilda and Olive had to go and get the cows in for milking and I went with them. When we got back down from the field, Hilda went first and opened the gate. She put the cows through the gate and we followed. There must have been a big puddle at the gate and it hadn't dried up properly. We stood on the mud and it squelched up in between our toes and it was warm and it was the loveliest feeling. I will never forget that feeling. It was time to go back to Ballyglass and the boys were first in the car so they could get the window seats and I would have to climb over one of them to get in the middle.

I was in the top field with Ray and Martin they were teaching me to ride a bike. Ray was at one side of the field and Martin at the other. Ray would start me off and then let go and I had to peddle across to Martin. Then he would do the same thing. I don't know how many times I fell off, but after about twenty goes I got it right and was very proud off myself. Willie was in the next field with the donkey and cart. He was moving stone's from one end of the field to another, He had loaded the cart and called the boys to help him unload them. I got in the cart to get as near to him as I could; to tell him I can ride a bike. "Well now, that's great news," he said "there will be no stopping you now." He told the boy's that was the last load and he brought the donkey and cart to the top gate and he started to take the cart off the donkey. The two boys were asking if they could have a ride on the donkey. Willie said they could but our Neddy here is a very contrary donkey, and if he doesn't want to go he won't. And if he does go, he goes like a bolt of lightning, so he told them to be careful. The boys were arguing about who was going to go first. Martin won and got up onto the donkey but it wouldn't move. Martin sat there for a while and still nothing happened. He turned his head to say something to Ray and the donkey bolted down the field with Martin hanging on for his life. When it got to the bottom of the field it stopped suddenly and threw him over its head and he landed on his back in the biggest cow clap I had ever seen, and the stuff splattered up in the air and fell back down on the front of him. He was covered in the stuff! He said, "Give us a hand up," but we moved away from him and told him to roll over on the grass and try to remove some of the dung. Ray was killing himself laughing. He told

Martin he could have his go as well if he wanted to. The donkey walked slowly up the field after us. As we passed the lean-too, close to the cottage, Willie was doing something with the cart. He looked at Martin and said; "Now I did tell you he was contrary, didn't I?"

We walked down to the cottage. Sue was outside and she took one look at Martin and said, "You're not coming in my kitchen like that. Down to the duck pond with you and rinse those clothes." Martin walked back from the duck pond naked carrying his wet clothes. Sue had a bucket of soapy water ready and told Martin to put his clothes in. Ray said it's all in your hair and on the back of your neck. Sue told Ray to get some water out of the rain barrel and she gave Martin some soap. Ray threw the bucket of water over Martin and told him to wash his hair and neck with the soap, Then Ray got another bucket of water for him to rinse off. Poor Martin was stood there shivering and we gave him a towel to dry himself. When we went to bed that night we were sure we could still smell the dung on him.

Days passed and I spent as much time as I could with the pig. It poured with rain one day, and I went out and sat under the tree with Pinkie. I wrapped a big waterproof cape around him and myself. I spent most of the day talking to him. I'm sure he understood everything I said. I was going home in a few days and I was going to miss him. The day before mam came for us we were all in the yard near the cowshed, and Sue came up to me with the small bucket and asked me to go to the well for water. I called Pinkie, but Sue said I was to leave him there. I went out the gate but then I needed the lavatory, and I went in the field next to the house. I was pulling my pants up when I heard Pinkie squealing, and I rushed back through the gate and up towards the cowshed. Ray and Martin were holding pinkie and Willie was putting a knife through his head, I will never forget the squeals from the pig. I started to scream, and they all looked up towards me. Willie said, "Oh no, I thought you had sent her to the well", Sue said she had. I ran into the house and to the bedroom and I sobbed my heart out, I remember Willie saying the pig had to go; but I thought someone was going to buy him. Now Pinkie would be smoked and cured and would be hanging from the beam in the kitchen. The more I thought about it the more I cried. Sue made the dinner and put it in front of us and we all ate in silence.

After dinner, Willie sat on his chair and called me over to him. He put me on his knee and tried to explain about being a farmer and how you have to live off the land. "It was survival; so that's what farmers have to do. Like when I killed the chicken for your mam to take home. I did it because I didn't want you to be hungry and you know what hunger is like, don't you?" I nodded. He said, "And what have you just had for your dinner?" I said, "Bacon, cabbage and potatoes." "Well there you are!" he continued. "You see the bacon came from that bit of pig that's hanging up there, and I did tell you not to get too fond of the pig." He gave me a hug and lifted me down from his knee.

Mam came for us the next evening. She was staying overnight and we were to go home early next morning. She kept talking to Sue about the job and how much she liked it. Then she was saying dad had no money the first week, but he got some the week after, and he had got drunk and beat her up. She was showing Sue the bruises on her arms and legs. She said, "I had to keep my hands up in front of my face because I couldn't go to work with a battered face." I wasn't looking forward to going home. I asked mam if dad was going to look after us while she went to work. She said, "No. Your granddad is coming home tomorrow." That cheered me up. Willie took us to Westport and put us on the train and we were on our way back to Ennis.

Chapter 13:
And We All Come Back!

Granddad arrived home a couple of hours after us and I was so pleased to see him. He said, "Well it's nice to have been missed!" He went in to his room and I followed. He put his bag on the bed and started to unpack it, "Well I had better find your present." He handed me a paper bag. When I opened it, there was a blue and pink necklace made from beads. I said, "They are lovely. Thank you." I told him mam had got a job. He said he already knew as she had written to him. "I am here to look after you so you had better be good! He said. "Oh we will and we will help you to do the work around the house." I replied. He smiled, and then he bent down and took his boots off and put them up the chimney. Now I knew we were going to get back to normal. Granddad was home. Dad came in later and I hoped he wouldn't start tonight as I was still upset about the pig and I couldn't stand any arguing. He didn't say much apart from, "I see your all back together like browns cows." He went into the bedroom and that's the last we saw of him that night.

We went to mass next morning. Afterwards, I went for my friend Miss and we went to see if I could take my cousin Maureen's little boy out for a walk. His name was Anthony and he was a lovely child, always happy. He looked like his mother and had the same nature. We walked a good way and I was telling Miss all that had gone on in Westport. About the car, the pig and donkey, and learning to ride a bike. She said, "In a way you are very lucky. I know you all have to run away sometimes but at least you are seeing a bit of life." When I thought about it, I suppose I was lucky, I was seeing two different lives; one in the town and one in the country. It would be awful if we had no Sue and Willie to run to.

We started back at school next day. I went up for my friend Miss and we walked up the Clare Road linking arms with Angela trailing behind us. When we reached Maloney's shop on the corner, there was this man standing outside Dolan's shop across the road. He looked like desperate Dan out of the comic book only he wore a flat cap and he looked very rough. I knew his name as Mattie because dad talked to him a lot. Miss asked me what I was looking at. I said

"That man. He's always standing outside that shop." Miss said, "I know. He is a bousie man." I asked her what a bousie man was. She said "I don't believe you don't know what a bousie man is! It's a man that is rough and won't go to work because they are lazy and just hang about all the time." Sometimes they do errands for the shops and the shopkeeper gives them a couple of shillings, they buy drink with it and when they have drunk it they come back and stand at the corner again." I wondered to myself if my dad was a bousie man, but he couldn't be because he did go to work every now and again. Even if he didn't bring the money home to feed us, so I thought I had better not ask any more questions.

When we got into the schoolyard, there were a lot of the girls in a group. They seemed to be talking about me. You could tell by the way they were looking at me. I asked Miss if she knew what it was all about. She told me, "It's because your mam is going out to work and leaving her children." I said "She isn't leaving us. My granddad is looking after us". She said, "I have already told them that but they say Grandfathers can't look after children and they said your mam is showing your dad up." The bell went and we went into school. Lunchtime came and we went to the hut. The nun gave me my cocoa and bun. She told me in front of all the girls that was the last I would be getting. "Your mother is working now so tell her you have to go home for your lunch or bring a packed one," she continued. I felt shown up. She could have got me to one side and told me.

When mam came home from work I told her what happened at school. She said, "God, they could give me a chance to get a wage first!" Then she told us all that the wage she was going to get wasn't very much. "If your dad gives me some money we will be all right. But if he doesn't, we are barely going to scrape through, but at least I will be able to feed you," she said. Mam was well talked about around the town for going to work. In those days women didn't work when they were married with children, but what else could she do when dad didn't give her any money? And to make it worse dad would go out in the road shouting out, "Look at her going to work and leaving her children. She is not fit to have children!" She would have to walk up to Captain Mack's Corner to get the bus with his voice bringing people out of their front doors to see what was going on. Things seemed to go from bad to worse. Granddad did all the cooking and making the bread. He had us up for school, making sure we were all washed and our shoes polished. He was going to cut the boy's hair, but mam said to leave it until she got a few shillings to send them to the barber. In the meantime she snipped a bit off the ends to make them look tidy. The boys gave a sigh of relief as they hated what they called the basin cut Granddad gave them. Granddad had to spend a lot more time in the kitchen now to get on with the cooking, washing, and so on.

Dad was horrible to him. He was always calling him names and complaining about the food, even though he wasn't giving them a penny towards it. I don't know how granddad put up with it. We were all in the kitchen one Saturday afternoon and granddad was making potato cakes. We were eating them as fast as he was making them, and Mam came in the back door and took one off the plate. She said, "I better have one before they have all gone!" Granddad was washing up the frying pan when the back door opened and dad came in. He was well gone with drink. Granddad put the pan away and started to walk towards the hall door to go to his room, when dad told him to stop, and pulled a gun out of his pocket. He told granddad to stand against the wall and put his hands up. Granddad did what he said. "Now you pagan bastard I am going to shoot you." We were all crying, so he told us to go and stand next to him and put our hands up. We were all terrified and he said, "I might as well shoot you all while I'm at it." I closed my eyes. I was saying a prayer under my breath when I heard the first bang and I knew it would be me next because I was standing next to granddad, I heard the second bang and I thought he must have missed me and I opened my eyes. Granddad was making a grab for dad, but he was too quick for him, and he was away out the back door and up the back path, Granddad went out in the back lane and he was shouting after him, "You bastard. How could you frighten the life out of your own children like that?" Granddad came back in and he came over and cuddled me and said, "Stop that crying now it wasn't a real gun, but it even fooled me."

Mam was fuming and said, "I have had enough of this. If he comes in tonight and starts, we will all have to have a go at him." He did come in late that night and started hitting mam. We all went for him at the same time, and I will always remember standing on the kitchen chair and hitting him on the shoulder with a ludo box. The rest of them got him across the kitchen table and were punching and hitting him with anything they could get their hands on. He was begging them to stop and said he would never touch a drink again. So this was my dad making his pledge for the second time. We would see how long it lasted.

My dad hadn't had a drink for a month. He was giving mam a bit of his dole money and the rest he was saving to get a ticket to go to England, he was going to show people that he could work and support his family. Then one day he said he had enough for a one-way ticket and that would do him, so off he went! We didn't know how long he would last over in England.

It was getting near Christmas. Mam took me up O'Connell Street and we were looking in all the shop windows. They all had their own decorations up and all the windows looked lovely. We looked in a toyshop in the middle of the street and Mam was pointing at this doll in the window. It was about twelve inches high and it had blonde hair in plats and you could undress it and take its shoes and socks off. She said, "She's beautiful, isn't she?" I said, "Yes she is." We went back down the street and did some shopping at Maloney's and then we went back home. Mam had bought some strips of coloured paper with glue at one end. There were green and red ones. She showed us how to make paper chains. We were all excited about this. We started to make a red one and she said, "You can mix them if you want and they would look brighter!" So we put one red and one green together. They looked lovely. Mam hung them up on the kitchen walls and it brightened the place up. We went and picked some holly from the back lane with loads of red berries on, and for the first time it looked like Christmas in our house it was so peaceful. Dad had sent a money wire; it was the first one we had received since he went away and Mam said it would give us a better Christmas.

On Christmas Eve afternoon she went up to town to get something for the Christmas dinner. She said the shops would be selling things off cheaper by this time. She came back with a turkey, but she didn't say if it was any cheaper or not. We went to midnight mass with mam and it was lovely with all the Christmas carols. My favourite one was Silent Night. When we got home, granddad was still up, and we all had a mug of tea. Then granddad said, "Did I hear a noise coming from the bedroom? I think it must be Santa!" I told granddad not to be silly as there was no such person. "Well," he said, "I had better go and have a look." He went into the bedroom and there was a big bang, we all went to see what had happened, and there was granddad on the floor. He was holding the doll with the blonde plats by the leg upside down, and was nursing his leg with the other. Mam asked him what had happened. He said "I went to reach for the box on the top shelf and the doll fell out. I tried to save the doll and lost my balance and fell banging my leg on the side of the bed. I managed to hang onto it, that's why it's upside down." Then he said, "I give in, there is no Santa!" Mam started to laugh, I took the doll out of his hand and the boys were pulling him up off the floor and then we all started laughing. He said, "Merry Christmas every one," as he limped back to the kitchen.

We had a lovely Christmas dinner, and every one was happy. Granddad got the wishbone off the turkey and let me pull it with him, He said if you get the biggest half you have to make a wish, and of course he made sure I did. I made a wish that dad would stay in England and never come back. Mam got a letter from

Chapter 13: And We All Come Back!

dad at the end of January. There was no money in it but he wanted her to write down all our shoe size's and send them to him. He also wanted her to send a copy of the Clare Champion newspaper. She wrote back and sent the shoe sizes and the newspaper, but she told him not to bother about the shoes, just send the money and she could buy them in Ennis. Then in February, he sent her a newspaper. She said, "What in gods name is this?" The paper was rolled up, and she opened it. It was the racing page and he had marked a few horses that were running, and by the side of their names he wrote. 'Back these!" Also, there was a tiny brown envelope which fell out. Mam picked it up and looked at it! It said "For Muriel's birthday" and when she got the contents out it was a little gold signet ring. It just fitted my little finger. I said to mam, "Maybe he has changed? He has never given me anything for my birthday before." She snapped at me, "You can't eat shoes and rings! Its money we need!" He did send her a bit of money at the end of February though. She said, "What am I supposed to do with that? There isn't enough to buy a couple of bags of turf!"

Dad arrived home at the end of March. I remember playing out the front of the house after school when I saw him coming up the road. He had a suitcase in one hand and a great big bag in the other. I ran in the house and told mam, her first words were, "Is he sober?" I said, "I think so!" He came in the kitchen and he was sober. He gave mam a kiss and a hug and he patted me on the head and said, "My you're getting big!" I told him I was nine. He said, "I know. Did your ring fit?" I showed it to him. He said, "It looks like we will have to have it made bigger!" My brothers came in the back door. Dad said hello to them and told them what big fellows they were getting. He told us he was home for two weeks and then he was going back to his job in England. He put the suitcase and the bag on the table, and he opened the case first and he handed each of us a pair of shoes. Mine were black with a silver bar across the front of them, and there was the shape of a flower punched onto the front of them. The boy's shoes were black brogues, we were trying them on and we asked if we could wear them now. Mam said no and that we could wear them too mass on Sunday. "But mam it's only Monday today! That means we have to wait a whole six days," we pleaded. But she wasn't giving in so we had to take them off. Dad opened the other bag and took out two pairs of shoes for mam, a pair of walking shoes and a pair of black suede high heels; with peep toes. I thought they were beautiful. I asked mam if she would save them for me after she had finished with them. She put them on and said, "I don't think there will be much left of them by the time you grow up!" Then dad brought out two dresses and he gave them to her, she was holding up one of the dresses in front of her and twirling round, and she looked very pleased with herself. Dad gave her some money. I don't know how much, but it looked a lot.

When we got home from school the next day mam wasn't in, she was on early shift at work and finished at two o'clock. I went in to granddad's room and asked where she was. He said dad was meeting her off the bus in town. We played out for a while and then we saw them coming down the back path. Dad was carrying two chairs and mam had loads of bags, and we ran to meet them. Dad gave Ray one of the chairs and Martin and I took some bags off mam and carried them home. We put all the bags on the table and couldn't wait for them to be opened. Dad said he was going out to see someone and that he wouldn't be long. Mam flopped down on one of the chairs she had just bought. She said, "They don't match the two we have, but they were a bargain at the second hand shop!" Then she opened one of the bags and brought out six cups saucers and plates. There was a chip out of some of them here and there but they were all right. At one time mam was always buying cups and saucers, but she gave up because dad would come home drunk and break them all. That's why we had tin mugs. Granddad was the only one with a pot mug; he took his in his room when he had finished with it. He wasn't taking any chances, so his mug lasted a lot longer. She opened another bag and took out two pairs of grey trousers; one short pair and one long pair, two grey shirts, two ties and two sleeveless Fairisle pullovers, four vests and four pairs of socks. The boys were all excited, and it was Ray's first pair of long trousers. I couldn't wait any longer, for what I had got. She took out two vests, two pants and two pair of socks, when she said, "I wasn't going to pay the prices they were asking for those dresses, so I bought some material to make you two" One piece of material was navy with a white stripe, the other was a faded looking pink with a grey stripe. I was disappointed; I wouldn't mind her making them if the material had little flowers on or something bright. The boys were trying their clothes on and they looked very smart. Mam told them they could wear them too mass on Sunday with their new shoes. She told me she would have one of my dresses ready by then.

Mam decided to make a skirt and top instead of a dress, she cut it out that night. She was going to take it to work with her and sew it in her dinner break. It was almost finished when she got home that day. She tried it on me when I came home from school. The skirt kept slipping down and she was loosing her rag with it. "I don't know what sort of shape you are at all." I said, "Can't you just put some elastic in it?" She said, "No, it will throw all the stripes out! I will have to join them together by putting buttonholes in the skirt and buttons on the blouse." I felt like bursting into tears but I daren't. I didn't like the material to

Chapter 13: And We All Come Back!

start with and now I had to have a skirt that buttoned on the top like a baby. She came home next day with the buttons and buttonholes done and I had to try it on again, "There now, that's better. I have put the buttons higher up so as you grow I can move them down. It will fit you for a couple of years. There's a nice big hem on the skirt as well so that can be let down too." I thought, oh god am I going to have to wear this for years, and I was fed up with it all. Mam asked me had I seen anything of dad and I said, "Oh I forgot to tell you. I saw him in O'Connell Street when I came out of school. He told me to tell you he would be home in about an hour." The hours past and there were no sign of dad, in fact he didn't come home at all that night. Mam went to work next morning and granddad got us off to school. I don't know what my brothers were thinking, but I had a very frightened feeling inside me as we walked to school.

When we got home from school granddad was in the kitchen peeling potatoes; he must have been miles away, because when I went to him and said, "Hello granddad," he nearby jumped out of his skin. We could hear mam crying in the bedroom, we asked him what was wrong, He said, "Your dad came in while your mother was at work. I was in my room and I heard some noise. I came out into the hallway and he was going out the back door with a big bag. I told your mother when she came home from work, so she went and checked the bedroom. He had taken all the new shoes and your mothers dresses. She has been in a bad state ever since, so you had better leave her alone for the time being". So that would be the last we saw of our shoes. He came home that night, I don't know what time it was all I know is that we were woken up with mam's screams, He never went back to his job in England.

We went to mass on Sunday without our new shoes. Then Martin said, "I wonder whose feet have gone to mass in our new shoes?" Mam looked at him and said, "And don't you be looking at everyone's feet in church! We have pride you know!"

Mam received a letter from my uncle Bert, He said he had a week's holiday and he wanted to bring his wife over to meet us all. Mam was in a bit of a state, she didn't know what to do. She wanted to see her brother but how was she going to cope with dad. She asked granddad what she should do. He said, "Well you can't very well write back and say they can't come, can you?" So she wrote back and said they would be welcome, she was a nervous wreck all week. We only had four cups and saucers left; she was wrapping them up in paper and hiding them at the back of the sideboard, she would get them back out just before they arrived in case they got broken, so it was back to our tin mugs again. Granddad had to move in with us and Ray was going to sleep on the floor. Granddad took his suit from under his mattress, his boots from up the chimney and put them in the same places in our room. Now every thing was ready apart from mam, she had to have a good talk with dad and she wanted us all to be there. She told us she had three days off and she was keeping them until the back end of the visit, and as we were on school holiday's, we could show them round for a couple of days.

When dad came in he was sober, he sat on a chair and started reading the newspaper. Mam said to him, "Massy, I was wanting a word with you. You know my brother and his wife are coming to stay with us tomorrow for a week?" He said, "Yes, I know." "Well," she said, "I am going to go down on my hands and knees and beg you to behave yourself just for a week. Please do this one thing for me!" He said, "Alright, I will." She asked him to cross his heart and hope to die and he did. Mam gave a sigh of relief and said, "Thank you." I felt sorry for mam, down there on her knees. She shouldn't have had to do that to a grown man. Next morning we were all up early. Mam was making sure everything was spic and span ready for their arrival. Someone came to the back door with a kid goat, and it had a bit of string tied round its neck. Mam took it from the man and paid him some money. I thought it was the most beautiful baby goat I had ever seen. Mam handed me the string with the kid at the end of it, then she told me to take the kid up to Mr Spellissy's house and say mam wants it killed skinned and gutted. Ray saw the look on my face and said, "It's alright mam, I will take it." She said, "No she will take it. She has to learn." I walked up the road as slow as I could, and knocked at Mr Spellissy's door. He opened the door. He was wearing a big brown apron covered in blood. His hands and arms also had blood on them, and I told him what mam had said. He took the string out of my hand and said tell your mam it will be ready this afternoon. He shut the door and I could hear the little kid bleating. I stood there and tried to think about what Willie said about survival, but it just didn't work. The tears were streaming down my face I was that upset. I just couldn't help it.

When I went back down the road Ray was stood at the gate. He didn't say anything and he just put his arm around me and we went in the house. Ray collected the kid later that day. My uncle and his wife arrived about four o'clock. She seemed to laugh a lot and her eyes twinkled, but we had an awful job trying to understand what she was saying. She was from Yorkshire in England and she talked very fast. They were all still talking long after we went to bed. My uncle had been in the air force for years but he was out now, and he and his wife were civil servants. He was also a part time photographer and he did weddings on a Saturday. Mam went to early mass next morning and she left the visitors in bed. They were still in bed when she got back.

Chapter 13: And We All Come Back!

She sent us to second mass and we all had our new cloths on, and there was a lot of fooling about on our way pushing and shoving. When we got there; mass had started. We sat at the back of the church. I was sat in between the boys. Then they started throwing bits of paper at each other. People were looking round at them, and then they started giggling. I was glad when mass was over. Martin was first out of the church and he was looking at everyone's feet. I told him, Stop it! You heard what mam said last week!" He said, "But I'm dying to know who has my shoes on, aren't you?" Ray told him to come on; "It wouldn't do you any good to know, they aren't your shoes anymore."

After dinner mam told us not to go away, as Uncle Bert was going to take some photos. My granddad was all dressed up in his suit and his boots were shining. My uncle told us to go across to the other side of the road to where the big wall is. I told him that was the cowshed at the back of the wall. Mam told me to be quiet. He took lots of photos of us all. There was a good few children watching what was going on and they were all dressed in their Sunday best. My cousin Joan was just coming up the road to our house, and asked me what was going on and I told her. I asked my uncle if he would take a photo of Joan and me. He told us to sit on our garden wall. All the other children were looking up at him, so he told them all to get on the wall, but Ray was missing. Martin said, "Oh he will be up at Captain Mack's Corner showing off his long trousers." My uncle took a couple of photos and said, "That's the end of the photo shoot you can all go and play now." and we all went out of the garden feeling like film stars.

Next day we got dressed up in our clothes like mam told us. We didn't know where to take my uncle and aunt so I suggested we went down the crags. My uncle said, "You're the guide, so we will follow you!" My uncle was taking lots of photos, not just of us, but the big rocks and the funny shaped ones. I showed him the flat ones that we used as the table and the ones we used as chairs. He said, "I will have to get a photo of us all on top of that big fairy rock. Ray said, "You can't take us all; there will be no one to take the photo!" "That's where you are wrong," he said. "I have a magic camera!" He told us all to get on top of the fairy rock. Then he did something with the camera and climbed on the rock with the rest of us then he said, "All smile." We heard a click and he told us we could get down now. My brothers were taken with it and my uncle was showing them how it worked. He told them the camera had cost an awful lot of money, so it had to be looked after. By the time we had walked home it was nearly time for mam to come from work, so we got changed into our other clothes again.

When mam came in from work, we asked her if we could go out and play now. Next day we took them into the town, and my aunt was interested in all the little narrow streets. I didn't know much about the town apart from O'Connell Street and Parnell Street and of course Abbey Street that led to the guard station. They were meeting mam off the bus in town. We hardly gave her time to get off the bus before we were saying could we go now. The next day mam was off work so they went to limerick to have a look around the shops. We stayed with granddad that night as they were going to the cinema, and we watched them go up the garden path. About an hour later we watched them come back down it. Martin and I ran in to tell granddad. He said, "I wonder what's gone wrong?" They came in the kitchen and mam was crying. Granddad asked my uncle what was wrong. He said, "We were sitting in the cinema when a message came over the loudspeaker. It said could Mrs Burns please come home and wash her husband's shirts as he hasn't got a clean one to put on his back!" Mam said, "Oh my god, that's Massy!" and she started crying. She was very upset so we came out. I just can't believe that he did that". Granddad said, "You don't know the half of it." My uncle asked him what he meant. Granddad replied, "You have seen nothing yet. Wait until he really starts." and went into the bedroom.

Next day my uncle asked mam, "What did my father mean when he said I didn't know the half of it? I know he keeps you short of money; but is there anything else I should know?" Mam said no everything was fine. But my uncle said, "Why would he do that to you in the cinema?" She said, "He was fed up because he couldn't get a job and it didn't help, me going to the cinema". We were all warned not to say anything to my uncle because she didn't want him to get upset as he was on holiday, but we didn't have to say anything because about nine o'clock that night he staggered in the back door and he was very drunk. My uncle, aunt, and mam were all sitting round the kitchen table having a cup of tea. He started shouting, "Oh we have cups and saucers this week. It was tin mugs last week." He swiped all the cups and saucers off the table and they hit the range and smashed into pieces. Then he got mam by the hair and pulled her off the chair and he was punching her in the face. By the time my uncle got round to her she had been hit a few times. My uncle, Ray, and Martin, were trying to get him off her. Then granddad came. It took the four of them to get him away from mam. My aunt was screaming, and I think she was in shock. I was crying and shouting at the same time, "You crossed your heart and hoped to die. You said you would be good." Mam went over to comfort my aunt, but she had blood coming from her nose and lip. I think that made my aunt worse. She was screaming, "I want to go home."

They managed to get dad into the bedroom, and put him on the bed, and my uncle and granddad sat on him. He was still shouting, "You get out of here you pagan Bastards" and still trying to fight. So my uncle punched him and it went quiet. He told Ray to go for the guards. Ray said, "There no point as they won't come." My uncle asked, "What do you mean they won't come?" Granddad said, "He's right, they will just say it's a domestic and there is nothing they can do." My uncle said, "I just don't believe this, how long has this been going on?" Granddad said, "For years. She has to go out to work to feed the children. He gets dole money, but he doesn't give her any. He just drinks it." Granddad told him the whole story. Dad was snoring his head off and he didn't have a care in the world. My aunt had calmed down a bit, but she looked terrified. Ray and Martin were picking up the broken crockery off the floor, and picked up a cup and it was only the handle that was broken. They said, "You can still use it," Martin gave it to mam and said, "It can be your cup." She took it out of his hand and told us to go to bed. My uncle and aunt left next morning, as my aunt wouldn't spend another night in our house as she was frightened. My uncle gave mam a big hug. He told her he was going to get legal advice when they got back, and then he gave her a box. She opened it and it was a watch. She thanked him and said it was lovely. They walked down the road to the train station. This was one visit I would remember.

We started back at school, and all went well for a week or so, and then dad started again. Mam told us he had phoned Shannon airport; he had said could they give Mrs Burns a message. One of her children had been in an accident. Could she come home as soon as possible? Someone gave her a lift home. When she got in the house she asked granddad what had happened. He said, "He didn't know what she was talking about. The children are at school." She just burst into tears. This happened a few times in the next five or six weeks. Mam was called into the manager's office and she said he was very nice about it. He asked her if she was having problems at home, she said I told him the whole story and said, "I don't want to lose my job. I have three children to feed." She asked him, could they just ignore the calls and not send her home every time. If there were an emergency; she would get granddad to call. So they agreed on that. Next time he rang they would say they would pass the message on. But dad was still going to the bus; shouting all sorts of terrible things. She tried to fox him by going up to Captain Mack's Corner one day and the next day she would get on the bus at the Old Ground Hotel. He must have had spies; because wherever she went he was there. One day when we got home from school she was telling us about this Blessed Martin that was in heaven. She said all the people at work prayed to him when they were in trouble and he helped them. So now, every night we had to pray to Blessed Martin to help us make my dad go away and never come back.

She said it would do no harm to say one during the day as well, "Are you listing to me?" We all said yes. Mam had great faith in Blessed Martin.

When we broke up for the summer holidays mam told us she was sending us to Ballyglass in a few days, because with us being off school dad would have an excuse to shout at the bus even more. I walked her to the bus on Monday; I thought my dad wouldn't shout if I were there. When we got to the bus stop across from the Old Ground Hotel, I could see Ray in the church grounds. When he saw us he hid from mam and put his finger to his lips to tell me to be quiet. I didn't say anything. I stood with mam until she got on the bus and she sat at the window and waved. My dad appeared out of nowhere and nearly knocked me down as he started banging on the window of the bus. Mam turned her head the other way; but he was shouting at her; "You whore, you bitch, leaving your children on their own!" The bus started up and he was still banging on the window as it moved away, and then he was gone.

Ray came over to me and asked if I was all right, I said, "Yes. I had just walked mam to the bus stop. I thought he wouldn't shout at her if I was there." He said, "You had better go home now and he went back to his friends." I watched him go across the road to the Old Ground Hotel. There were a lot of people coming out, so I went to have a look at them. I had hold of the bars on the gate and my head in-between the bars and watched all the people going in and out. They had bright coloured clothes on and they all wore peaked caps. I thought they looked like Leprechauns only bigger. They looked like a ray of sunshine. That's the only way I can describe them. They made me smile as they all looked so happy. I thought, when I grow up I am going to stay in this hotel and I might be happy too. My thoughts were interrupted when this couple came up to me and said, "Hi honey, do you want some gum?" They put a packet of chewing gum in my hand patted me on the head and then went out the gate. Ray and his friends were at the other side of the gate and they were asking all the people that were coming out for gum, they didn't get any. Ray came over to me and said, "I told you to go home." I said, "I just wanted to see the people. They talk funny, don't they?" Ray said, "They were Americans, and if mam finds out you were begging you'll get a good hiding". I said, "I wasn't begging. I only wanted to see the people and I don't even like chewing gum!" He said, "Give it to me then!" I gave it to him and he said, "Home now!"

Some of my Uncle Bert's (Paddy to me!) pictures: Me with Uncle Bert (Top), Uncle Bert, Raymond, Aunt Val, me and Martin (left to right) on the Fairy Rock (Middle) and Mam with Aunty Val.

Chapter 14:
Martin's Washing Disaster

Mam was on the late shift so she was able to take us to the train station. She put us on the train to Westport and Ray was in charge. She told us to be good and help on the farm and she would be up in a couple of weeks for us. And not to forget to say our prayers to Blessed Martin! Willie met us off the train and we went to Ballyglass. On the way he told us he had got a new tractor, so he didn't have the horse any more, but he still had Neddy the donkey. When we pulled into the farmyard, there was the new tractor. It was bright red and the boys couldn't wait to get up on it. Sue came out and made us all welcome, and we helped all we could for the next couple of weeks.

We went to the bog with Willie for a couple of days. He would dig the turf out and slice it into sods and then we would make stacks with it. We would place two sods one way about six inches apart and then two more on top of them the opposite way until you had little stacks. Then the wind could blow through them and dry them out. On the second day Ray was digging as well so it kept Martin and I busy building a lot more stacks. The only thing I didn't like about it; was when your feet were in the bog, there were frogs jumping all over your bare feet and I didn't like them. We went in to see Sue's sister Emily a couple of times. She had another little girl now and she had called her Olga. Hilda and Olive came out to see us at Ballyglass on their bikes and we all played for hours climbing the trees in the orchard and running all over the farm together.

Willies car didn't go very far, He got ready to go to town one day and we asked if we could go with him. He said, "Not this time." We were disappointed; but Sue explained that Willie took the farmers wives to town once or twice a week and they paid him. Willie would go and do what business he had to do, then pick them up a couple of hours later and take them back home with all their shopping, she said, "The car had to pay for itself!" She made us laugh one day. Willie was all ready to go and pick up the farmers wives, and he set off down the boreen. Then Sue got her bike out with the basket on the front. We asked her where she was going. She said she was going to town. "But why didn't you go with Willie?" we asked. "You're a farmer's wife?" She said, "There isn't a seat left in the car and it's cheaper to go on the bike. I can take as long as I like!" Willie took the boys on the tractor when he was going from one field to another and they loved it. He sat me on his knee and would let me steer if there was plenty of room. Willie never seemed to stop working, but having the tractor would make it a lot easier for him.

When we first came to Ballyglass, the cottage had a thatched roof and you would see him repairing it in the summer evenings for hours. The cats used to go up into the roof to have their kittens. One cat would go up and a couple of weeks later five or six would come down. They had a new roof put on; so that would be one job less for Willie to do, but it never looked the same. He had built a lean-to at the back of the house, and under it he put a piece of wood across with a hole in the middle, and then put a bucket under it. This was the lavatory now. There was no door on it, but it was better than going in the field. Mam came for us when it was time to go back home. Willie took us to the station but stopped at Emily's house on the way; so we could say good-bye to Hilda, Olive, Georgia, and little Olga. Mam had a few words with Emily, and they all waved as we set off for the station. Willie put us on the train and we were on our way back to Ennis.

Nothing had changed when we got home. Mam said it didn't make any difference us being away. He was still making a scene at the bus stop. It was alright when all the regulars were on the bus, they knew what he was like, but if there were strangers, she would get embarrassed. She took me to work with her a few times and I loved it. To walk into that linen room and smell the oil off the sewing machines and the smell of the linen it was very special to me. Everyone who came in the linen room seemed to like mam, a lot. It's no wonder she liked working here. It must have been another world to her. She gave me some scraps of linen and told me to cut them into squares and make some hankies. It took me ages cutting the linen into squares before I hemmed them. When I had finished, I had three lovely hankies. Mam pressed them with the iron and they looked like they had just come out of a shop. Then a man came into the linen room and said, "So where have you come from?" "I came with my mam. Look at the hankies I made." I replied. He said, "They are very nice. I wonder if you could make me one." I said, "If mam has any scraps of linen left". He turned to mam and asked her if there were any scraps left. She said, "Yes sir, I have a few." He said, "Well, will you give them to this young lady. She is going to make me a hankie. I will call back later for it!" Then he went out. Mam let out a sigh of relief and said, "I thought I was going to be in trouble." The woman next to her said, "He's very nice is Mr Patterson. I wish they were all like him!" He did come back later for his hankie and said it was the best one he had ever had and maybe another day you can make me a couple more. I was so proud of myself and what a nice man he was. I asked mam if she would take me again tomorrow. She said no, but she might take me next week.

When we got back home dad was in. He started as soon as we got in the door. It was hard to take after we just had two weeks of peace and quiet. Martin asked me if I was going out and I said yes. Ray was standing in the kitchen with his hands over his ears. He reminded me of Patrick. I followed Martin into the back yard. He had two very rusty bike wheels. He gave me one and he had the other. He had a stick and he told me to go and find one in the back lane, which I did. We set off up the back lane hitting the wheels with the stick and trying to keep them going without bumping into anything. Martin said, "Let's go on the road. It will be better. The back lane is too uneven." So we went on the road; and it was a lot better, we were having races between each other. A few more children joined in. They were all taking turns at having races, and the onlookers were shouting for who ever they wanted to win. You would never think you could have so much fun with a couple of rusty bike wheels.

That night we were woken up with mam screaming and dad shouting. We all got out of bed half-asleep and went towards the kitchen. Granddad was behind us. We opened the door and mam was stood there in her nightdress and dad was accusing her of trying to sneak out to see someone. She was shouting at him; "I got up to make myself a cup of tea. I have a thumping headache. As if I was going out like this to meet someone? You're mad. And you can tell you have had no drink tonight because if you had, it would take the devil himself to wake you". Then she shouted at us, "Get back to bed!" We went back to bed and Ray said, "What's she shouting at us for? We only got up to help her. I'm fed up with all the shouting and swearing and being hungry half the time and everything getting broken or sold." I had never heard Ray go on like that before, I think he was crying, but I couldn't see because it was dark, but I heard a few sniffs.

When we got up next morning, Ray wasn't there, we thought he had gone out early, and we asked granddad if he had seen him. He said, he hadn't; and he had been up since eight o'clock. I said, "I know where he will be. He will have gone to work with mam because she starts at seven o'clock." Martin said, "That's not fair you went with her yesterday." I said, "Well maybe she will take you tomorrow and then we will all have had a go." Mam came in from work and she was very upset. She said there had been a phone call for her just before she finished work and it was a woman that phoned, so the girl in the office had passed it on. It said, could Mrs Burns come to Limerick and collect Ray as he had run away from

Chapter 14: Martin's Washing Disaster

home. It was Auntie Jo who had phoned. Mam had to come home first because she had no money. She asked dad if he had any money. He said he hadn't, and if you were home to look after your children they wouldn't be running away would they. She looked at him and said, "And if you got off your lazy arse and got a job they wouldn't be going without would they? So shut your mouth!" She went in to granddads room. He said he only had a few coppers. She was getting herself in a right state, "What am I going to do?" I said, "Do you want me to go and ask Mrs Riedy if she could lend you some money?" She said, "No, I will go and ask her. This is awful, how did Ray get to Limerick?" We said, "We didn't know; we thought he was at work with you." She plucked up the courage and went to ask Mrs Riedy, and she hated having to do it. She came back in with the money and went to see what time the next bus was to Limerick.

It was getting late when they got back, and Ray was very quiet, and so was mam. She told us to go to bed. She was tired and she had to be at work by seven. When we got in our room Martin said, "What did you run away for? Mam had to borrow the money from Mrs Riedy to get you home." He said, "I know, and I don't want to talk about it. I've had enough today." A couple of day's later Ray got a part time job selling ice cream. He had to ride this bike with two wheels at the front and one at the back. There was a square box in between the two front wheels and it was full of ice cream. His boss would count the wafers so he knew how much money Ray had to hand in when he got back. Sometimes when the boss wasn't looking, Ray would take a few extra wafers so Martin and I could get one free. The first time I saw him coming down our road ringing his bell, I was very excited. He looked great in his white jacket and hat, I was telling everyone that's my brother, as though they didn't know, but I was so proud of him. Whatever money he made from his work, he gave to mam, to help her out. A couple of week's later granddad wasn't well. I had only ever seen him ill once before, that was when we got chased with the axe. Mam wanted to get the doctor but he wouldn't have it. She told him he was to stay in bed, and he did what he was told, so he must have been ill. Mam told us we had to help in the house and see to granddad, as Ray was going to work.

Martin was giving the orders. He told me to wash the dishes, sweep the floor and make the beds. I asked, "And what are you going to do?" "The washing" he replied. He was out in the yard with the big bath and the scrubbing board. I said, "Mam doesn't do it in that; she uses the smaller one.", "Well," he said, "I need the smaller one". He put some water in it but he couldn't lift it. "Will you give me a hand?" he asked. "Where do you want it?" I said. "On top of the range." He replied. We got it on the range, but it was a struggle. I carried on with my work.

I washed-up the three mugs and one cup without a handle, swept the floor and sort of pulled the top blanket straight on the beds. I left Martin to it, and I went out for a while.

I came back about an hour later and called in to see if granddad was alright. He wanted a drink of water and I took his pot and went in the kitchen. Martin had a pan in his hand and was emptying the hot water from the small bath on the range, a bit at a time, and putting it into the big bath in the yard. He said it was red hot. I said, "It will be, if it's been boiling for an hour!" The floor was soaking wet and Martins face was all flushed with the steam. He said, "There isn't a lot of water left in it, so can you help me lift it down." I told him off and said, "You could have scalded yourself!" I gave him a hand to get it off the range and into the yard. He had the big bath ready with clean water to rinse the clothes. I left him to it and went to get granddad his water. I sat with him for a while; but he didn't feel like talking. He said he would feel better tomorrow and he was falling to sleep, so I left him. I went back into the kitchen; Martin had cleaned the floor and now he was hanging the washing on the line.

Mam came in the front door with Ray behind her and she came into the kitchen. Martin went up to her with a big smile on his face, "Look mam I have done all the washing for you; I even boiled it like you do!" Mam went to the back door and looked up at the clothesline, "Oh Jesus, Mary and Joseph. Please tell me I'm having a bad dream!" We all looked at her, and then looked up at the line, Martin had boiled the two-Fairisle pullovers, Rays long trousers, his short ones, the wool socks and the two shirts that were like a glazed material, and my skirt and blouse. They had all shrunk, apart from my skirt and blouse. Ray's long trousers were so small they wouldn't even fit me, and the pullovers and socks were all matted. They wouldn't fit a two year old. Mam looked at Martin and said, "Get him out of my sight before I kill him." Martin shot out the back gate as fast as his legs would carry him. Mam started crying and said, "In god's name how am I going to replace those clothes?" We all had to suffer for Martins washing disaster for days after.

The school holidays were over and we went back to school. Ray's job had finished as it was the end of the season. He had given mam all the money he had made, so she could buy clothes for us. He was looking for another job but he could only work weekends. He said he was going to see about one after school today. When he came home he told us he had got the job. It was in O'Connell Street working in a shop and he would get two and six for the weekend. "That will be alright won't it mam? It will help out a bit." Mam said it would and that she was proud of him.

Chapter 14: Martin's Washing Disaster

Time passed and it was nearly Christmas again. We got the paper chains out that we had made last year, and went and picked some holly. It brightened the place up a bit. Dad was still the same. As soon as he got his money, he would drink it, and if he got an odd days work on top of his dole, he drank that as well. Mam kept on at him to go and see if he could get free boots for the boys. She told him, "I only get a small wage, and it's not enough to support a family! So you will have to give me some money or I will have to stop feeding you!" He just laughed at her as he knew she wouldn't do that. Mam got a piece of pickled beef for Christmas dinner and we were looking forward to that as and we hadn't had any for ages. The chef at mam's work gave her some bits and pieces that were left over from the restaurant to take home. There was a quarter piece of cake with cream in the middle and icing round the top, a few little cakes and some sausage rolls. So we had a feast on Christmas day! Martin and I got new school bags for Christmas because ours were on their last legs and Ray got a jumper to keep him warm at work. We were all still praying to Blessed Martin, but we weren't having much luck!

Chapter 15:
Dad's Final Journey

At the end of January mam got a promotion at work to the head linen keeper. She was very pleased as it would bring in a few extra shillings a week, and of course it was all down to Blessed Martin. So we prayed harder! There was a pearl factory in Ennis. I don't remember where it was, but you could work from home, so that was all of us threading strings of pearls. There were a lot of other families doing it as well to make a few extra shillings. It was very boring work as you had to get the right pearl in the right place. If you didn't you would have to take so many off and start again. That came to an end, when the factory had enough pearl necklaces made and closed down.

Mam took me to work again, and I made Mr Patterson two more hankies. He was very pleased with them, and asked me how old I was. I told him I would be ten in two weeks. He asked me what I wanted to do when I grew up. I told him I wanted to be a dressmaker. "Well I think you will make a very good one," he said. He put this big red curtain on the counter, and a pair of trousers that had gone a bit shinny. He asked mam if she could get rid of them for him. She asked if she could have the curtains as she could make good use of them. He said, "Well yes; but there are a few faded parts on them." She said, "I could cut round them!" He said he would let her have a docket so she could take them out of the airport.

It was my birthday; I was ten years old today. The chef at Shannon had sent a cake for me. It had lots of cream on it and he sent lots of small cakes, jam tarts, and sausage rolls. Mam brought some party masks that you put on your eyes in all different colours and hats and streamers that were left over from Christmas. She said I could have a party. I was very excited and asked all my friends. When they arrived, I gave them a hat and mask each, and then we all started eating. When we had our fill, we all stood their looking at each other and saying nothing. The boys were away as soon as they were full! Mam was falling asleep on the chair. I asked her if we could go out and she said, "I thought you were having a party?" "I don't know what you do at parties. I have never been to one!" I replied. "Away you go out then," she replied. We all made for the door at the same time, and we were glad to get out. We had great fun outside with the masks, and the streamers, and we were playing all sorts of games. I asked the girls what you do at a party, but they had never been to one either. Anyway we had more fun outside.

Easter came and I got my first chocolate Easter egg. It was in a box and had a lovely pink ribbon tied around it. It took me three days to take it out of the box as I didn't want to spoil it. The boys kept on at me to open it, so that they could have some. When I did open it, I kept the empty box for ages.

I was out picking blue bells to put on my altar. They smelt lovely. I left my friend Miss at our front gate and told her I would see her later, and went in the front door. I saw the back of dad going into granddad's room. I peeped in. He was kneeling down at the fireplace, and was putting paper and sticks in the grate. There was a lace hanging down the chimney from granddad's boots. I thought, "Oh no, he has found them!" I ran up the hall, threw the bluebells on the table, and found granddad in the yard fixing someone's pot. I shouted at him, "He has found your boots, and lit a fire!" Granddad rushed past me. Dad was just coming out of his room and said, "I have lit a fire for you. I thought you might be cold," then started laughing. Granddad dashed into the room. I was behind him and the flames were shooting up the chimney. Granddad got down on his knees and put his hands up the chimney. I was screaming, "No, no, please, you'll get burnt!" He managed to get the boots down onto the hearth, and he was stamping on them. He got the fire out but his hands were all burnt. He got on his knees again and he was looking at his boots. I felt so sorry for him. All those years he had those boots up the chimney, and he thought they were safe. Mam came in, "What's that smell?" she asked. I ran to her and was trying to tell her what had happened in between crying. "Calm down," she said. "I can't understand a word you are saying." I took hold of her hand and pulled her into granddad's room. "Oh my god! What's happened? Your hands are all burnt." I stopped crying, and told her what dad had done and he wasn't drunk. He just did it out of spite. Granddad said, "That man is a lunatic, and he wants putting away. There's something wrong with him."

Mam got granddad off his knees. He was covered in soot and she led him into the kitchen. He called back to me to look under the mattress and see if his suit was still there, I checked and it was. Mam was washing granddad's face and hands and he said, "I can manage myself!" He hated being a burden. Mam said, "You just shut your mouth and do as you're told!" I looked at mam and I couldn't believe she was talking to her father like that. The boys came in and asked what had happened. I told them what had gone on and told them mam is in a very bad temper. She finished with granddad and told him to go and lie down. He said he had to go and clean the mess up, and see to his boots. Mam shouted at him again, "I told you to go and lie down! Will you do as you're told? We will clean the mess up." She told the boys to go and see if his boots had cooled down. If they were they were to put them in the shed, and they were to clean up the soot in the room. She said, "I'm going to take my uniform off and then I'll come and wash it all down."

Dad came in, and sat on a chair, then opened his newspaper. Mam went over to him and tore the newspaper out of his hands and said, "You fucking bastard! How could you do that to an old man? You have tried to frighten him with a gun and your children were frightened. You have gone after him and your daughter with an axe. You have done so many bad things to him; when he was only trying to feed your children and keep them warm. You are scum! You shouldn't be allowed on the streets, you big lump of shit! And if it hadn't been for her coming in the house when she did, the house would have burnt down and your children wouldn't have a roof over their heads." "Well," she said, "I have had enough now, and I am not going to take any more of it, do you hear me?" He looked at her in disbelief, and then he said to her, "Is my dinner in the oven?" That did it. She looked at him and shouted, "If you want to eat here, get yourself a fucking job, and put some money on the table, because I am not feeding you any more until you do!" Dad went out the back door and banged it. We all stood there with our mouths open as we had never heard mam swear before, and for the rest of my life I never heard her swear like that again.

She cleared the dishes off the table and threw them in the sink. I started to cry and she said, "What are you crying for?" But I couldn't tell her as I didn't know myself! She said in a softer voice, "I will be alright now. I've got it all out of my system. It should have been done years ago." All we were worried about now was dad coming home drunk and starting on mam as granddad wouldn't be able to help with his burnt hands. I didn't think us three children would be able to do much, because he was so strong. I went in to see if my granddad was all right. He asked what all the shouting was about and I told him. He asked about his boots. I told him we would look at them tomorrow!

Ray had an interview in Northern Ireland for the Air Force, and mam didn't have the money for his fare. The only thing she could do was sell the few clothes she had and try to get enough money together. She managed to scrape enough by selling most of her clothes, and Ray was sent for his interview. He was all right with the written work, but when it came to the medical, it was a different story. They said he was under nourished and needed building up. They told him they were very sorry but if he came back in a year they would see him again. Ray was very disappointed. Mam told him not to worry as we would get him built up for next year. Mam wore her uniform all the time for the next two weeks as she told us money would be very tight. She would have to get to a sale of works, and see if she could get some second hand dresses that she could alter, as she might get reported for wearing her uniform when off duty.

A couple of days later I was looking out of our bedroom window and I saw the insurance man coming. I went in the kitchen and told mam. She said, "I have no money. Ray, you go to the door and tell him I'm out." Ray said, "Can't someone else go? I hate going!" Martin said he would go, so when the knock came on the door, Martin opened it. The man said, "Is your mam in?" "No, and I don't know what time she'll be back," he replied. The man started talking to Martin, asking him how old he was. He told him he would be fourteen in November. The man was saying what a big lad he was, and then he said, "I wonder if you could tell me when your mam will be in?" Martin had got carried away with all the praise he was getting and shouted up the hall, "Mam, when will you be in?" Mam came down the hall and her face was scarlet. Martin put his hand to his mouth. She told us to go in, and stood talking to the man. She came back in the kitchen, Mam said insurance wasn't a depth, and she would pay him next week, and she did. Martin said he was sorry and the man had mixed him up.

The beginning of June was like a nightmare in our house. Dad had received a letter that morning to say he had to appear in court on the tenth of June. My mother was taking him to court. One of the charges was for not maintaining his children. I don't know what else there was, but she must have witnesses. We children didn't know anything about it until dad got the letter. He was going mad, throwing things about, and shouting and swearing. We wished mam had told us. She had gone to work and must have made the charges a while ago, so we were getting his bad mood. It was the longest week we had ever lived through! On the morning of the tenth, we were in the kitchen; Dad was shouting at us all and we were very frightened. He had got a full time job starting today. I suppose to show the judge he was working. He was saying that he would have to ask them for time off to go to court, but Mam wasn't taking a bit of notice of him, and she knew he couldn't hit her today. He went out the door, then he came back in. He was pointing his finger at mam and said, "I am going to tell the judge you give those children margarine!" Those were his last words, as he went out the door. Those words have always stuck in my mind, because it was such a childish thing to say, as we were lucky if we got margarine! Mam told us to get ready for school and not to worry.

I sat at my desk at school and all I did was worry. I was thinking about what was going to happen after the court has finished. He might come home and kill us all! We would have to pray extra hard to Blessed Martin today. The classroom door opened and a nun came in. She went over to the nun that was teaching us and said something to her, and then she went out again. The nun who was teaching us said, "Mary Burns you're to go home. Your father is dead!" Those words will always stick in my mind. She could have had a softer way of telling me, but she was so abrupt. I was going to tell her she had made a mistake, that my dad was in court, but I thought better of it. I walked out of the classroom, and everyone's eyes were looking at me. I closed the door quietly behind me, went down the stairs and across the playground. There was a nun stood at the gate. My two brothers were at the other side waiting for me, but she wouldn't let them in because of what dad had done. She unlocked the gate and let me out and I went over to the lamppost where they were stood. They put their arms around me and said, "Dad is dead. He can't hurt us anymore." We started dancing round the lamppost! Although we didn't know how he had died, someone had been to the boy's school and told them and they were told to come and get me.

When we got home mam and granddad were in the kitchen. I looked at mam she was dry eyed. She told us to sit down and said, "When your father got to work this morning his job was to catch a horse and put it on the cart. He was running after it and he had a heart attack and died. That's all I know at the moment." She said we were to act upset. There were people in and out of the house all day, and I was thinking about how strange it was! He was in court on the tenth June; he died on the tenth June; and he was only forty years old. What a waste of a life, and all through drink! I had been praying hard to Blessed Martin, but I only meant for him to send him away, not for him to die. It was late when we got something to eat that day, with mam making cups of tea for everyone. Someone had brought some cups in. I don't know who it was, but she was glad of them because she only had the tin mugs. We went to bed all tired out, but I couldn't sleep. I couldn't get all that had happened that day out of my mind.

We all went to see dad's body at the mortuary. There seemed to be more than just dad's there, because there was a group of people down the other end of the long room that we didn't know. There was a line of wooden chairs along the back wall. Mam had warned us before we went in, that we were to look and act upset. She said, "My Nana and Granda will more than likely be there." I felt really sorry for them that two of their children that had died, so they must be very upset. Everyone just sat there. I sat at one side of mam and my brothers at the other side. The boys were starring straight ahead, they looked like statues. I stood up

Chapter 15: Dad's Final Journey

and was walking towards my dad, but mam called me back. Someone else said, "Let her go and see him." I went over to him. He wasn't in a coffin. He was just on a trolley bed. I looked at him. He looked so peaceful. Why couldn't he have always been like this? It was then I noticed that the tuft of hair was down on his forehead, so I tried to put it back, but it wouldn't go. I went back to mam and asked if she had a comb. She opened her bag and gave me one, but she looked very cross. I went back to dad and I combed his hair and the tuft was gone. I said, "Now you can rest in peace." I kissed him on the cheek and said, "Goodbye", and with that I burst into tears and walked back to my chair. My two brothers were also crying. They were making funny noises in their throats, because they were trying not to, then everyone was crying.

When we got home, mam gave us all a slap! Ray said, "What's that for?" She said, "For all that wailing and carrying on up there!" "But you told us to act upset didn't you!" She shouted at him, "Not that upset!", and then she went into the bedroom. The boys said it was my fault; you went and combed his hair and that set everyone off crying. I thought I can't do right for doing wrong. We went to the funeral, and all the family were there. When they took him through the gate of the little cemetery I thought, this is the end of his journey. There was a slit in the wall by the side of the gate. You could get one person at a time through. It had a couple of steps up, and steps down the other side into the cemetery. This was where I stood and looked down onto the service. My sister Patsy was buried in the same grave; she had died three years before I was born and she was only nine months old. Then there was little Patrick, who was also with Patsy and now dad was going to be with them. The people started to walk towards me; so it must be all over. We could all go home and I was glad, and so were the boys.

In the next few weeks our lives started to change. We got new cups, saucers, dinner plates, and two electric rings on a little stand, a lovely electric sacred heart lamp, and a wireless. Life was a lot happier now! There was no one coming in breaking everything in the house, and we could go to sleep without worrying about if we had to get up in the middle of the night.

Chapter 16: Where Did You Put the Winkles?

Mam asked for two weeks holidays from work and we were all going to Ballyglass. She had been very quiet for the last few weeks, but when we got to Ballyglass she seemed to be her old self again. The day after we arrived in Ballyglass, we went to the bog with Willie, and as he dug the turf, we stacked it for drying. We helped him to load the cart with turf that had dried, to take home. When we got back we piled all the turf neatly by the side of the house, and I will never forget the smell off it. We went hay making, which was a lot easier now that Willie had the tractor. We would rake all the hay into a pile, and then the men would make it into big cock of hay. It was three or four times the size of me! When the hay was ready, Willie would tie a big rope around it and drag it from the field to the barn with the tractor. The men that helped were other farmers, and they would go to each other's farms in turn until all the work was finished. We went to one farm with Willie, and we worked all day.

When we got back to Ballyglass, Mam looked at me and said to Sue, "What's up with her?" They all came to look at me. I was covered with black 'Ticks', from the hay! Sue went and got a sheet and spread it out on the kitchen table, they laid me face down and started to squeeze them out of my body. Then they turned me over and started on the front of me. Martin was telling me that the 'Ticks' sucked all the blood out of your body and if you didn't get them all out you would die. I started to shudder with the thought of it. Then he said, "Will you look at the size of this one?" Mam told him to shut up. I asked why no one else had got them. Willie said it was because they liked me the best! I said, "Well I wished they wouldn't like me the best!" My body was sore for a couple of days; with all the squeezing, but after that I was all right.

Another day we asked Sue if we could borrow her bike to go and see Emily and the girls. She asked, "How are the two of you going to go on one bike? The hills around here are bad enough for one to get up, never mind two!" Martin told her he had worked it out. He would cycle up all the hills and leave the bike at the top, when I had walked up the hill I would get on the bike and cycle down, and leave the bike for him. Sue let us go but I don't think she knew what Martin was on about! I told Martin he could go down the first hill because it was the boreen and it was very narrow and full of big potholes. He waited for me on the road. As it was a steep hill down, Martin said he would give me a craggy down as the road was straight at the bottom until we got to the turning for the church. When we got there we took it in turns for the four miles to Emily's.

We stayed there a couple of hours and played with the girls, and then we set off again and did the same thing back to Ballyglass. Our two weeks were nearly over; but before we left, Sue and Willie were having a 'Shindig' for us. They asked all the farmers and their wives. One of the farmers had two daughters; one was called Aggie, and the other was called Baby. We had been to their house once before, to a 'Wake'. Martin got on well with them and they were always kidding around together, but I think Martin had a little crush on Baby! They were a few years older than him, and we all teased him. We all had a great night singing, dancing and eating. But a couple of days later we had to go home, as Mam had to be back at work. We called in to see Emily and family on our way to the station, and her husband Harry was there. We got out of the car and Harry grabbed mam and started twirling her around, He was always kidding her on and making her laugh and the rest of us as well, with the antics he got up too! Emily would say, "Put that woman down!" and she would laugh. We were going to miss them all. They were such a happy family! We got back in the car, and we could see them waving until they were out of sight.

We were back in Ennis again. We had two weeks left of our holidays. We were walking down the road early one morning and we saw Florrie at her door. We asked her if she was going to milk the goat. She said she no and that she was going to Lahinch for the last dip in the sea because it was near the end of the season. We asked if we could come with her. She said, "Have you got money for the train?" "No," we said, "But we would go and ask granddad." She said, "Go on then, and be quick, and bring a bottle of water". We dashed up the road and asked granddad for the fare, but all he had was a shilling. Ray was in the kitchen and said, "You won't get there for a shilling". We got our bottles of water and went back to Florrie. We showed her the shilling and she said, "It would have to do!"

When we got to the station, she said, "We have to go in with a crowd of people." We got on the train and Florrie told Martin to get under the seat where she was sitting. Martin said, "What do I have to do that for?" Florrie said, "Do as you're told; it won't be for long." The guard came and looked in all the doors of the carriages, Florrie held her tickets up. He counted the people and then he banged the door shut. The train set off very slowly, it had a bad bend to go round, and Florrie told Martin he could come out now. He got out and he was all black and full of dust. He said, "Look at the state of me!" Florrie said, "Ho, it will wash off when you have a dip in the sea." Then she said, "I will have to have a word with the cleaners for not doing their job!" Then she started to laugh. I went over to the door of the carriage and put the window down, and looked out. There were boys standing on the steps outside the other doors of the train, clinging on to the windows and Ray was one of them. I told Florrie to come and look, but she told me to come and sit down. I said, "But Ray was outside the train and he might fall!" "He wont", she said. "He will get in one of the carriages in a minute. Then he will get out again when we are coming into Ennistymon because he has to help to push the train up a big hill!" I believed every word Florrie was telling me! And sure enough, when we were coming into Ennistymon, the train slowed down and the boys that were hanging on to the outside of the train got out, closed the carriage doors and started to run. I asked Florrie what they were doing now. She told me that Lahinch was only two miles away, and they were going to see if they could race the train there!

When we got to Lahinch, Florrie usually waited for the other people to get off, but today she was pushing us in among them, she told Martin to stay behind her. When we got to the ticket collector, she was talking to him and at the same time pushing Martin out the other side. We had a great day in Lahinch. We went picking winkles, and climbed all the grassy hills, playing hide and seek. Florrie and the boys went swimming, while I paddled. Ray and the other boys set off for the train, and I got a bit worried. I thought we were going to miss it, but Florrie said, "Don't worry! We'll be going shortly. They have gone now because they are going to race the train back to Ennistymon." When we got to the station, we waited outside until there was a crowd going in and we got in the middle of them. Martin had to hide behind Florrie until we got in and got on the train. This time Florrie gave Martin a towel and said, "It's a bit wet but its better than getting all dirty again!" He laid it down under the seat and got in on top of it.

When we were coming into Ennis, the train slowed down at the bend, and then we saw Ray and the other boys get off and run. Florrie told us to get our things together and when we got off, we were to get in with the crowds of people. That's what we did, and we got out of the station. As we walked up the road, Florrie said to Martin, "It's a nightmare trying to hide you with that red hair!" and then she laughed and ruffled his hair. We had a great day for our shilling and Ray

Chapter 16: Where Did You Put the Winkles?

had said it wouldn't get us there. When we got to Florrie's house she got the towel out of her bag with all the periwinkles in it and said, "I only want a couple of handfuls of them." She got her little pan out that she warmed the tea in, and we filled it with winkles. She wrapped the towel back up and told us to put them in something when we got home and put some water on them.

When we got in the house we emptied them in a bucket and put some water in. Granddad was talking to Mr Riedy out in the back lane, and I asked him where mam was. He said she had gone out, but she wouldn't be long. He said," I will be there in a minute to get your tea." Ray came in, and I asked him why he had jumped off the train before it got into the station. He said, "It was a dare!" Granddad came in and dished up our dinner and left us to it. It was stew and we were all ready for it. Mam came in just before we had finished. We told her we had a great day. She said, "And where did you get the money to go?" I told her granddad gave it to us, and I said "We brought lots of winkles back!" She said she would see to them later. I didn't know what was wrong with mam lately. She seemed to be going off in a daydream all the time and she kept going off for half an hour and we didn't know where. We finished our tea and went out to play. Ray was first in bed that night. He said he was tired and it was no wonder trying to race the train two miles there and two miles back for a dare! What if he had missed it?"

We all had a sleep in the next morning, because mam was on late shift. We were woken up with mam shouting, "Oh Jesus, Mary and Joseph! What's happened in here?" We ran out to see what had happened. We couldn't believe our eyes, all the walls and doors and the ceiling were covered in winkles. They were everywhere and Mam was going mad. She said, "Where did you leave the winkles?" We told her in the bucket under the sink. She went to get the bucket, there wasn't one winkle left in it. She said, "Why didn't you put a lid on the bucket?" "We didn't know we had too! Florrie never said anything about a lid. She just told us to put water on them, and you said you were going to see to them last night". "Well", she said, "I forgot!" We spent all morning picking winkles off the walls and doors. Granddad got the sweeping brush and knocked them off the ceiling onto the floor and told us to pick them up. We asked him where we had to put them, He told us to put them in the big pot, and don't forget the lid. When we had collected all the winkles we could find, Granddad washed them, put clean water and some salt on them and put them on to boil. When they were cooked, he strained them. Then he said, "We can have some nice sandwiches for tea, so get some pins and start picking them out." We all went off winkles for a long time after that!

Ray stared work at Shannon airport. He had got a job as apprentice confectionery Chef and he seemed to like it. There was a Swiss Chef there, and he took a shine to Ray and they got on well together. He was going back to Switzerland soon because his wife couldn't settle in Ireland. He kept asking Ray to go back with them. Then he asked my mother if they could take him, they said, he could live with them and they would look after him. But mam said, "No. He was too young." Ray was upset about it, but he got over it in time.

I found out where mam was going for her half-hours! I was walking up the Clare Road with my friend Miss, when mam came out of the back lane gate onto the Clare Road. She was going up towards town, and I shouted her but she didn't hear me. We walked on behind her but she was walking very fast, she stopped at the corner and she was talking to a man. When we got nearer, Miss said, "That's the man that works in the grocery shop." We went up to her and she said, "What are you doing here?" and he started to flap and couldn't get away fast enough. Mam looked very cross, and we walked back home in silence. I left Miss at our back gate, and we went in the house. Mam was very nervy. She said, "You are not to tell your granddad that I was talking to that man." I asked her was that where she went when she was missing? Talking to that man? She said, "Yes, but I wasn't to tell anyone."

I wished many a time that I hadn't seen them together, because now that I knew about it, she took me with her every time she went to meet him. She would tell granddad that she was taking me to visit her friend from work, and she lived at the other end of town. Then he would pick us up in a lorry and go for a drive. I got so fed up with it, as I couldn't go out to play with my friends when I wanted to. One day she took me up to the end of his street where he lived. I can't remember where it was; but I know it was a red brick house with a little front garden and we were stood behind a wall. I got fed up of waiting and started to go down the street. Mam called me back. I said, "Why can't we just go and call for him?" Mam said, "Come off that street. I don't want his mother to see you." I asked why. And she said, "She wouldn't like it. You must never go down that street again." I didn't like this man at all. He was very false, and if mam weren't looking, he'd stick his tongue out at me, and if she turned round, he'd put a big smile on his face for her. When he did come out of his house I said to him, "Aren't you allowed to talk to women? Mam says your mother wouldn't like it?" With the look on his face he could have killed me. My mam wasn't too pleased either.

Another afternoon we got picked up at St Flannon's College. When I got in the lorry I could see through the little window. There was a man sitting in the

Chapter 16: Where Did You Put the Winkles?

back. We stopped near a river and there was a wood at the other side. We got out of the lorry and the man got out of the back. I nearly passed out as it was the bousie man, who always stood on the corner when we went to school. Mam laid a rug out on the grass next to the river, and we all sat down. I was that close to mam I was nearly on top of her. After a while mam said, "Mattie is going to take you for a walk in the woods and you can look and see if you can find any rabbits." She pulled me up and put my hand into the bousie mans hand. I was so frightened, I was shaking. We got half way across the field and all I could think about was the tramp down Scabby Lane. I pulled my hand free of his and I ran as fast as I could back to mam. When I got there they looked shocked and there was a fumbling of clothes and buttons. Mam was furious and so was he. I said, "I want to go home to my granddad!" There was silence on the way back. Mam didn't say anything until the lorry pulled away, and then she said, "What is wrong with you?" I told her I was frightened of the bousie man. She said, "You are not to say anything to your granddad. Do you hear me?" I said, "Yes."

Another day mam said he was taking us out in the lorry for the day, so we have to tell Granddad that we're going to Limerick. I went to bed that night dreading the morning. I woke up with earache and I went into the kitchen. Mam and granddad were there and I told them I had earache. Mam said it was just the way I had been laid in the bed and it would soon go off. Granddad said, "I think you had better cancel Limerick today." But mam insisted I would be alright. We were picked up at St Flannon's College. He said he was going to take her around the Ring of Kerry. It was the worst day of my life! My ear was getting worse, and I was crying all the time. I couldn't help it and I kept thinking if only I could go to sleep. I tried but I couldn't. I don't know if we got around the Ring of Kerry or not, but when I saw Captain Mack's Corner; I was so relieved. He said to mam, "Well she has spoilt the whole day with all her whining and crying and I bet she was putting it on." Mam started shouting at him, "She wasn't putting it on. Have you never had earache? Well I have so I know what its like." "Right," he said, "if that's the way you feel." She said it was and banged the door of the lorry and he took off.

When we got back in the house granddad said, "You're back early." Mam told him we had to come back early because my earache had got worse. He said, "Well, I told you not to take her, didn't I?" He took my hand and said, "She can lie on my bed. I will stay with her". He laid me on the bed and went out again. "Back in a minute." He came back in with a warm towel, and placed it under my head so the bad ear was on it, then he stroked my hair and kept stroking it until I fell asleep. When I woke up next morning the towel was stuck to my ear, Granddad took it off very gently, He said, "Look at that! Whatever was in there has burst, so you will start to feel better now." A few days later mam was taking me to the hairdresser, I said, "Please don't get my hair cut. It's nearly long enough for plaits." She said, "What have I told you about plaits? I am going to get your hair permed." I said, "Oh no, I don't want it permed!" She said, "You will do as you're told." We went into this house, just a couple of doors away from my nana's, and this woman started cutting my hair. After she had finished she was putting some sort of lotion on that smelt awful and then she put big heavy clamps all over my head. They were a ton weight and I had to sit with those in for ages. When it was finished and I looked in the mirror; I just wanted to burst into tears as I was like a golliwog.

There was a Fancy Dress at the convent gardens on Saturday. Mam was making me a fairy outfit at work, with crepe paper and cellophane. She said she would bring it home tomorrow and told me to remind her to get some white socks and pants. The day before the Fancy Dress, I reminded her about the socks and pants, but she didn't come home and it was gone teatime. My friend called for me and said, "You were supposed to come up for me." I told her I had been waiting for my mam. She said, "I saw her about half an hour ago talking to the man from the shop." I thought, oh no, she must be friends with him again. I went out to play with Miss, and when I came in a couple of hours later she still wasn't home. It was time to go to bed and by this time granddad was looking very cross. I couldn't sleep for ages as I was worried about mam. I eventually got to sleep; then I was woken up again with someone shouting. It was granddad; he was going on at mam for coming in at this time of night. "You have three children," he said, "and you would think you would have had enough with the man you had without staying out half the night with another. Have a bit of decency! He has only been in his grave a couple of months!" She said, "Don't you talk to me like that. It's my life and I will do what I like."

Mam with a work friend at Shannon Airport c.1947 (Top Left), Shannon Airport c.1947 and me in my fairy outfit for the Fancy Dress competition.

She came into the bedroom and I pretended I was asleep, so couldn't mention the socks and pants. When we got up next day mam and granddad weren't talking to each other. Later on I was getting ready for the Fancy Dress, and I asked mam where my socks and pants were. She put her hand to her mouth and said, "Oh I forgot to get them!" She came in the room and she was searching for socks. She found a pair that weren't very white looking and they had red stripes on the top of them. She said, "If we fold them down below your ankle, you won't be able to see the stripes. I said, "I can't wear navy blue pants." She went into her own drawers and pulled out a pair of yellow knickers. They had wide legs and on the front and back of them it said Wednesday, in big blue letters, I had to put them on she was telling me to hurry up or we would be late. I was ready and Granddad wished me luck. We were walking up the road when the lorry stopped and Mam told us to get in. He dropped us off at the convent grounds, but mam didn't get out. I said, "Mam, I'm supposed to have a parent with me." She said she would be back in about fifteen minutes before the judging started and told the boys to look after me. But she didn't come back, and it was time to go in front of the judges. We had to walk in front of the judge's one at a time, you gave a little twirl and then you had to bow to them. When it came to my turn I was shaking like a leaf. I was frightened that when I had to bow, that the people standing behind me would see my yellow knickers with Wednesday on them, so I bowed and hoped for the best. I ran to my brothers.

It was about fifteen minutes before they announced the winner. It came over the loud speakers, that I had won first prize! My brothers were jumping up and down with excitement. They took me over to collect my prize and the judges asked me where my parent was and I said my mam wasn't here. So they handed me second prize; which was a big box of chocolates. Ray said, "Excuse me, but she won first prize. It was announced over the loud speakers and everyone heard it." They told us to take our prize and go. We were walking up the road with Ray going mad when the lorry pulled up. Mam opened the door and the boys were talking at the same time. They told her, she would have to go and see the judges. Mam said, "Get in. It doesn't matter. She won a prize." Ray said, "It does matter and those judges are supposed to be Holy people." Mam told him to get in and shut up. I was disappointed. I thought for once in my life I had achieved something, but it wasn't to be.

After the row with granddad, Mam didn't go out very much. She only went out about twice in the next month, but I didn't have to go with her and I was glad about that. She got Ray some new clothes and a sports jacket. He was growing up fast and growing out of everything. She took Ray to Paddy Con's Ballroom to teach him how to dance. I remember the first time she took him because about an hour later Martin said, "Let's go down and see if there is any way we can see them." We got outside the building and Martin was looking round and said, "We can't go in the door or we will get caught, so that's out." Then he pointed to the roof. "We could climb up there and have a look." I said, "It is very high, we might fall." He said, "We wont if we're careful". We started climbing and we reached the top. There was a window in the roof. Martin got at one side and I got at the other. We looked in and could see all the people dancing. They looked very small because we were so high up and then we saw mam and Ray. They seemed to be gliding across the floor and I though they looked great together. Martin said, "Look at him swanking. I bet he thinks he is great. I'm going to call him Lord Haw, Haw from now on." I asked him who Lord Haw, Haw was. He said, "I don't know who he is, but I bet he looks like Ray!"

There was someone across the road. He had seen us and shouted at us to get down. We got down as fast as we could, and this man said, "Are you trying to break your necks? Get along home and don't let me see you up there again!" We ran as fast as we could. Martin said, "I hope that fellow doesn't know mam, or were in for a good hiding!" Mam took us to the cinema one night and we were getting all sorts of treats that we had never had before. On the way home as we walked past the Church we could smell this lovely smell. It made you feel hungry and we asked mam what it was. She told us that Dolan's Shop had started selling chips and I said, "I've never had a chip." "We could have a bag between us, in case we didn't like them." Mam replied. We walked down the Clare Road with our bag of chips. I had never tasted anything like them. They were lovely!

The following day Martin and I went down the crags. Ray and his friends were there but they didn't see us so we watched what they were up to. Then we saw all this smoke and we thought they had a fire, so we went over to them. But it wasn't a fire. They were all smoking. Ray said, "You aren't going to tell mam, are you?" Martin had a big grin on his face and said, "Well I don't know." Ray said, "I'll give you three pence each if you don't tell her." Martin said, "It's a deal!" We went off our own way. Martin said, "He's just wasted his money." "You are not going to tell mam, are you?" I said. "No," he replied, "I wouldn't have told her anyway!"

Chapter 17:
At the End of the Rocky Road …

It was mid October when mam told us that Ray was going to England. We were shocked. I said, "But Ray is the man of the house now. What does he have to go to England for? He has a job at Shannon and we are all happy!" I burst into tears and said, "I don't want Ray to go to England!" Mam said, "That's enough now. I don't want to hear any more." Martin and I were very upset about it as we didn't want to be split up. But why was Mam being so calm about it? At the end of October, Ray was packed. He didn't look old enough to be going to England as he was only fifteen and a half. He went out to say goodbye to his friends and Martin and I were standing outside the front gate when he came back. He said, "Cheer up you two. There is something I want you to do for me. When you hear the train setting off, you can tell mam that I smoke!" He went into the house and got his bag. He didn't have a lot in it. He gave mam a kiss and a big hug. Then he went over to granddad and shook his hand.

We were walking down the road with him. He said we could come as far as nana's house and then we were to go back. He told us we were to be good for mam. He went into nana's to say goodbye to them and that was the last we saw of him. Martin put his arm around me and said, "Don't worry. He will come back to see us, and anyway you have me, haven't you? I will look after you." We walked slowly back to our house. We listened until we heard the train go and then we went in to see mam. We told her that Ray said we had to tell you that he smoked. She said she already knew as she had opened his bag to put something in and found some packets of Gold flake. Martin said, "What do you think of that then? She knew he had Gold flake, and never even hit him? If it had been me, I would have got a good hiding." I said, "Maybe it was because he was going to England and she might never see him again."

I had slept in mam's bed since dad had died, but when she was on the early shift she had to be up about six in the morning. She was complaining that I kept her awake with my nightmares. I told her it would be better if I moved in with Martin now Ray had gone and that I could have one end of the bed and he the other. Martin was glad. He didn't want to sleep on his own because Ray had told him that many ghost stories he was frightened.

Christmas came and went. Mam seemed to be very quiet, but we didn't know what was wrong with her. She seemed to be waiting for something to happen. If anyone deserved to be happy it was mam. After all she had been through, I hoped she would meet a nice man and settle down. She had bought herself a second hand sewing machine and that kept her busy. She was making herself a blue dress and was putting braid round the neck and sleeves. I thought it was to long for her, but she said it was the fashion, it was called the new look. When she had finished the dress, she was going to make me a coat out of the red curtain that she got from Shannon airport, and she was going to make me some slacks out of Mr Paterson old trousers. I asked her what slacks were. "They're like trousers but they are for girls and are very fashionable." She replied.

Granddad was very content with himself. He was always polishing his boots, since they had been charred in the fire, but he said the more you polished them the better they got. Mam wanted him to get some new ones but he said there was years of life left in them. So they were still granddad's best boots. Mind you he was the same with the range. I think we must have had the cleanest range in Ennis. I think he just liked things to be shiny.

We went back to school in January. My friend Miss and I were walking up the Clare Road and the bousie man was standing on the corner. I had told Miss about him; that day he was taking me for a walk. She said it was lucky I had got away from him as you don't know what could have happened. We had a penny each and we went into the shop as you could get two toffees for a penny. We picked up our sweets and were going out when I said to Miss, "I'm glad that man wasn't there." She said, "Oh, he left a while ago. I heard he went to live somewhere else." I let out a sigh of relief. Thank goodness for that.

February came and it was my birthday. I got a bike and I couldn't believe my eyes. It was brand new. Not second hand and I was very excited. It was great at first cycling here there and everywhere, but I was on my own all the time as none of the other children had a bike. I was stood outside our front gate one day and I asked one of the girls if she wanted a ride, and before I knew it there was a gang of them. Martin said, "Just a minute. You are doing this all wrong. Look, I will be in charge of the bike because it's my idea. If someone wants a ride I will charge them a penny for half an hour. That way we can make some money out of it. But

I get a free go." I let him get on with it as he liked to be in charge. I think we made six-pence in the end.

May came and we were off for a couple of days. Martin and I were wondering what to do with ourselves. I said, "Let's go down to Maureen's and see if we can take Anthony and Finbar for a walk. We met Billy Pigott, who was Maureen's husband, and we asked if she was in. He said she was. Maureen let us take them for a walk. Anthony was always chatting, but Finbar was only a toddler and he was a bit shy of me, but he was great with Martin. He would put his hands up for Martin to lift him up. I think it was because Martin had red hair like Maureen. Martin loved children and they always took to him. We walked for a bit and then we would stop and play with them, and start to pick bluebells for the children to take home to their mother. Anthony thought this was great and he was trying to pick some, but he was only pulling the heads of them. We walked back to Maureen's with Anthony clutching the bluebells. We met Billy again. I had never seen a man walk as fast as Billy Pigott did. He stopped and talked to the children and then he was off again, like a Hare. Maureen said she had got lots of housework done while we were out. We handed the children back. Maureen said, "Thanks," and took the bluebells out of Anthony's hands and said they were lovely and that she would put them in water. Anthony was very pleased with himself.

One-day mam brought my cousin Sheila's little girl, Moira, to our house for the day. We were playing in the back yard when I asked mam if I could take her for a walk. She said yes but that I wasn't to take her far. I told mam I would just take her up the back lane out the gate onto the Clare Road and round to our front door. She said, "That's alright." We had just come out the gate to the Clare Road, when the heavens opened and it poured down. I had never seen rain like it and I didn't know what to do. If I took her back down the back lane; it would be all muddy, so I went down the front way. It was lashing down now and I took my cardigan off and put it around Moira, but it didn't help much. The rain just went straight through it and she looked up at me and smiled. We got over half way down the road when we saw mam coming towards us with a coat. She wrapped it round us and we hurried back to the house. She stripped Moira straight away as her clothes were soaking. She had a towel around her and was drying her hair with another. I was stood there shivering and she said, "Get those clothes off." I took them off and dried myself, then got some dry one's and put them on. Mam wrapped Moira in a blanket and dried her clothes in front of the fire. Later that day mam took her home. A few days later we got a message that Moira had died and we were all in shock. All I could see was her little face; looking up at me and smiling, and to this day I can still see her. I was in a terrible state with myself. It was my fault she had died. If only I hadn't taken her for a walk? She might still be alive.

Mam took me up to Sheila's. She had a little sweet shop and they lived at the back of it, I couldn't go in. I sat on the ground outside the shop. No matter what mam said to me, I couldn't go in. Mam went in and a few minutes later Sheila came out. She took my hand and told me it wasn't my fault. She pulled me up and led me into the house. She said, "You want to come and say goodbye to her, don't you?" When I saw her lying there, she was like a little angel and I was expecting her to open her eyes and smile at me. She looked so beautiful. Sheila gave me Moira's little gold bracelet. Every time I looked at it I saw her face looking up at me and smiling.

The summer holidays came, and mam told us we weren't going to Ballyglass this summer. We were very disappointed about that. Martin and I were sitting on our front-step thinking what we were going to do today when Maude from next door came out and sat on her step. She looked a bit sad today, which wasn't like her. I thought she was a bit lonely. Ninie, her sister, had got married a long while ago, and she had a pub in the town, so she didn't get to see her very often. Nan, her other sister, had gone to England with my cousin Francis, and her sister Bridie went as well. Everyone was going to England. Maude asked us what we were going to do with ourselves today. I told her I didn't know but Martin was thinking about it. Maude said, "Why don't you go and get your friends together and take a picnic down The Rocky Road? That would be a nice day out! We said, "That is a good idea!" We went for our friends and when we ended up, there were six of us. We asked granddad if we could have a picnic. He made us a sandwich each and a big thick slice of mam's bit of old cake, and another one of seedy cake, that mam had made last night. We all met up and went to The Rocky Road. We had a great time playing games of one kind or another and when it came to lunchtime we all sat down to eat. When we opened ours, everyone was looking at the two thick slices of cake we had each. We ate our sandwich and then we shared the cake six ways, and they all thought it was lovely. I was picking the seeds out of mine as I didn't like seeds in it. We all started to play again, and when it was time to go home, we were all tired out but content. We slept well that night!

We went to Lahinch a couple of times with Florrie and mam. Martin didn't have to hide under the seat this time and we didn't pick any more winkles, but we all had a good laugh.

About the middle of August mam told me we were going to Westport for a few days. There was only mam and I going and we were taking my bike on the train. I thought this was great. When we got on the train, mam told me we wouldn't be bringing the bike back. We were going to give it to Olive because we were going to start a new life in England! I was shocked and I wondered if Martin and granddad knew about it. When we got to Westport, she told me to ride the bike to Emily's and she would meet me there. It was only a mile out of Westport.

When I arrived, they all seemed to be expecting us. Willie came for us after milking. Emily and mam were hugging each other and there were tears. Then they were all giving me a hug. Emily told us to look after ourselves, keep in touch and to have a good life, and then we went to Sue's. Mam and Sue were talking long after I went to bed, but I don't know what about because they were talking very quietly. We spent a few hours there the next day, and then we said our goodbyes. Willie hugged me that tight I thought I would burst. Sue gave me a big hug, then mam and Sue were hugging each other for ages and there were more tears. Willie took us to the station but he didn't come to the train this time I could see he was upset. When we were on the train mam told me I wasn't to say anything to anyone for a couple of days until she had a talk with granddad. I fell asleep on the train and the next thing I knew we were in Ennis.

Martin was out playing when we got home, and granddad was in his room. I went in and gave him a hug and I was dying to tell him that we were going to England, but I kept my mouth shut. He said, "I thought you weren't back until tomorrow?" I said, "Well, we were here now." Martin came in and said the same thing, "I didn't expect you until tomorrow." He was asking how everyone was in Westport. I said, "They're all fine." Martin and I always talked to each other. No matter what it was, we had no secrets, so I couldn't keep this one from him. When we went to bed, I told him I had a secret, but if I told him he wasn't to tell anyone. He crossed his heart. I said, "We're all going to live in England." "When?" he asked. "I don't know. But I think it's very soon. That's why mam went to Westport. To say goodbye to them all." "Well I didn't get to say goodbye to them, and what's all the secrecy about anyway?" I said, "I don't know. Mam has been acting odd all week and she said she wanted to talk to granddad first." We lay there. Martin said, "Maybe we will live in a big house with a lovely garden." I said, "It would be all shiny like that big shop in Limerick." We fell asleep thinking about all the lovely things we were going to have.

Mam was trying to get us out of the house the next day. She told us there was a sale of works on at the hall, and she gave us four pence each to go. I told Martin she was trying to get rid of us so she could talk to granddad. We spent ages going round the stalls looking to see what we could buy. I saw this red hat and I asked the woman how much it was. She said the hat was nearly new and thought it was to go with a school uniform and that she couldn't take any less than two pence for it. I bought the hat as it would match the red coat that mam had just made for me. I went along to another stall and they had lots of handbags, but another woman was looking at the one I liked. I stood there for ages waiting for her to make up her mind. In the end she put it down and I grabbed it. It was red and very shiny. I asked the woman how much it was. She told me it was three-pence. I told her I only had two-pence. She must have felt sorry for me as I had stood there that long, so she gave it to me for two-pence! I saw Martin at one of the other stalls, I showed him what I had bought, and he said I had got a bargain. I asked him what he had got, and he unwrapped this piece of newspaper and showed me a little ornament done in a basket of flowers. He said, "I got this for mam." I felt awful now as he had spent all his money on mam, and I had spent mine on myself.

We went home and granddad and mam were in the kitchen and Granddad didn't look very happy. I thought that maybe he didn't want to go to England. Maybe he thought he was too old at seventy. I showed mam my hat and bag and she said they were very nice. Martin went up to her and gave her the little ornament and she thanked him and said it was lovely. Mam told Martin to sit down as she wanted to talk to him. All three of us sat down. "Martin," she said, "We are going to England next week." Martin had a big grin on his face and so did I. She continued with what she was saying, "But I can't take you or granddad with me because you are not old enough to work, but I will send for you both when you are fifteen." Our faces dropped and we were nearly in tears. I butted in, "But you are taking me and I'm not old enough to work." She said, "You're different. You are only a child." Martin said, "I'll be fifteen in November. That's only three months away." I said, "Why can't we wait until November and we can all go together?" She said, "If you butt in one more time, I'll give you a slap!" I started to cry and said, "If Martin isn't going, I don't want to go!" She said, "Well you can't stay here, so you better get it into your head that you are going." Then Martin burst into tears, although he was trying hard not too, but he couldn't hold them back. We went to bed, two very unhappy children. I told Martin I was sorry, as I thought when she said we were going to England she meant all of us. I didn't want to leave him, and he said he didn't want me to go. We cuddled each other and we fell asleep crying our eyes out.

We had a talk with granddad next day while mam was out at work. I said, "Can't you talk to mam? You're her father and she should listen to you!" He said, "I have already talked to her but she wouldn't listen. She is making a big mistake. She should know better after the first one, and there is nothing I can do or say that will change her mind. I have been told that when the time comes for us to go, I have to sell everything in the house". I said, "She has just bought a lot of new things for the house. Why did she do that then?" Granddad pointed to his mouth and said, "I'm keeping this shut, so don't ask me any more questions."

A couple of day's later mam told me to give my Fairy Dress to one of my friends. I took the dress out in the back lane. There were lots of girls playing, and my friend Miss was one of them, and I gave it to her. The day arrived for us to leave and mam had the case packed. I went out into the back lane to say goodbye to my friend. I would miss them. I had the grey pinstripe trousers that mam had made into a pair of slacks on. One of the boys said, "Is she turning you into a boy now?" I said, "They are not trousers. They were slacks and they were all the fashion." I went back in the house, and put my hat and coat on. I picked up my bag. Then I thought, "Look at me! A red curtain from Shannon airport made into a coat, Mr Paterson's trousers made into slacks; a hat and bag from the jumble sale, and I was going to England."

We went out the front door. Granddad was standing on the step, and Martin was standing at the gate. I think granddad must have kissed me about six times, and he kept giving me hugs. Martin gave me the biggest hug he had ever given me. He had his mouth tightly closed, but it was quivering. Then he let it all out and there were tears streaming down his face. I had never seen my granddad cry, but I did that day. I felt as thought someone was pulling my heart out, and I was trying to get back to them but mam was dragging me away. I kept saying, "I want to stay with Martin and granddad!" She was saying, "You'll see them soon."

We got to Aunt Fanny's. She said, "Look at the state of you. Hush now, you will be coming back soon to see us." She gave me a kiss and a hug. Then we went to my nana's. She gave me a big hug and told me to keep my faith and to go to mass and I told her I would. My Granda patted me on the head. We went to the station and got on the train. Then we got to the boat, and when I saw the size of it, I didn't want to get on it. It was like a big hotel sitting in the sea. Not like the one's we had seen in Clare Castle, and Mam was dragging me on. I was alright when I got settled, and I sat on a wooden bench and I thought, that my life up till now had been a Rocky Road, but now I would have to try and put all the bad memories behind me, and remember all the good ones. I was going to England to start a new life.

Chapter 18
A New Start in England

I had left Ireland with my mother in 1950 to start a new life in England. We had to leave my brother Martin and my grandad behind because Martin wasn't old enough to work. He had another three months to go until he was fifteen and it broke my heart leaving them behind. Mam said she would send for them as soon as Martin was fifteen. I couldn't understand why she was in such a rush and couldn't wait the three months when we could have all gone together. My older brother Ray had already gone to England ten months earlier when he was fifteen and a half. I was eleven and a half now and wasn't looking forward to starting a new school.

We were on the train now and I asked Mam if we were in England. She said we were. I don't know what I expected, but there seemed to be rows of red brick houses and the people looked the same as we did. I asked Mam if we were going to see Ray now. At least that would cheer me up. We were all that upset when he went away last October. We three children were very close and we had been through a lot together.

My dad had died in June 1949 of a heart attack on the very day my Mam was taking him to court for not maintaining his children. He was always drunk and he only ever worked for short periods at a time and he didn't give my Mam any money to keep us, so we were often hungry. He beat her up all the time and she was always covered in bruises. After his death, Mam was seeing this other man who worked at the grocer's shop. I was always with her when she saw him, but he didn't like me since I always seemed to be in the way. I thought he was silly and acted like a child.

After a couple of months she didn't see him anymore and my friend Miss told me he had gone away. I was glad and hoped I would never see him again.

I asked Mam again if we were going to see Ray. She came out of her daydream. "No, we're not," she said. "I have something to tell you—we're going to Harrogate in Yorkshire to see your uncle Bert and you are going to live with him for a while. I have to go back down to Salisbury. That's where Ray is."

I was shocked. "But I want to go with you," I protested. "I want to see Ray!"

"Now, don't start," she said. "I'll come back for you in two or three months."

"Two or three months! I could have stayed with grandad and Martin."

"You like your uncle Bert, don't you?"

"Yes," I said, "but I want to live with *you*."

"I don't want to hear any more about it," she said firmly. "It's been settled."

I wanted to cry. Our whole family would be split up now.

I was pleased to see my uncle Bert and aunt and they made us very welcome. They had a meal ready for us on arrival. They were all talking and I was falling asleep. Mam took me upstairs and I got into bed and I was out like a light.

Mam stayed for a few days and we got to know our way around Harrogate. We went and looked at all the shops. It was nice spending time with her but I was dreading her leaving me. She went to the school to get me registered; school didn't start for a few days so I was spending every minute I could with her.

The day Mam left I was very upset and she warned me not to be crying or clinging to her, as it would upset my uncle and aunt. She told me to be good and to do everything I was told. When she left I bottled it all up inside me until I went to bed that night, and let all my feelings go, crying under the blankets so no one would hear me.

I started school in September and tried my best to fit in but I couldn't understand half of what the other children were saying. I don't suppose they understood me either. I got through the first week and felt a bit better. I was missing my brothers and my grandad but I always had to wait until nighttime to cry under the blankets.

The second week I had two very bad nightmares, so an appointment was made for me at the Doctors. The Doctor asked my aunt what symptoms I had.

"She's having nightmares," she said. "I think she must be missing her mother."

The Doctor spoke to me and asked how long I had been having nightmares. I told him I had been having them for years. The Doctor told my aunt there was nothing wrong with me and there was nothing he could do about the nightmares.

On the third week I got a bit of a cold. It wasn't a bad cold, just a runny nose—so back to the Doctor again. The Doctor examined me and told my aunt there was nothing wrong with me. I had a bit of a cold and that was all.

At the end of the fourth week I was at the Doctor's again. I was feeling very embarrassed and I don't think the Doctor was too pleased either. My aunt told him the nightmares were getting worse.

"I think it's because she's missing her mother, don't you?"

"She's bound to miss her mother," the Doctor replied, "but there is nothing wrong with the child."

That was enough for my aunt. When we got back home my aunt got pen and paper and wrote to Mam and told her I wasn't well and that the Doctor said it was because I was missing her and could she come and collect me?

Three or four days later Mam arrived. My aunt was out and I was in the kitchen with my uncle. He was tickling me and making me laugh when the door opened and Mam came in. Her face changed from Concern to Fury.

Uncle Bert & Auntie Val

"I thought you were supposed to be ill!" she said, glaring at me.

"No, I just had a bit of a cold," I replied meekly.

"I want to talk to you upstairs!" she said decisively.

I went upstairs and she followed me. When I sat on the bed she pulled me off it and started hitting me and throwing me about the room; then she took off her shoe and continued to hit me with that. I was screaming with the pain—I couldn't believe this was my mother! She was as bad as my father was, though he never hit me. She kept hitting me until I nearly collapsed on the bed. Then she started to cry. She told me to put my nightdress on and get into bed and went out of the room and down the stairs. I could hear raised voices from down below but I couldn't tell what they were saying, and I didn't want to know.

I was trying to get my clothes off but the pain was making it difficult every time I moved. I managed it in the end but I couldn't stop crying—I was in awful pain. At that moment I hated my Mam. She wasn't the same person! I got into bed and faced the wall. I couldn't go to sleep and I couldn't get warm. I curled up in a ball.

When Mam came to bed a couple of hours later, I hadn't moved. She got into bed next to me and after a couple of minutes she jumped out of bed and put the light on. She touched my shoulder, saying, "Oh God, have I killed her?"

Then she turned me round and was shaking me, saying, "Oh God, you're ice cold!"

I turned back around to face the wall and said, "I'm all right"—and she let out a sigh off relief.

"Oh thank God!" she sighed. "I thought I had killed you. I know now you were telling me the truth." And yet she didn't say sorry.

I did go to sleep eventually, keeping as far away from her as I could.

When I woke up next morning I ached from one end of my body to the other. Mam wasn't in bed and I was glad about that. I lay there for about half an hour, longing to be home in Ennis with my grandad and Martin, and all my friends. I thought I'd better get up and go downstairs to get washed.

Mam was in the kitchen and asked if I was all right. I nodded without speaking.

"I've put some hot water in a bowl for you to get washed," she said.

So I took my nightdress off and went to the sink. She looked at me in horror.

"Oh God in Heaven, what have I done?" she said. "What came over me to do something like that?"

I wanted to shout at her, 'Why don't you tell me you're sorry!'—but no words came out of my mouth. I picked up my nightdress and was going back upstairs when she called after me: "Put those slacks on and a long sleeved jumper to cover those bruises."

When I came back down, she gave me some cornflakes and a piece of toast.

"We'll have to be going soon," she said. "We don't want to miss the train."

We got to the station with time to spare. The train was waiting on the platform so we got on and not long after we were on our way to Salisbury. Mam started talking to me. She told me they wouldn't give her any time off work to come to Harrogate for me so she had to give up her job and she would have to go and look for another tomorrow. Then she told me about Martin. The day after we left Ireland Martin ran away to Ballyglass in Westport, and went to Willie and Sue's farm. We don't know how he managed it but they were going to look after him until it was time for him to come to England. I thought to myself, lucky Martin, I wish I could run away to Ballyglass or Ennis. I asked Mam if we could go and see Ray when we got off the train.

"No," she replied, "we'll have to wait until tomorrow. It'll be late when we get there."

It was getting dark by the time we got into Salisbury. We walked from the station to where Mam was renting a flat. We stopped and walked up the path of this big red brick house. She let herself in and we were in a hallway. She started to go upstairs, and when we got to the top she opened another door and we went in. It was a very small room but it seemed to have lots of things in it. I asked Mam if this was my bedroom?

"No," she laughed, "this is everything—it's the kitchen, bedroom, living room, and you and I have to share it. The lavatory is next door and it's used by all the other tenants as well." As she said that, I could hear the lavatory flush; it sounded as if it was in our room. I couldn't believe Mam had left our house and a good job in Ennis to start a new life here!

Mam gave me something to eat and drink and then she told me to get ready for bed. I got my nightdress out. I hadn't had a nightdress before—my aunt and uncle had bought me two and I was very proud of them. I was told to sleep at the bottom of the bed and Mam would have the top. It was a very narrow bed but it wasn't long before I fell asleep.

Next day we went down to town. Mam was taking me to the hotel where Ray worked and lived. By this time my dreams of us all living in a big house with a big garden were shattered, but I was longing to see Ray.

"That's the hotel." Mam pointed across the road.

So we made our way across and down a side street to the back entrance. There was an outside door with a step up into a little porch and then another door. It was painted white and the top part was frosted glass.

Mam told me to ring the bell, which I did and I stood there with my heart thumping. I saw a shadow on the frosted glass and the door opened. There stood Ray, but he wasn't the boy that had left us a year ago. He had turned into a man and oh, I was so pleased to see him! He gave me a big cuddle. The bruises on my body were hurting but I didn't care. He said he had to go back to work but he would see us tomorrow. I went away a lot happier now that I had seen him.

We walked around the shops and there was a big market place in the centre of town. Mam told me about ration books and you had to have coupons to buy food, clothes and sweets. She showed me where the Co-op was and told me I would have to do the shopping while she was at work. Then we went to the school, and she told me to wait outside. When she came out she told me I was to start next week. Then we went to the hospital and she told me to sit on a chair until she got back. She was away for about half an hour. She returned with a smile on her face and said she'd got a job and would start next week. She looked happy now so we went back to our little room and had our tea. After that she showed me where everything was kept, in little cupboards, scattered here and there.

Later that evening there was a tap on the door. It opened and a man walked in. I looked at him and thought, 'Oh God, no, it's the man from the grocer shop!'

"She doesn't look sick to me!" he said, looking at me with hate in his eyes. "What she wants is a bloody good hiding."

Mam stood in front of me. She told him I had already had a good hiding. "In fact," she continued, "I thought I'd killed her and none of it was her fault. It was all a misunderstanding—she was having bad nightmares and they thought she was sick."

"You *would* stick up for her, wouldn't you?" he said.

She was begging him to calm down. "Come on Cove, sit down and I'll make you a drink."

He sat down at the table and I sat in the armchair, which was as far as I could get away from him. I was thinking, Please God tell me he doesn't live here with us as well! And what a name! Cove! And she was saying it so lovingly to him! It made me feel sick.

Now I knew what all the rush was about—why we had to come to England and why she couldn't wait another three months for Martin and grandad. How I wished they were here with me now.

Chapter 19
Homesick and Feeling Alone

THE weeks went by and I went to school. It was hard at first—they spoke differently again, here, than they did in Yorkshire! There was a lot of name calling to start with, such as, "Have you just come from the bogs?" and, "You're too late for the potato picking, it's finished!" And so on. I didn't take a lot of notice of them and they soon got tired of it and left me alone.

I saw Ray a few times a week and that made me happy. He told me he loved it in England. I asked him why.

He said, "I have a room in the hotel, with lovely white sheets and pillowcases and they're changed every week. I get four meals a day and I've never been hungry since I came here, and it's always warm in my room. What more could I ask for? I never want to go back to that awful life of poverty again. I'm going to block it out of my mind and get on with life."

My Mam & big brother Ray in Salisbury

It was getting near Christmas and there was still no sign of Martin or grandad. I was told they had to wait until April or May for the season to start in the hotels, so that Martin would get a job where he could live in, like Ray did. Mam hated her job at the hospital; she would come home after work crawling up the stairs on her hands and knees. Sometimes she would be crying. She said she had to scrub floors and other heavy work, and she wasn't used to it after working at Shannon airport. I would say to her, "We'd be better going back home to Ennis. Grandad is still in our house and maybe they would give you your job back?"

"No, we can't do that?" she would say. I didn't understand why.

Her boyfriend came to see her about four times a week. He worked at Newbridge Hospital as an orderly and had a room that came with the job. I hated it when he came to see us; he would completely ignore me when he came in, but if Mam went to the toilet (as I was told to call it now), he would make all sorts of faces at me and call me a little bitch and say I was nothing but a bloody nuisance. I wished I could go outside for a walk to pass the time but it was dark and cold and I didn't know any other children around there. When Mam came back into the room he would give her a big smile as if butter wouldn't melt in his mouth. When it was his day off he would stay the night. I would be told to go to bed early and I would go down to the bottom of the little bed and curl myself up in a ball and try and will myself to sleep.

Sometimes I couldn't, and after about an hour or so I would hear him say to her, "Is she asleep?" Mam would say, "I think so," and then they would get into bed and I would cringe. He would leave in the early hours of the morning and they thought I didn't know anything about what had gone on.

Christmas Eve came and mam and I were in the little room.

"Cove might not make it tonight," Mam said, "but we will see him at midnight mass."

I asked her why they had started calling each other Cove.

"It's because we love each other and that is our pet name for each other," she said.

Well, I was hoping Cove didn't turn up so that Mam and I could spend Christmas Eve together—but it wasn't to be. I opened the door to go to the toilet and there he was at the top of the stairs making faces at me. He walked past and into the room, and I could hear Mam greeting him with enthusiasm.

"Oh Cove, you made it after all!" she said.

I went out into the toilet and wished I could stay in there all night, but I knew the other tenants would be trying the door to get in soon. I came out and sat on top of the stairs for a few minutes. Our room door was open a little bit. I couldn't have closed it properly when I went out, and I could hear raised voices.

"I've told you I'm not going to do it," I heard him say.

"If you loved me you would!" she said. "All you have to do is give her the bag and say, Happy Christmas."

I went back into the room and sat at the table where Mam was. He was sitting on the bed. He threw the bag at me and the zip caught me on the chin, and it stung.

"There was no need for that, was there?" Mam said.

He didn't answer her. Then she turned to me: "What do you say to Cove?"

"Thank you," I said, but all I wanted to do was hit him with it, even though I knew it was Mam that had bought it. (It was a round shoulder—tartan—bag and it lay around the flat for a long time after and I never knew what happened to it.) Mam had got me a hat, scarf and gloves, all matching.

Ray had got me a little box of Sharps toffees. We all went to midnight mass; I kept as near to Mam as I could get and I prayed to Blessed Martin, to make this man go away; but I didn't want to kill him—just send him away!

About two weeks after Christmas we had started back at school and when I got home I was trying to light the fire before Mam came home from work. It was one of those days when the fire just wouldn't start. I was blowing and blowing it, but it was no good; in the end I put a sheet of newspaper across the front of it. At last! There was a glimmer. I held it there for a while longer and it started burning. I took the paper away and went to put on some more coal. The bucket was empty, however, so I went down the stairs to get some more. I had to go through the kitchen of the tenant's flat below to get into the back yard for the coal. I always knocked and she would let me out the back door. I struggled back up the stairs with the bucket full and put some more coal on the fire. It was going well now, so I washed my hands and started to lay the table. It had an oilcloth to cover the table and it was great, because if you spilt anything on it you just mopped it up and didn't leave any stains. When I'd finished I sat on a chair by the table and was playing around with a bottle of brown sauce.

My mind went back to Ennis and I thought about Martin coming in the kitchen at home. I remembered how my friend and I were playing hairdressers, and Martin was complaining about some boys outside who were calling him names and going on about his red hair. He was fed up about his hair being red, and I asked him what colour he would like it to be. He said, "Blond, like Ray's, or dark, like Mam's." I noticed he didn't say mousy like mine! I was looking around for something to put on his hair, when I saw the tea leaves in a dish, but thought better about using them because they had to be dried out and used again. Mam would kill me if I touched them! I looked in the cupboard and all I could see was a half bottle of brown sauce, so I got it out and started to pour it on Martin's hair; then I rubbed it well in. I poured a bit more on and rubbed it in again and wiped all the sauce off his face and neck with a towel. Then I got our half mirror and showed him his hair. It was like a maroon colour, but Martin said it was all right—he liked it and it was better than red! I put the mirror back on the windowsill and went back to where Martin was sitting. There was a very strong smell of sauce coming from him!

The back door opened and Mam walked in. She stood there at first just looking at Martin. Then she grabbed hold of him and took him over to the sink and put his head under the tap! She scrubbed his head vigorously and all you could hear was, "O'ha o'ha!"

She was shouting: "You haven't a stem of sense, child, letting your sister do this to you!" She picked up the towel to dry his hair. There was sauce all over it! That was it—she roared at me, my friend flew out the door, and Martin and I got a good hiding. The way she was going on about the waste of brown sauce, we were glad to get in our room away from her.

I came out of my daydream when I heard footsteps on the stairs. The door opened and Mam came in; she looked in a bad mood and threw a little package on the table. Then she looked at me.

"Look at the state of your face!" she exclaimed. "It's all black!"

I told her I had a job getting the fire going.

"Go and get you're hands and face washed," she said.

I went to the wash-hand basin in the toilet and got cleaned up, then went back in the room. Mam was banging the little package on the table and then started crying. I asked her what was wrong. She said that she had been to the butchers and the little package was all she could get. She was opening it and there were four sausages—well squashed after the banging she'd just given them. I don't think it was just the sausages that were making her cry, however; I think everything had got on top of her and she was fed up with it all. She didn't like her job—that had a lot to do with it.

"Mam, why don't we just go home?" I said when she'd stopped crying.

"We can't go home," she sniffed.

I asked her why not. She said she couldn't leave Cove.

"But if he knows it will make you happy, he'll go with you," I argued.

"No, he can't," she said. I asked her why. "We could never be together in Ennis because his mother wouldn't like it," she said. "That's why he left and that's why we're here, so we can be together."

I couldn't believe a man of his age could be frightened of his mother. So Mam had left her house and a good job for this man who she was besotted with. As my grandad had said, "She's making a big mistake; but she wouldn't be told."

Mam told me I wasn't to mention Cove's mother when he was here; it would only start trouble. This man had split up our family when we were happy and it was his fault we were here. I knew now I would never be able to talk my Mam into going back to Ennis. While grandad was still in the house I had that chance, but not anymore. I realised now that Cove had won and I would have to get used to it. I loved my Mam very much and as long as I was with her I would be all right. I thought about Martin and grandad—it wouldn't be long before they would be here too and then I would settle myself down

Chapter 20
New Hobbies and Interests

FEBRUARY came and I was twelve. I would be glad when spring and summer came so I could get out. Cove was still coming around and he was still ignoring me, apart from pulling faces at me every time he got the chance. I would sit there all evening reading a book, and if Mam went to the toilet, I would hold the book up in front of my face so that I didn't see him at all; but I could hear him, and he would say, "Bitch. Bitch," and then he would go, "Hee, hee, hee." I hated being left on my own with him.

Ray paid for me to have piano lessons once a week. That got me out of the little room for one night. But I wasn't very musical at all. After six weeks the music teacher was getting very cross with me because when she pointed her little stick at the notes, I couldn't tell her what they were called. I didn't go back after that, and anyway I didn't have a piano to practice on.

Ray was a bit cross with me as well at first, but he soon came round. "Well," he said, "we'll have to find you something else to do, won't we?"

One of the girls at school was telling me she went to tap dancing lessons. "I think you would like it," she said, "I've been going for a long time and I enjoy being there and meeting other girls, and so will you." So off I went to see Ray and told him all about it. He agreed to pay for the lessons and take me down to Salisbury market and get some second-hand tap shoes from there. I was all set and ready to go.

On the first night of my lessons I was very nervous. I saw the girl from school—she told me I would be fine. Then she told me this was her last day at the dancing because her family was moving away from Salisbury; her father, being in the army, was always moving to somewhere else. I was sad about that, for I thought I'd made a friend; anyway, I was glad she was here that first day, and I looked forward to the dancing every week.

By the end of six weeks we were practising for a little show they were holding for the beginners. The song we were dancing to was called 'How

Much Is That Doggie in the Window?' The teacher said, "Next week we'll do a full dress rehearsal."

When I got there the following week, the teacher was telling us that at the end of our dance routine we'd all do a cartwheel. I was in a panic! I couldn't do a cartwheel; all the girls did their cartwheel together, and I was standing there like a spare part. The teacher came over to me and asked me what was wrong? I told her I couldn't do it, so she told me to stand on the floor and she would hold my body. I started to do it and it seemed to work. "Now you do it by yourself," she encouraged me. I tried and I fell over! All the girls were laughing at me. I tried another couple of times but it was no use, I couldn't do it, and burst into tears. So that was the end of my dancing lessons, and I never went back. I tried and tried over the years to do a cartwheel but could never master it.

We had been having swimming lessons with the school and I was determined I was going to learn to swim. It was only once a week but I kept trying and wouldn't give up. It took a while but by the end of term I got my swimming certificate. I had achieved something at last and was very proud of myself. I was getting on better at school, and I got to know some of the other girls much better, as well as a good few orphans from the convent that was next to the school. A lot of the boys and girls would call them names, especially the boys; they would shout, "Here comes the Orphan Annie's!" I felt very sorry for them and I would go and play with them whenever I could. It took my mind back to my school in Ennis, where there were a good few orphans. I remembered the day before Pancake Tuesday; the nuns told us all that we could all take one of the orphans home with us for a pancake tea—with our parents' permission, of course. One of the orphans was called Phyllis. She was supposed to be one of the roughest girls in the convent; she was always in trouble and all the children would stay clear of her, but she kept on at me to pick her. I was a bit frightened of her. She was a lot bigger than I was, and she had a very red face and rough skin. I think she came from the country. Anyway, I picked her and when I got home I was too frightened to tell Mam that we would be having someone to tea the next day.

The next day after school, Phyllis and I set off to our house, and as we came in the gate off the Clare Road; there was a load of barrels stacked next to each other so we went to play on them for a while, jumping from one barrel to the other; we were having great fun, and she kept shouting, "I'm free! I'm free!" At this moment I plucked up the courage to tell her I hadn't told them at home that she was coming; and I didn't think there would be any pancakes for me, never mind anyone else. I was waiting for her to punch me! (I had noticed she had very big fists.) To my surprise, however, she was fine about it; she didn't care if she starved as long as she was out of the convent for a couple of hours.

We went into the house. Mam and grandad were in, and I didn't know what to say. Mam looked at Phyllis, and said, "And who is this?"

"She's one of the orphans from the convent," I explained. "The nuns said we all had to bring one home for a pancake tea."

If looks could kill I would have been dead in a moment! Mam went down the hall and out the front door. I looked out to see where she was going and she went into Florrie's house. A few minutes later she came back up the road with some things in her hands. I ran back inside the house. She came in and was banging things about.

"Where's the frying pan?" she said.

"Oh," I said, "Mrs Hogan borrowed it yesterday."

"Well, get down to the Hogan's and get it back!" she said.

Phyllis and I went down the back lane to Mrs Hogan's and told her my Mam wanted her frying pan back.

"I'm using it!" she said.

"Mam said she wants it now!" I told her.

She wiped the frying pan out with a cloth and gave it to me. It was still very hot and I had to carry it with both hands out in front of me all the way home.

Mam made the pancakes and put them down in front of us and sprinkled a tiny bit of sugar on them. It was almost time for Phyllis to go—she had to be back for six.

"I've had a great time," she said, and added, "If there's anyone bulling you at school, you've to tell me and I'll sort them out!"

I walked with her back to the convent and was pleased I'd made a friend.

When I got home I got a slap on the shoulder from Mam.

"Don't you ever do anything like that again!" she said crossly.

Chapter 21
Martin's Here At Last

IT was the beginning of May, and I wouldn't be able to go and pick bluebells this year as there weren't any fields around where I could go to collect them; but then again, I had nowhere to put them! My little alter had gone and all I had left of it was my holy pictures. I joined the Guild, at the church hall—it was like a youth club for girls—and there were all sorts of things to do; you could play netball, table tennis, and even dance if you wanted to, but I enjoyed the embroidery and sewing best of all. It was every Tuesday night from seven till nine and it got me out of the little room for a couple of hours away from Mam and Cove.

The church hall was about five minutes walk from the school, so every lunchtime we would walk from the school to the church hall for our school dinners. I loved the school dinners and the puddings. I couldn't understand why a lot of the girls said they were disgusting! I ate everything that was on my plate and I was glad of it too.

The following week Mam told me Martin was coming over from Ireland and should be arriving in about a week.

"Is grandad coming as well?" I asked.

"No," she said, "grandad will be coming in July."

I was that excited I thought I would burst! Over the next week I had problems sleeping at night with all the things going over in my mind that I was going to tell Martin and the places I was going to show him. I just couldn't wait!

At last the time came and I was allowed to go and meet him at the station with Mam. When the train pulled in I watched all the carriage doors open—and then I saw him! I hadn't seen him for eight months so I thought he would have changed into a man like Ray; but he hadn't; he was still my Martin and was still wearing short trousers—and they looked odd on him! Suddenly he spotted us, and that lovely slow smile appeared. Then his whole face lit up. I ran down the platform to him; he opened his arms and I ran into them and we were both laughing and crying at the same time. Then he started twirling me around like he used to do back home. Mam came up to us and told Martin to calm down. He got hold of Mam and was squeezing her that hard she could hardly breath and he gave her a kiss; then he would hug her again. She had a big smile on her face and looked happy.

Martin had always been her favourite. He wouldn't be pushed away; he could always make her smile and he always tried to help her even though it went wrong most of the time. We all pulled ourselves together and started to walk back up the platform, and then Martin said, "Oh, I forgot my trunk!"

He turned back and I followed. I was asking him what he had in the trunk. He burst out laughing.

"I'm only kidding you! I haven't got a trunk."

I asked him where his case was. He said he didn't have one. I asked him where his clothes were. He opened this brown paper bag and showed me: there were two pairs of socks and a vest.

"You'll have to take me like this or not at all!" he laughed again.

Mam told us to stop messing about and get a move on, and Martin talked all the way to Albany road where our little room was.

"God, this is very small, isn't it?" Martin said when we entered the room.

"It'll have to do for now," she said. She told him he would have to sleep on the armchair that night and that the next day we'd have to get him some new clothes before he went to see his employer at the hotel. Martin was going to be a pageboy and he would get a uniform as well. Now Mam was telling him he had to be very polite to all the guests at the hotel and he would have to open doors for them, and he wasn't to be cheeky to anyone.

"Okay," he replied, "I'll do all that." Then he said, "Mam, I need to go to the lavatory."

"That's another thing you're not to call it—lavatory! From now on you have to call it toilet."

"Okay, but whatever it is, I need it now."

I went with him and showed him where it was.

"Oh, fancy that, an inside lavatory!" he said.

When he came back in Mam put a cardboard box at the bottom of the armchair and took a blanket off our bed. She told him to get in and settle down. She and I got into our bed but Martin was talk, talk, and talk! In the end Mam told him to shut up—he was like a gramophone! We had a bit of a giggle and then everything went very quiet. I still couldn't get to sleep because I was so happy. Martin was asleep because I could hear him grinding his teeth—he always did that when he was asleep!

My big brother Martin

I had to go to school next morning. Mam and Martin were going down to Salisbury market to get him some clothes and he had an interview that afternoon at the hotel. It seemed to be a very long day at school, and I had taken a photo of Martin to show all the girls. At last it was time to go home. I went out the school gate, and there was Martin! He had long trousers on and a new shirt and new shoes, and there was a big grin on his face. He looked older. I ran up to him and we started talking. He said he had got a job and was to start in a couple of days and he could move into his room tomorrow. I asked him if he was to get a whole room to himself.

"No," he said, "I have to share one with Ray, but there's plenty of room and I've got my own bed—isn't that great?"

We walked along towards Albany road, and I asked him if he knew about the grocer man.

"Sue told me," he said. "She said they were going to get married when they had saved enough money."

I told Martin he was a horrible man. "He never speaks to me, and when Mam goes out of the room he calls me names and makes faces at me; when she comes back in, he smiles at her. She calls him Cove and he calls her Cove."

"What sort of name is that!" Martin exclaimed.

I told him it was their pet name for each other. When we got near the house, Martin said, "Mam's getting chips for tea and I'm looking forward to them; I haven't had chips since you left Ireland."

"Well, they don't taste as nice as Dolan's in Ennis," I replied.

Cove came round that night, and when he came in he said hello to Martin and asked him if he'd had a good journey. Martin said he had and then he started to tell him all about it. Cove looked board stiff, and Mam was trying to catch Martin's eye to tell him to shut up, but Martin just talked on and on. Mam butted in and suggested to Cove that they went for a walk, and I think he was glad. As they went out the door, we heard him say, "God, he's like a parrot! He never shuts up."

"He's only trying to make friends," Mam said.

Then we heard the front door shut. Martin looked very hurt.

"I was only trying to be friendly with him, but if that's the way he wants it, fair enough, I'm glad I don't have to live with him."

"No, *you* don't, but I will have to when they get married!"

Chapter 22
Martin's Disasters Continue

THE next couple of months were great! Martin came round to see us a lot, but on his second day in Salisbury he left our room in Albany road to go into the town. I was at school and Mam was at work and he got lost. He was walking across the road and walked into a man on a bike and knocked him off and Martin landed on top of him. The man had a few scratches but otherwise he was all right. A policeman who was nearby came over and pulled Martin off the man; then he helped the man up who started shouting at Martin.

"You should look where you're going, you stupid boy!"

"I'm very sorry Sir," Martin said. "I didn't see you."

"I might have known you were Irish!" The man replied. He got on his bike and went.

The policeman asked Martin if he was all right.

"I'm fine, but I'm lost," Martin said.

"Well, where is it you want to be?" the policeman asked.

"My Mam and sister live in a room of a red brick house, but I don't know the name of the street or the number. I'm to start work tomorrow at a hotel."

"Which hotel?"

"I don't know; but my brother works there," Martin said.

"Do you know where your mother works?"

"She works at the main Hospital in the town."

The policeman told him he would take him to the police station, then go and check the Hospital to see if his Mam was there. He came back with Mam and asked her if this was her son. She said it was.

"You'd better teach him where he lives and what number," the policeman advised.

The other policemen were having a laugh about it all. Mam took Martin back to Albany road and told him he wasn't to move until she got back from work. When I got in from school he told me the whole story. By the time he had finished telling me, Mam was home. She told him to get pen and paper and to write down the name of the street, the number of the house and the name of the hotel.

"Martin," she then said, "I don't know what I'm going to do with you! You haven't got a stem of sense!"

Well, at least no one was hurt, and we all laughed. It was funny, really.

I would have loved to be a fly on the wall when he began work the next day.

Martin came round one night and Cove was there, so he asked me if I wanted to go out for a while. He would take me to this little café in the market place and have a cup of tea and a bun. He told me it was great working at the hotel, where he got loads to eat.

"You've never known me to refuse food, have you?" he grinned.

"No Martin, I haven't," I smiled.

"Well, I did today! They were giving me an extra pudding and I had to refuse, I was that full." He added: "The guests they have there must be very rich! They ask me to do a little job and tip me sixpence, and the odd guests give me a shilling! I have loads of sixpences in a dish which I keep in our room."

I told him he was very lucky. There is one thing when you were with Martin—you didn't have to say much because he never stopped talking.

"Well," he said, "I'd better walk you back home; I won't come in while Cove is there but I'll come and see Mam when she's on her own. I might see you tomorrow. It depends on what duty I'm on."

I said goodnight to him and he waited until I was in the front door before going back to the hotel.

When Ray and Martin had a day off together at the weekend, we would all go to the swimming baths. It was great! About the third time we went together all the boys were messing about and were pushing each other under the water. Ray and Martin pushed me under and that was the end of my swimming days; it frightened me that much, I would never go back.

Chapter 23
Grandad Comes to England

JULY came and grandad would be arriving in a couple of weeks. I was very excited again and knew that when my grandad came I would feel safe again. Mam said we would have to move out of our little room so grandad could move in. She said it was only meant for one person anyway. I asked her where we were going? She said she didn't know, as she hadn't found anywhere yet. She changed her job and went to work at the same hotel as the boys, as a chambermaid, and after she had been there a few weeks they said she could have a room and live in and I could stay with her. It wasn't in the hotel, though—it was a stone building at the annex part of the hotel. We went to have a look and it was on the second floor. We went upstairs to see the room; it was a bit bigger than the one in Albany road but it didn't have as many things in it. At least the bed was a bit bigger.

"Its only three-foot wide but we'll manage," Mam said. "We'll have to get an electric ring, kettle, and a frying pan."

On the day my grandad was due to arrive, Cove had a couple of days off work, and he was helping mam with the cases and the bags and took them up to our new room at the hotel. I thought to myself, this is the third time I've moved in the ten months I've been in England. While they were taking the luggage away I stayed in Albany road making sure everything was ready for grandad's arrival. When they came back it was nearly time to go to the station to meet his train. I asked Mam if I could go on my own to welcome him; I knew grandad wouldn't want any fuss. She said I could.

"But you'd better get going now or you'll be late," she advised.

I was off like a shot. On the way I called into Salisbury market and bought grandad a bag of cherries. There were all sorts of fruit in the market and very cheap. I made my way to the station and waited. The train he was supposed to arrive on came in and I watched everyone get off, but grandad wasn't among them. I thought he wasn't coming, that he must have changed his mind and I was very upset. I walked home slowly. The brown paper bag the cherries were in started to get soggy and the red was coming through the bottom of the bag onto my hands. I got home, feeling very sad and sorry for myself. I opened the door (of what was now supposed to be grandad's room) and said, "He hasn't come," and burst into tears as I walked into the room—and there he was, sitting on a chair! I couldn't believe it! I was lost for words and held out the bag of cherries, and said, "I've got you a present."

"And I've got you one!" he said, holding out a brown paper bag! I took it from him and gave him mine. We had both bought each other the same thing—cherries!

"What happened?" I asked him. "I watched everyone get off the train."

"I had a chance of an earlier train and took it," he smiled, "so I thought I would have a look around the town and get my bearings—and here I am! You know I don't like a lot of fuss."

He sat me on his knee and gave me a big cuddle.

"We're going to do a bit of shopping," Mam and Cove said. "We'll be back later."

I was glad they had gone—now I could have grandad all to myself! I asked if he could still play the bugle? He put his hands together and gave me a demonstration: it was just as I remembered it and then we sang 'Sweet Rosy O'Grady' together. We laughed and clapped each other, and I knew this was the happiest I had been in the last ten months! I never wanted to be separated from him again.

When Mam and Cove came back from the shops she put a few things on the table for him, a tin of this and that, bread, margarine, tea, and sugar.

"It's up to you now to keep that lot topped up," she said. "If you use one, just replace it—it'll be easier that way."

I asked Mam if I could stay with grandad that night so I could show him where everything was.

"It's a small room, not a mansion," she said. "I have taken all your things up to the other place now."

"I've taken my nightdress, a dress and pants out of the case," I said. "I thought you might want me to look after him tonight as it's all strange to him?"

I could see grandad smiling to himself.

"Oh, all right then," she sighed, "but you make sure you go to mass in the morning."

"Don't worry, I will."

They said goodnight and went. My grandad and I could talk all we wanted now and I didn't have to sit there all night with that stupid man making faces at me every time Mam turned her back. One of these days she'll turn round quickly and catch him, I thought. I showed grandad all the little cupboards here and there and where different things were kept, and put all the things on the table away. I told him the coal for the fire was downstairs; it was kept in a shed in the back yard and I would take him down tomorrow and show him.

"I think that's everything I have to tell you," I said. Grandad and I talked for ages and I told him all about Cove and the way he treated me.

"It was because he thought you would be staying in Harrogate with uncle Bert and his wife," he said. "He thought that because they had no children of their own they would keep you there. The boys have living-in jobs and it hasn't worked out the way he had planned."

"Do you believe, at his age, he's frightened of his mother?" I said. "It seems to me he thinks that Mam isn't good enough for him; otherwise he wouldn't care what his mother thought? And another thing, I'm not to mention his mother when he's here. Mam says it'll only start trouble."

"He's a Mamma's boy," grandad smiled. "I think he still sends money home to her. I have just given your mother the money for the things I sold in the house. I believe they're going to use it for the wedding. I've told her she's making a big mistake but she won't listen. Anyway, they can't be short of money, they're both working full time."

I told grandad that Mam had changed. "She isn't like she used to be, and she believes everything that Cove says."

"If he ever hits you, you're to come and tell me," grandad said.

I told him I would.

"It's time we were in our beds now," he said. "It's been a long day."

I got in bed and rolled myself into a little ball. I told grandad to keep his feet to the outside.

"Right," he said, "are you settled now?"

"Yes," I said.

"So goodnight."

Grandad was asleep first. I wasn't long after him.

My Grandad

We got up for mass next morning. Grandad made sure I was all spick and span. He said he'd walk to the church with me and while I was in mass he'd have a look round. We came to the church, and I showed him the church hall where we came to have our school dinners and pointed to where my school was near the end of the road. "And that's the convent at the very end," I said. He said he would look them over and be back in an hour for me.

When I came out of mass he was waiting for me. I linked my arm in his and we walked back up the road. I asked him if he had a look around.

"I went to have a look at the Cathedral as I was so near. It's a fine building."

We went to the town and into the little café and had a cup of tea and scones. When we had finished, I said, "I'd better be getting back home. I'll walk home with you first and pick up my clothes and then you won't get lost."

"Oh, I don't think I'll get lost," he smiled.

"Well, Martin did, and Mam had to go to the police station for him."

Grandad laughed and we went to get my clothes and I made my way back to our room in the hotel.

We were on holiday from school and spent the next week with grandad. I would walk to work with Mam, then make my way to grandad's. I would stay with him all day and make my way back when Mam had finished work.

That Saturday Mam said she had met some friends from Ennis and they had been in Salisbury for a week. They had children about my age and they were going back to Middlesex on Monday and asked if I would like to go back with them for a couple of weeks.

"I'll take you to meet them tomorrow and see what you think?" Mam said.

I went to mass next morning and straight to grandad's afterwards. I told him about going to Middlesex.

"I don't want to go," I said. "I'd sooner be here with you."

"Look, it will do you good," he said. "You should be with children of your own age and not hanging about with an old man all the time."

"I'm frightened to go in case no one comes for me."

There were all sorts of things going on in my mind: were they trying to get rid of me again? Were they going to leave me there?

"If you are not back here in two weeks I'll come for you myself," grandad said, and added, "That's a promise."

That was good enough for me—I could trust grandad. If he said a thing, he would do it.

Ray and Martin were very busy at the hotel and I didn't see much of them at all, but Mam told them I was going away for a few weeks.

I had two great weeks in Middlesex. I went ice-skating a couple of times and to the pictures. There was a big field just across from where I was staying and I could run wild like I used to back in Ennis and Westport. We made a tent out of old curtains and called it our den. There was a load of big pipes you could hide in or jump from one to the other along the top. There was a boy called Eric and he asked me to be his girlfriend.

"Yes," I said with my heart fluttering. There was a song out at the time called, 'They Tried To Tell Us We Were Too Young." He said that would always be our song but my two weeks were up next day and Ray was coming to collect me. I think that must have been the shortest romance in history. I said goodbye to Eric, and he gave me a little kiss on the cheek and said he would always be thinking of me.

I got back home thinking of my lost love and wishing he had asked me to be his girlfriend at the beginning of my holiday and not the day before I went home. Anyway, I had a good time.

I went down to grandad's again while Mam was at work. "I bet you had a great time?" he asked.

I told him I had and that I'd got a boyfriend but it was too late, as I had to go home the next day. "Plenty more fish in the sea," he said.

When I went down to grandad's on Friday I told him, "Mam said she has the day off on Saturday so you can have a lie in and she would be able to look after me."

When she came home on Friday she said, "Now they want me to go in for a couple of hours on Saturday. I'll have to think what am I going to do with you."

"I'll just go to grandad's," I said.

"No," she replied. "He won't be up because you told him I would be here and you can't be banging at the door; you'll be getting the tenants out of their beds." As she went out of the door she said, "I'll be back in a minute." She came back in and said, "It's all right, I've got someone to watch you in the morning."

"Can't I just stay here by myself?"

"No," she said, "not in this place; there's lots of men live here and some of them aren't very nice."

She got out her sewing box. She had made me a skirt and top about two years ago. The skirt buttoned to the top at the waist and I hated it; it made me look like a baby. She was moving the buttons on it once more, and said, "Well, that will be the last time I'll be able to move the buttons, but you have had plenty of wear out of it."

Well, I thought, thank God for that!

I must have grown a good bit in the last two years but I was still small for my age.

Next morning Mam was fussing over me. She was making sure my hair was done just right and my socks were folded down right. She gave me a light cardigan.

"You can put it on or have it over your shoulders," she said.

I put it on and asked, "Where am I going?"

"Just down the corridor. The chef is going to look after you so you are to be very good."

We went down the corridor and Mam knocked at the door. There was a grunt from the other side. She opened the door and he was still in bed.

"I'm going now, chef," she said. "See you in a couple of hours."

She told me to go and sit on the chair at the end of the room, closed the door and went. I seemed to be sitting on the chair for ages swinging my legs, as my feet didn't reach the floor. I thought I should have brought a book to read.

Eventually the man in the bed stirred; he popped his head up and looked at me.

"Hello, and what's your name?" he asked.

"Muriel." I didn't like the look of him at all.

"Do you want to get in bed with me and get warm?"

"No, I'm not cold." I was horrified.

"Oh, come on, just for five minutes."

"No!"

He swung his legs over the side of the bed and I was a frightened sick! He had a bald head with bits of hair on the sides and big buckteeth and white stuff coming out the sides off his mouth.

"Come on, get in this bed," he said again.

"No!"

I thought about making a dash for the door but I would have to pass his bed.

Then he stood up. He was over six-foot tall and had no clothes on, and his penis was standing up towards the ceiling. He came towards me and I jumped up off the chair, but he grabbed the back of my cardigan and it came off. That seemed to make him angrier. I was trying to get to the door but he grabbed me and flung me onto the bed. He pulled my pants down and he was putting his fingers inside me. I got the heel of my shoe and dug it into him. It must have hurt him because he let go of me for a few seconds. I got off the bed and was back where I started.

All I kept saying was, "Oh God, please help me."

He told me to sit back on the chair. I had to lift my skirt up to get on it. There was only one button left on my cardigan and it was dragging along the floor. I sat there shaking.

He stood up in front of me and opened his legs. He pulled his penis down.

"Put this in your mouth," he said.

With his other hand he was pushing my head down towards it. I ducked down in between his legs and ran for the door, trying to hold my skirt up. I got out and down the corridor, screaming my head off. There was no one around so I ran down the stairs and out the front door and made for a clump of bushes. I sat down trying to get my breath back. There was slime that came from him in my hair and I could feel it on my face. I was shuddering like I saw Mam do years ago, and I felt dirty. I resolved not to move from there until Mam came. I could see the road from where I was and just waited.

When I saw Mam coming along the road I jumped out of the bushes and frightened the life out of her. She took one look at me.

"Oh mother of God, what's happened to you?" she said.

I was crying and at the same time I was telling her to get the police.

She took me to the other side of the bushes away from the road.

"Now I want you to calm down and tell me what happened."

I told her what that awful man had done to me.

"Oh my God! I can't believe this."

I asked her again to get the police.

"We'll have to go to our room first," she said. "We need to get your clothes changed and get you washed."

"You can bring the clothes out here!"

"Don't be silly now." She reached into the bushes to grab my arm and pulled me out. "You have to come and get washed." She began to drag me towards the door. "Now you'll have to calm down."

She put her hand on my head and was patting it. Then she pulled it away quickly and said, "What's that on your hair?"

"It's slime off him!" I was screaming at her now.

"Oh God, we have to get you in and in the bath!"

I was too exhausted to fight with her anymore. There was a toilet and a bath just down from our room. She took me there and gave me a bath and she washed my hair a couple of times. She wrapped a towel around me and we went back to our room. I asked her to lock the door. She was drying my hair with a small towel and a big one wrapped around me, but I still felt dirty. She got me clean clothes and I put them on. I asked her if she was going to get the police now?

"After you have a lie down."

She said I was tired. In fact, I was *very* tired. Mam covered me with a blanket and picked up the skirt and top or what was left of it. "Well, I think that's beyond repair," she said, and put it in the bin.

My eyes were just closing when there was a knock on the door. I sat up in bed begging her not to open it. She went to the door and asked who it was. She looked at me and said, "It's only Cove and he won't hurt you."

I asked her not to tell him what happened.

"All right, you lie down and have a sleep, but I will have to let him in."

I fell asleep in no time at all.

When I woke there was only Mam in the room. She was putting some things in a bag. I asked her where we were going.

"You are going to stay at grandad's until I can find another room for us. Now I want to talk to you. You're not to tell anyone what happened here today because I could lose my job—and your brothers could lose theirs too; then we won't have anywhere to go. You're not to tell your brothers or your grandad—do you understand? If your grandad knew what's happened, he'd be up here like a shot. He's an old man and they would beat him up."

"But can't you tell the police?"

"What have I just told you?"

"But he might do it to some other girl if you don't tell the police."

"No, he won't, and that's the last I want to hear about it."

She took me down to grandad. She told him they weren't allowed to have children staying in the rooms anymore, so could I stay there with him for a week or so until she found somewhere else for us to live?

"Cove is coming with a sponge cushion off an old armchair," she said, "so you can put it on the box at the end of the chair to make a bed; he's also bringing a blanket and a sheet."

"Is there anything wrong?" grandad asked. "The child doesn't look well at all."

"No, she's fine, aren't you, Muriel?"

"Yes," I said.

So I stayed with grandad for over a week and I felt safe. My little bed with the sponge was very comfortable. I wished I could stay with grandad forever. He kept asking me if I was all right.

"Is there anything you want to talk to me about?" he asked.

"No, I'm fine."

I was longing to tell him what had happened to me but I was too ashamed and I still felt dirty and, anyway, Mam would kill me if I said anything and they would all lose their jobs. So I would have to learn to live with it. Maybe it would get better in time. Mam came down mid-week; she said she had tried all over to get a room in the town, but had no luck. She said she would have to try further afield.

"I don't know why she can't stay here?" grandad asked.

"This room is for one person," Mam replied. "I was taking a risk when I had her here and you wouldn't be able to have a fire. It's warm enough now, but in another month or so you will have to have a fire, and the bed is right up against it. I will have to find somewhere else."

She came down again at the weekend and said, "I've found us somewhere to live but you'll have to get a bus to and from school."

I asked her where we were going.

"To Laverstock," she said.

This would be my fifth move since I came to England a year ago.

Chapter 24
Mam Gets Married

WE moved to Laverstock, to live in Melvin Close, which was a couple of miles out of Salisbury. The lady letting the room was a widow and she had a daughter that was about a year younger than I was and her name was Jean. Mrs Goodman told us she had to rent a room out to help pay for the house. She was a well-built woman with white hair. I think she must have had Jean late in life.

She was a very pleasant person and showed us to the room. The first thing I noticed was the double bed, which gave Mam and me more room. The room was lovely, decorated and clean. The only thing I was going to miss was grandad. I would only be able to see him on a Saturday.

I started back at school and had to be up earlier in the mornings as I had a bus to catch. The first morning we got up we got washed and went into the sitting room for breakfast. Mrs Goodman had the table laid and told us to sit down. The wireless was on; it was a big wooden one and it was highly polished. The news was on and the sound of the man speaking sounded as though he was reading a poem! I'll never forget that sound. Mrs Goodman told us not to be shy and help ourselves to the Cornflakes; then she gave us some toast.

Mam and I set off for the bus. She gave me a note to give to my teacher to ask him to let me out five minutes before school finished to get the bus because there wouldn't be another one for two hours.

When I was going home I asked the bus conductor if he would tell me when we got to Melvin Close, as I was new here, which he did.

I didn't see a lot of Ray and Martin now, but I saw grandad every weekend. He was always pleased to see me and would tell me how much he missed me and that made me very happy. We went for walks and loved looking round Salisbury market to see what bargains we could get for a shilling.

Mam seemed to be in a bad mood in the last week. With everything I said to her, she seemed to snap my head off. Like, this morning—all I said was, "It's lovely living out here, isn't it? And Mrs Goodman and Jean are great; they make you feel like family."

"Oh yes," she snapped, "it might be great for *you*, but Cove and I have had a big row because we can't see each other, and he can't very well come out here, can he?"

I felt as though it was my fault we had to move out here.

When I got home from school that day, I was talking to Mrs Goodman; she mentioned that Mam wasn't very happy looking these days. I told her she had a row with Cove.

That night I heard Mrs Goodman talking to Mam. She was saying to her, "Anytime you want to go out, Muriel will be fine here with me."

Mam thanked her and said, "It would be nice to get out now and again."

Next day Mam told me she was going out that night.

"That would be nice, it'll cheer you up a bit," I said.

"What do you mean!" she snapped. "There's nothing wrong with me!"

I thought I had better not say any more. A few days later Cove and Mam made up and she was happy again. I knew now that I would have to accept this man she had given up everything for, and there was nothing else she had to give. I wanted her to be happy and this was the only man to make her feel that way. So be it! I would have to try harder to get on with him.

He came to Mrs Goodman's a couple of times for his tea. Jean and I would be sitting there together and he would talk to Jean all the time and if I tried to join in the conversation he would cut me dead. Mam would give him a stern look and I would think to myself, 'Leave it be, Mam, it doesn't matter. It will only start another row.' He had everyone wrapped around his little finger. He was a ladies' man and he could turn the smile on and off for them whenever he wanted to. Now he was saying to Mrs Goodman that it was a beautiful tea and she was a lovely baker.

"All those lovely cakes!" He was holding her hand and patting it as he was saying it. "I will see you again sometime."

Mrs Goodman was flushed with pleasure at all the praise he was giving her.

"You'll have to come for your tea on your next day off," she gushed.

The weather was getting very cold now, so there wasn't a lot of playing outside. Jean and I got on very well and we would do our homework, and then play board games together, and laugh a lot. I was glad I would be able to stay there for the winter. It was cosy.

It was the middle of November now, and I was getting ready for bed, and Mam came in the room and said to me, "You will have to take that ring off your finger, it's getting too tight." It was a little gold signet ring my dad had sent me in a newspaper from England a few years back. I took it off and gave it to her.

"Are you going to get it made bigger?" I asked.

"No, I'll get you another one later on," she said. "Why don't you give that one to Jean? Her fingers are smaller than yours."

I went out and gave Jean the ring and she was over the moon with it. It fitted her perfectly.

Mam and I went to mass next morning and when we came out she was talking to someone. I went over to talk to some of the girls from school and they were asking me, "Is it your Mam that is getting married?" They pointed to a poster on the notice board and said, "Didn't you hear the priest reading out the banns during mass?"

"I heard the getting married bit, but I didn't take any notice to the rest," I said. "I didn't know anyone called, Joseph, or Lydia."

I went over to Mam and asked her.

"That's right," she smiled, "we are getting married in a few weeks."

I thought she could have told me and not make me feel stupid in front of the girls. What would they think of me now, not knowing my own mother was getting married?

I made my way up to grandad's.

"You look a bit upset," he said. "What's wrong?"

"Did you know Mam was getting married in a few weeks?"

"No, I didn't," he frowned, "but I don't see her for weeks on end; but you knew they were going to get married sometime?"

I told him what happened after mass. "I felt awful in front of my friends, not knowing my own mother was getting married!"

He told me to cheer up.

"But Mam has changed that much," I said. "I wish she would go back to the mother I had in Ireland."

The wedding got nearer, and Mam was going out a lot. She told me she had things to see to. Mrs Goodman was going to see to all the food for the reception and it was to be held in her house. Jean was wondering what to do.

"I'm trying for the best attendance certificate at the school," she said, "and I haven't had a day off school up to now. If I stay off for the wedding I would be breaking it." Then she added, "I might just have the afternoon off."

I was worried because I would have to spend every day of my life with Cove. Then I thought he might change after they were married and he had a family. He would be my stepfather then, but it wouldn't matter, I told myself, because I would have Mam.

The big day came and they were married on the fifth of December, 1951. We weren't all at church. It was all grown ups that went. They all arrived back at the house, and there were a few of Mam's friends, a few of Cove's, and my grandad. There was none of Cove's family there at all and Ray and Martin were missing too. We all went in the house and everyone was chatting. Grandad was over in a corner as usual so I went over to talk to him.

"Did you go in the church?" I asked.

He said he had. He told me he would be going shortly. Grandad wasn't his usual self that day. Was there something wrong with him? I asked him if he was all right, and he said he was, so I put it down to him being shy. He left a short time after that. I went over to Mam and Cove.

"Well, you have a new dad now," she smiled.

"Stepfather," Cove corrected.

"Does that mean I'll have a new nanna now?"

"What do you mean?" Mam asked.

"Well, Cove's mother will be my step-nanna now, won't she?"

His face went white. He looked very angry.

"My mother is nothing to do with you," he said. "She's not your step-nanna or anything else to do with you, do you hear me? Don't you ever mention my mother's name again!" And he went out.

Mam looked at me. "What did you do that for? Haven't I told you before you are never to mention his mother?"

"But I thought it would be different now that you were married."

She went outside to Cove and I was wishing my grandad hadn't gone home. The party broke up and they all started leaving. Everyone said they all had a great time. Mam went and got a little bag out of the bedroom. Cove was thanking Mrs Goodman for the lovely spread. Mam came out of the bedroom and spoke to me.

"We're staying in a hotel tonight," she said. "You'll be staying with Mrs Goodman. I'll come for you tomorrow." She went over to Mrs Goodman and said, "Thank you for having her tonight," and they went.

Next morning I asked Mrs Goodman why our cases were packed. She said it was because my Mam had got a flat. I hadn't thought about that—I just assumed we were going to live there. I would be very sorry to leave there, and I wondered what the flat was going to be like.

Mam and Cove came back just after twelve. I will always remember them standing there in front of me; he had hold of Mam's hand and kept patting it.

"We have something to tell you," he said. "You won't be coming to the flat with us. You're going to live in a convent. It's for your own good. There isn't enough room in the flat for all of us."

I stood there looking at them. I couldn't believe what I was hearing! I looked at Mrs Goodman who was standing behind me. She had her hands up to her face and she looked very upset. I knew then it was true what they were saying.

"No, please Mam, no!" I cried. "You can't do this to me! Why do you want to do that to me?"

I turned to Mrs Goodman and grabbed hold of her. "Please don't let them do this to me!"

She was cuddling me. "There's nothing I can do about it, darling," she said.

I was begging her to let me stay with her.

"I can't darling," she said. "I have to let the room. I need the money to help pay for the house."

I turned to Mam and begged her. "Can't you pay the rent on the room and then I can stay here?"

"No, and that's enough of that carry on," she said. "You're upsetting Mrs Goodman." Cove kept squeezing her hand and was looking at me with a smirk on his face.

They had ordered a taxi to take them to the flat to drop off Mam's things and her case before we went to the convent. We got out of the taxi in St Nicholas Road and went in the gate of this big house. There were steps up to the front door. We went in and up three flights of stairs. Cove unlocked the door and we went in. There was a big living room and a sofa in it. Cove went to this other door and put the suitcase in. I could see it was a bedroom. There was another door, but I didn't know what that was. Their living room was more than twice the size of grandad's room.

"Are you ready?" Mam shouted to Cove.

"Should I just stay here?"

"No," she said. "You said you would come."

I knew when we left the flat there was plenty of room and it was me they didn't want. The flat was near Salisbury Cathedral. We walked up the road by the side of the Cathedral, and across the road was the convent. We went in the gate and up to the big black door, and Mam rang the bell. A nun answered the door and asked us to come in. There was a big hall with a highly polished floor and there were other doors leading off the hall. We went through one of them and we were outside at the back of the convent. There was a door to the right of us and the nun took us in there and into a long narrow room. On the left-hand side were a lot of dark green cupboards. The nun unlocked one of the cupboards and spoke for the first time.

"This will be your locker and you will be responsible for the key," she said.

Mam was handing the nun my case, but the nun said, "No, you take that away with you. You can leave her coat and shoes, but orphans have to wear the clothes supplied. They will be put in her locker and she will get clothes for her age group."

By this time I was so terrified. I burst into tears. The nun told Mam she had better go now—one of the other sisters would show them out.

They started to walk away and I was shouting after her: "Please don't leave me here, Mam! Please don't leave me!"

But she just walked on and she didn't look back. Cove did and tutted, putting his head up. I knew now that I had lost my Mam because the Mam I had in Ireland would never have done this to me. So Cove had got his own way.

The nun told me in a very stern voice to stop crying, I was acting like a baby. She then took me into this big room with a polished floor. There were toys scattered here and there and some children playing.

"This is the playroom," she said. "I will leave you here and Sister Catherine will show you where everything is."

I sat down on a chair and a couple of the children came up to me. They were the ones I played with at school. One was called Ann and the other was Betty. They asked me what I was doing there. "Are you an orphan now?"

I told them I had a mother. They said they had mothers as well, but they were still orphans. Ann said her mother had put her in the convent a few years ago. "Sometimes she comes to see me, not very often though, and sometimes she says she is coming and I wait all day and she doesn't turn up."

Betty said she might see her mother once a year, but I've heard some of the big girls talking and they were saying that when you're fifteen the mothers come and take you home because you can go to work then and bring their wages home. "We have some boarders here," she said. "We only have two at the moment, but they aren't orphans; they go home on Friday after school and come back on Sunday night, and spend all the holidays at home."

They said we would be getting our tea soon and then we would be going to chapel for the Angelus and evening prayers. There was a nun coming towards us. She told the two girls to go and help set the tables. She turned to me.

"I am Sister Catherine. I will be looking after you."

I stood up and looked up at her. "Hello," I said. She was small and plump, and wore glasses that were very small. She had the most kindly face I had ever seen on a nun. She told me not to worry.

"You'll soon settle in," she smiled. "I'll go through all the do's and don'ts after chapel. It will be strange for the first few days." She patted my hand. "I'll see you later."

Shortly after that, Ann and Betty came back over to me.

"Come on, tea is ready."

I went with them into the dining room. We all said grace. I don't know what we had for tea or if I ate it or not—everything seemed far away. I must have gone to chapel because I can remember coming out. Then we went to the playroom for a while and sat as far away from the others as I could get. My head was throbbing and I wanted to go home, but I didn't have a home anymore. Sister Catherine came back over to me. She took me to see the dormitory. It was a very long room with about seven or eight beds down each side. She showed me where my bed was. There was a fireplace a couple of beds up from mine and a fire had been lit. Then she took me to the washroom where there were lots of sinks, and showed me where the baths were. And there was another dormitory where all the older girls slept. Then she told me, "We get up at half past five in the morning and go to six o'clock mass. When you came back from mass, which is about seven, you go up and make your beds. When you have finished that you go downstairs and help with the cleaning, polishing all the big cupboards and tables and chairs." We would take turns polishing the big playroom floor. Then, about eight-fifteen, we would have our breakfast and clear away our dishes and then it would be time for school.

"I don't expect you to take in all this at once," she said. "It will take a couple of days to get used to it." She looked at me. "Now, is there anything you want to ask me?"

"I don't think so." Then I said, "Yes, there is." I asked her if I could lie down on my bed for a while because I wasn't feeling very well and my head was thumping.

"It's almost bedtime, anyway," she said. "I'll get you some toiletries and a nightdress. You're twelve, aren't you?"

I said, "Yes."

She went off and she was back in a few minutes.

"There you are. Now go and have a bit of a wash and clean your teeth."

When I came back she was still there.

"There now, that's better, isn't it? I will leave you now and don't forget to kneel beside your bed and say your prayers."

I said my prayers and I asked God why he was doing this to me. It had been the worst fifteen months of my life, and I would never forgive my mother for putting me in here. But she must have arranged it all a while ago, when she was still a widow. I thought back to Ennis, to when times were a lot worse than this, but we all stuck together and all helped each other. There wasn't any money most of the time, but we got through and we were all together then. Before we left Mrs Goodman's, I asked Mam to take me to see Ray and Martin before we went to the convent.

"They are both working away somewhere else," she said.

So that was why I hadn't seen them for a while. My grandad must have known yesterday, and that's why he was so quiet. I wouldn't see anyone, unless Mam came to see me. At that moment I just wanted to die. My head was so full of all the things that had happened the day before and now I had to remember all I had been told on that day. I kept thinking about Mam walking away from me and never looking back. I got into bed. It was very cold, and I curled myself up in a little ball, put my head under the blankets and cried, and cried. Eventually I fell asleep and I didn't know another thing until someone was shaking me, saying, "It's time to get up."

I did what all the others were doing, getting washed and dressed and we all went to six o'clock mass in the chapel. When we got back we did our chores, and had our breakfast; then it was time to get ready for school and this was the part I was dreading. Ann and Betty were telling me not to take any notice when they started calling us names. I went to school with the rest of the girls, and as soon as we walked in, a few of the boys started shouting: "Here come the orphan Annie's!" So now I knew what the other girls felt like.

Some of the other girls at school were asking me why I was in the orphanage. I couldn't tell them it was because I wasn't wanted and a nuisance and in the way. So I made up this story: "I'm only in here for a few weeks because my Mam is buying a new house and it isn't ready yet."

The first week was the worst. When we were all in bed one night I got up and climbed out onto the window ledge. I always remember that when you looked down you could see the wall that went all round the convent and all the broken glass was shining on top of the wall. I wanted to jump—I felt as though I couldn't cope with all that was going on in my head. I badly wanted to see my Mam; she hadn't been to see me at all and I hadn't seen my grandad. Before I knew it there were three or four girls at the window holding me. Then a nun appeared, and I was taken back to the dormitory and put to bed. I got a good telling off next day. I was told never to do anything like that again.

The following week when I went to school, the boys didn't shout Orphan Annie's and that made me feel better. It was only a few of the boys that shouted, but it was very hurtful. At lunchtime we walked up to the church hall for our dinners. And when we came back out, my grandad was standing there. I didn't know whether to laugh or cry, I was so happy. I ran over to him and we put our arms around each other. Oh, I was so pleased to see him! He put his arm out for me to link on, and we walked back to the school.

"I didn't come last week because I wanted you to settle in first," he said.

I asked him if he knew they were going to put me in the orphanage.

"They told me on the way back from the church after they got married," he said. "We had words about it but there was nothing I could do. I haven't seen your Mam since."

We got to the school gate and I had to go in.

"You will be breaking up for the Christmas holidays in a few days," grandad said, "so I will come and see you at the dinner hall tomorrow."

That night kneeling by my bed saying my prayers I said an extra one to God for sending my grandad to see me. I slept like a log that night.

Grandad was there the next day and the day after that. Now I had something to look forward to but that day would be the last time I would see him until after the holidays. I knew he wouldn't come into the convent. He was outside the church hall when I came out. He was holding something wrapped up in Christmas paper, and gave it to me and told me I wasn't to open it until Christmas day.

"It was only a little thing," he said. "That's all I could afford."

"Thank you," I said and I told him I was sorry I couldn't give him a present because I had no money. I asked him if my Mam was coming to see me.

"I don't know, I still haven't seen her." He told me to settle down now in the convent and be good. "I'll always be here for you," he promised.

I watched him walk back up the road and I thought I was very lucky to have someone to love me like he did.

We had a couple of days before Christmas to put up the Christmas tree and the decorations. We were making little things to go on it out of empty matchboxes or anything else we could find that was small, and wrapped them up in Christmas paper, and put string round them and hung them on the tree. Then we put all the lovely coloured baubles on and lots of cones we had painted and then a fairy on top. We put decorations up in the playroom, and we were all singing carols as we were doing it. The crib was set up and the whole place looked lovely.

Christmas morning we all got up and got washed and dressed and ready for mass. I had been left out a brown dress with long sleeves; it had my age on it but when I put it on it was miles too big. It must have belonged to a fat child! I turned the cuffs up again so that it would fit me in the arms. It was like a wool dress outside, but inside it was all hard, and making me itch all the time. After mass we all went and did the chores. We had the big buffer to do the floor. It was as big as we were and we took it in turns pushing it up and down the floor. We left it all looking spick and span and then went for our breakfast. After breakfast I asked sister Catherine if I could go upstairs and get the present grandad had got me.

"Of course you can, child," she said, and she was very happy looking as she usually was. Her cheeks were rosy red and she was smiling all the time.

When I came back down I went into the playroom. There were lots and lots of presents under the tree and four more nuns with Sister Catherine. They started calling out names and when your name was called you went up to the Christmas tree, and they would ask you how old you were and then give you presents suitable for that age. The other nuns weren't anything like Sister Catherine. They handed you your presents, and you would say "Thank you" and they would say, "Next!" They never smiled—they just had a stern look on their faces, and I was sure that God wouldn't want them to look like that. I went back and sat down with my presents, and opened grandad's first. He had got me a box of hankies and they had small bunches of flowers in the corners. I thought they were too nice to use and I started to open the others. They were things that people sent in for the orphans that they had finished with. The first one I opened was a book called 'Little Women'. It looked new, but when I opened the cover it had someone else's name on it, but I was sure it had never been read. I opened the next one; it was a colouring book and some pencils and only one picture had been coloured in. The next one I opened was a little teddy bear that looked new also. All that was wrong with it was its ear was torn a bit, but I would soon stitch that. I opened the last one and it was a box of sweets. There were no presents from Mam, but I told myself she would bring it this afternoon. It had been a lovely Christmas day. I had never had a Christmas day like this, and all the children had presents. Now I was watching Sister Catherine, in among all the children: she was as excited as they were! I thought about grandad who was all on his own, but as he said, he didn't mind his own company.

Mam didn't come that day, or the next day. In fact, she didn't come at all. I was glad when it was bedtime and I could get this brown dress off, as it was the only thing that spoilt the day. I hoped they would lose it when it went to the laundry, so I didn't have to wear it again.

Chapter 25
My Convent Experience

THE school holidays seemed to drag. I felt closed in. At least when you were at school you were getting out of the convent. I missed the walk to the dinner hall, and you couldn't go on the swings in the yard because it was too cold. So we were inside all the time and seemed to do a lot of praying. I liked night times best because Sister Catherine would come to our dormitory, and she would sit us all around the fire and would tell us stories or read a book to us. It was lovely watching the flames of the fire; you could see all sorts of shapes in it. When she was reading a book she would stop at the most exciting part and say, "Well, that's all for tonight girls, we'll finish it tomorrow," and would close the book and clap her hands loudly, followed by the words: "Time to say your prayers."

We would all kneel down by our beds and pray. There was a little room at the bottom of the dormitory and Sister Mary slept in there. She was a teacher in our school. To me she always looked embarrassed when she walked down the dormitory. We would all say goodnight to her, and she would nod her head and give a little half smile. When she got to her room the lights would go out and we would all settle down for the night.

Just before we started back at school, we had just come out of the chapel when Sister Catherine came over to me and said, "You have a visitor." I was surprised as it was nearly seven o'clock. She continued: "You can take your visitor into the playroom for ten minutes."

I went to the front hall and there stood Ray! I was so happy to see him. He gave me a big hug and asked me how I was and said, "You've grown a lot since I last saw you." He told me he was back in Salisbury and had got a job at Newbridge Hospital. "The nuns don't like anyone coming at this time," he said, "but I've only just found out you were here!" He gave me some pocket money and said, "I'll come and see you next week and try to be earlier."

Sister Catherine came over and said, "Your time is up. I'll give you five minutes extra." After that she smiled at us and said to Ray, "I'll see you out."

I was so happy! Seeing him had lifted my spirits no end. I knew now I had a family—I had Ray and grandad. All the girls were asking who he was, and I told them very proudly that he was my big brother.

We started back at school, and I was longing for lunchtime. It was a cold miserable day. We kept getting heavy showers of icy cold rain. I thought when I was walking up to the dinner hall, 'He'll never come today in this weather, and I shouldn't expect him to.' I ate my dinner as fast as I could. One of the teachers had just come into the hall and came over to me and said, "Your grandad is standing out there in this terrible weather." I asked the teacher if I could be excused, and she let me go. I ran out to him. He was soaking wet!

"You should have stayed at home," I smiled. "You shouldn't have come in this weather."

"I've been in that room long enough," he replied. "I've had a bad cold since Christmas and it knocked the stuffing out of me, but I'm all right now." He asked if I'd had a good Christmas and I told him all about it and the presents I got.

"So it wasn't that bad after all?" he enquired.

"No, it wasn't," I said and thanked him for the hankies.

February came. It was 1952. On the eighteenth of February I was going to be thirteen. I would be a teenager! We were sitting at our desks one day when the teacher said he had an announcement to make and we were to be quiet. Then he told us the sad news—the King had died. There was silence in the class, and everyone looked shocked. Even me. I had an awful feeling in my tummy. It was a terrible thing to happen. I didn't know a lot about the King, but in my mind kings lived forever, and you didn't expect them to die. I said a little prayer under my breath and I said, God rest his soul. There wasn't much work done after that; everyone was talking to each other about it. When we went back to the convent, all the nuns seemed to be walking here and there and ending up where they started, and were praying all the time. Even at teatime we said more prayers before we said Grace, even though we had just finished prayers before we left the school. After tea we got about an hour in the playroom, and then it was the Angelus at six, then evening prayers. We went back in the playroom for half an hour, and then we were sent to bed. We all sat around the fire as usual. Sister Catherine came in and told us there would be no stories tonight because of the King's death. She told us we were to go to our beds and to say extra prayers for the King and his family. Sister Catherine joined us in prayer.

Time went by. Ray was still coming to see me whenever he could and always brought me some pocket money. Grandad came every school day, whether it hailed, rained or snowed. All the teachers knew him, and would all say "Hello" to him. I don't know what I would have done without Ray and grandad—they were my whole life now; I hadn't seen Martin for ages because he was working away somewhere else.

June came, the weather was nice and we could get out into the garden. I was having a bath in one of the cubicles one Sunday to be ready for school on the Monday. I had been in the bath for a few minutes and noticed my body—my arms and legs were covered in red blotches! I shouted to one of the girls in the next cubicle and asked her if she would go and get Sister Catherine. She asked what for? I told her what was wrong. She came back with Sister Catherine and came into the cubicle. I was standing in the bath with a towel wrapped around me (we weren't allowed to show our naked bodies); she took part of the towel away and had a look at me. She told me to dry myself and she would go and get me a nightdress. I dried myself and wrapped the towel around the top of my chest. She came in with the nightdress and put it over my head. When she got my arms through, she told me I could take the towel off now, and took me to this little room, which had a bed in and told me to get into bed. I asked her what was wrong. She told me it looked like chickenpox and I would have to stay in isolation for ten days.

"Now, if any of the girls try to come and see you, you tell them to get out. The Doctor will be in to look at you tomorrow."

It was lovely in that little room; the only one I saw was Sister Catherine. She came in next morning with some porridge. I didn't feel like eating. I felt very hot and a bit dizzy.

"Just try a little, it will do you good," she said. "I'll go and get a bowl of water and you can have a wash. The Doctor will be calling in this morning." I had my wash and Sister Catherine looked at my spots. "Oh dear, they've got worse! I don't think I could get a pin between them this morning." I asked her if any one else had them. "No," she said, "that's why we have to keep you away from the others."

The Doctor came and had a look at me. He told Sister Catherine she was right, it was chickenpox. He told her to keep me warm and to give me plenty of fluids to drink. And he told me not to scratch the spots, as they would leave scars. I was worried about my grandad. He would have been waiting outside the dinner hall, and would be worried about me. I asked Sister Catherine if she could give a message to one of the teachers, to tell grandad what's happened. She said she would, and told me the next day that a teacher had passed the message on to grandad for me.

"Maybe he'll come and see you?"

"I don't think he will," I replied. "He's very shy, and won't come into a strange place where there are a lot of nuns."

She smiled and went off about her business.

On the third day I heard footsteps in the corridor. They stopped outside the door. It opened and Sister Catherine came in. She said she was just going to chapel for the Angelus. About five minutes later I heard footsteps again and the door opened. A nun came in with grandad. She didn't look very pleased with him, and said she would come back later to let him out. He sat down on the chair beside the bed and looked at me.

"Oh dear, you do look spotty, don't you? Are you feeling any better?"

"I am now that I've seen you. I feel a lot better today." I asked him, "Did you ring the bell?"

"Yes, and I wish I hadn't now—that nun was very sharp with me!"

I told him it was because they were all going to the chapel for the Angelus. "They go to chapel every day at this time. It's a very long day in here. I get very lonely, although I do read a lot, or try to. It's the night time that's worse—I can't sleep; with lying here all day, I'm not tired, and when I did eventually get to sleep last night, I had a bad nightmare. I was so frightened. Someone came in and calmed me down, but I don't know who it was."

The nun came back to get grandad and show him out. The next day when it was time for the Angelus, I heard footsteps outside and the door opened and in walked grandad. This time he was on his own.

"Oh grandad, have you rung that bell again?" I said. "You will be getting me into trouble!"

"Don't worry, I didn't ring the bell," he smiled.

"How did you get in then?"

He said he climbed over the gate and up the fire escape.

I was horrified. "They will get the police if they find you!"

"It'll be all right, don't worry!"

So that's what he did for the rest of the time I was in there. I'm sure Sister Catherine knew!

When I came out of the isolation room and was put back into the dormitory, Sister Catherine gave me the bed next to the fireplace. The girl who was in the bed before had been taken out of the convent. I got back to normal, and started back at school. They didn't call me Orphan Annie; in fact, they were asking me if I was feeling better. There was a girl at school called Valerie, and she used to get all the Enid Blyton books. They were about five children and the things they got up to. I loved those books. Valerie would lend me one at a time until I finished reading them all. I imagined I was in all the adventures with them and it stopped me thinking about being closed in at the convent.

Grandad was still coming every school day, and Ray was coming when he could. I was still heartbroken about my Mam not coming to see me. I would keep asking grandad or Ray if they had seen her. They said, very rarely. Ray said he had seen her at mass a couple of times, and it would be a couple of times because Ray wasn't very fond of going to church if he could get out of it. I thought to myself, she would have to pass the convent to go to mass, so it wouldn't have hurt her to call in and see me for a few minutes.

Ray told me years later that he asked Mam when he got back to Salisbury why I was in the convent. She told him it was because I was ill and that he wasn't to go and see me, as it would make things worse. I'm very glad that Ray disobeyed her!

Chapter 26
The Garden Fête

JULY came. We would be breaking up for the summer holidays in a few weeks. There was to be a garden fête held at the convent. All the girls were very excited about it; a couple of them had written to their mothers about it and their mothers were coming. A few more said they didn't know, but they had asked them. They asked me if my Mam was coming. I said I didn't know.

The next time grandad came to the dinner hall, I asked him if he would go and ask Mam if she would come to the garden fête. He said he hardly ever saw her but he would call at the flat and ask her. When he came back the following day, he said he'd been to see her, and she said she couldn't because she was working.

"But couldn't she just get an hour off work?" I asked.

"I told you what she said and I can't do any more." I could see that grandad was getting all chewed up. I asked him if he had a row with her.

"Yes, and now I don't want to say any more about it."

All the children at school were bringing in clothes they were finished with, books, tins of this and that, homemade jam, lots of toys for the toy stall, and a lot of their mothers were doing lots of baking for the cake stall. At the convent, the nuns told us they wanted the whole place shining like a new pin. Then they had to decide who was doing what. They were to serve tea and biscuits in our dining room. The children at school were talking about the garden fête and were saying that the priest had said at mass that he wanted to see all his parishioners there and that he would be watching out for them.

"My mother didn't want to go," one of the girls said, "but now she will have to show her face, since the priest is going to be watching out for *all* his parishioners!" All the girls laughed.

Saturday came and it was a beautiful day. They were putting all the stalls up around the garden and we were all helping the women who were going to run the stalls. We were carrying boxes full of things, and when we got to a stall, the woman would display what was in the box. Twelve o'clock came and the bell went for the Angelus, so everything stopped. After that we went in for our lunch. The fête was to start at two o'clock. Sister Catherine looked tired out now and it hadn't even started yet. I think it was the heat and she had been out in the sun a long time. After lunch she was telling us what jobs she wanted doing, and wanted the older girls to help the women on the stalls. The girls put their hands up and she picked so many of them. Then she picked up a tin. It was quite big and it had written on it, 'Please help the orphans.'

"Now," she said, "whoever's going to hold this tin will stand by the side door and shake it. I have put a couple of coins in it already. All you have to do is smile and shake it and say, 'Please help the orphans.' And when they put something in you say, 'Thank you.' Now who wants to do that? Hands up?"

Not one hand went up.

"Come on now," she said, "we need it to keep the orphanage going."

I put my hand up in the end and she said, "That's a good girl."

Then she said she needed some help with the tea and biscuits, and had a full show of hands for that. I had a nice cotton dress on that fitted me; it was a bit faded but you could hardly tell. It had little flowers all over, and I loved flowers. They had left me out a cardigan but I didn't put it on. It was all matted.

The garden fête opened at two-o'clock. There was a man opening it—I don't know who he was but anyway he cut the ribbon and declared the fête open. I went back inside to Sister Catherine. I asked her if there was anything she wanted me to do. She said no, everything was ready. "Don't you want to go and have a look around the stalls until it's time for your job?" she asked. I told her I had seen them all when we took the boxes over and helped to put the things on the stalls. I went and sat in the playroom. After a while she came over to me and asked if there was anything wrong. I wasn't myself today, but I told her I was fine and away she went. The time came and they announced it over the loudspeaker, adding that tea and biscuits would be served in the dining room.

"Please make your way to the side door." (That's where I was to stand.) I stood at the door with my tin box. Sister Catherine moved me a couple of yards along the side of the wall. She said if I stood at the door people might not see me and if I stood here, the queue of people would see me all the way down. "So that's when you rattle the tin! It gives them a chance to get their money out and ready." The people were coming. I started to shake the tin and say, "Please help the orphans." They were putting money in the tin and I would give them a smile and say, "Thank you!"

About half way down the queue I thought I could see my Mam. I was trying to keep my mind on what I was doing. As she got nearer I looked again—and it *was* my Mam! She had a white blouse and skirt and a pair of white high heel shoes and a white handbag; her dark hair was down below her shoulders and she looked beautiful! My heart was fluttering. I was so exited I thought she would never get to me. Cove was with her. He tapped her on the arm and pointed to me. She looked at me, but I couldn't make out what her eyes were saying. It was as though she were looking straight through me. She turned her head away as she walked past me, and never said a word. I couldn't go after them because there were a good few people still coming in. I was saying to myself, 'Please hurry up!'

My Mam when she turned up at the garden fate, at the convent

The last of them went past and I ran with the tin to find Sister Catherine. I found her and gave her the tin. There were lots of people in the dining room and in the playroom. I was looking all over for Mam and I couldn't find her.

There was a nun standing by another door. I ran to her and asked if she had seen my Mam and told her how she was dressed.

"Yes," she said, "I've seen her, but she left because she wasn't feeling well."

I thought, '*Why* is she doing this to me? I haven't done anything wrong!' She might as well have stuck a knife in my heart and twisted it. I will never be able to describe the pain I felt. I wanted to cry, and I felt angry as well, but I bottled it all up inside me. She hadn't come to see me—she had come because the priest had told them all to come. I would be glad when this day was over. We all went out and helped clean up the garden and put the things that weren't sold into boxes for the next time they had a fête. I was really fed up with myself. I kept seeing my Mam standing there and turning her head away. What kind of mother would do that to a child? They must have come in at the last minute to show their faces, because they hadn't bought anything. All Mam was carrying was her handbag and they didn't put anything in the tin box, and it was the orphanage that was feeding and looking after me. I was so mad! When I was kneeling down by my bed that night, I wasn't so sure there was a God, but I said my prayers anyway and I wished my mind would stop thinking because it felt as if my head was going to burst.

Next morning we were all seated having our breakfast, when Sister Catherine clapped her hands and said, "Quiet, everyone." She thanked us all for helping yesterday, and said, "Yesterday was a great success and we have made a good bit of money." Then she walked over to me and said, "And I also want to thank this young lady here for doing a great job with the tin box!" She smiled at everyone and continued, "Thank you, and a lot of people remarked on it so I am going to give her a shilling, because no one else would do the job she did."

There were a few moans from some of the girls. They didn't know you would get paid for it! Sister Catherine did not say anything further and she started to walk away. Then she turned to me and said, "And you can come up and get an extra slice of bacon dip."

At any other time I would have been pleased with what Sister Catherine had said, but not that day. I went up and got my extra slice of bacon dip—and I needed it that day! We were all in the schoolyard and I was up near the gate. When no one was looking, I ran out the gate and up towards the town. I looked around the town for a while. I thought about going to grandad's. Then

I changed my mind. I didn't want to get him involved, so I made my way to the railway station and I sat on a bench just watching all the trains coming and going. I still had the shilling in my hand; I would have to find out how far it would get me. I looked up and I saw my grandad coming towards me and there was a policeman with him. I thought, 'Oh God, the policeman is going to put me in jail!' They both stopped a short distance away and grandad was saying something to him. I was just getting ready to run when grandad came towards me. He was on his own. I stood where I was and he came up to me.

"Now my wee ducksey," he said, "what do you think you are doing?"

I told him I was trying to get home to Ireland. He looked at the shilling in my hand.

"That's not going to get you very far, is it? And what about me? Were you going to leave me here on my own?"

"No, I would have sent for you."

"Now you listen to me. There're nothing left over there. Everything has gone and there is no house to live in. I am here for you, and I am not going to leave you."

I started to cry, and then I let it all out. I was trying to tell him about Mam and how much it hurt me.

"I'm going to do something about it, but it will take time," he said kindly. "So you will go back now and face the music?"

I asked him if the policeman was going to put me in jail.

"No," he laughed, "but people were worried about you so you are never to do anything like this again. The policeman had been to your mother's flat, but there was no one in, so they came for me. I brought them here because I knew you had a liking for railway stations after you played truant from school years ago."

He put his arm out for me to link and we went up to the policeman, who took me back to the convent. We went in the front door and the policeman handed me over to a nun, who then took me into an office, and I got a good telling off. I was told to hold my hand out and the ruler came down on my hand three times. Then I was told I was to go straight to bed and I wasn't to get any tea. It was a good job I got that extra slice of bacon dip that morning!

There—I had faced the music! I had got a lot out that was bottled up inside me and I felt a lot better for it. Sister Catherine came up to see me; she asked me if I were all right, and said she was going to the Angelus and that I was to behave myself. She put her hand in the pocket of her Habit and brought out three biscuits and gave them to me. Then I felt awful for making this lovely nun worry. I think God had made her special to look after children. She told me not to get crumbs in the bed, and then left.

I got up next morning feeling a lot better. One of the girls came over to me and asked me if I'd run away because my mother hadn't come. She said her mother hadn't turned up either even though she had said she was coming.

"But I'm used to it, so it doesn't bother me anymore," she said. "You'll get used to it in time."

I swore then that it wasn't going to bother me anymore and I would get on with life. As grandad said, he would always be there for me, so I settled down and got on with it.

Chapter 27
The School Holidays

WE were to break up for the summer holidays at the end of the week, and I asked grandad, "What are we going to do now? Will you come in and see me now and again?"

"Well, you know what I'm like," he said. "I don't like going in there, but we will work something out." We walked back down to the school and I left him at the school gate. He started to go straight on and I shouted after him:

"You're going the wrong way!"

"It's all right," he said, "I'm just going to have a look down here."

The next day when I met him, he told me he had found somewhere; it was down at the back of the convent garden at the right-hand side.

"It looks like an iron gate," he said, "and it's overgrown with climbing rose bushes and weeds. There's a little grass bank at the other side of the gate and a little stream. I could sit on the bank and you could talk to me." He smiled. "You won't be able to see me but we can talk to each other. The trouble is, what time would be best? You always seem to be praying in there."

I told him about half eleven, before the Angelus, or two o'clock after the lunches.

"We'll make it two o'clock then," he said, "but if it's raining you know I can't come. Now when you get back after school, go down the back of the garden and have a look."

After school most of the girls were playing outside. There were two girls on the swings and two more waiting for a go. The others were playing with a ball on the concrete bit. We weren't allowed to play with balls in the gardens. I came out with my book and walked down to the bottom where grandad had said, on the right-hand side. I kept stopping to have a look at the flowers, so no one would think I was up to something. I made my way along the flowerbeds and when I got to the bottom there was a big tree. I went to the side of the tree and looked to see if I could find the iron bars. I couldn't see them at first—they were well covered over—but I found them right opposite the big tree. I went closer and made a hole in the weeds and looked through and saw the little bank. It was very narrow so I made another couple of holes, just small ones, and then I went back up the garden. I felt very exited; it was like a big adventure and I couldn't wait to try it out!

When I met grandad next day, he asked me if I had found the bars. I told him I had and made some holes in the weeds and I could see the bank.

"Do you think that was a gate into the garden?" I asked.

"It could have been—a long time ago," he answered.

"I can't wait to try it out!" I said.

"Neither can I."

It was our first day of trying our plan. Thank goodness it wasn't raining. I took my prayer book and the book I got for Christmas and started off down the garden looking at the flowers on the way. I sat myself down under the big tree and it was lovely and peaceful. All the girls were playing at the top end of the yard. I could see little bits of grandad through the holes I had made, but couldn't see his face, just a bit of his leg or hand when he moved.

"Are you there?" I said in a voice as loud as I dared.

"Yes, I'm here."

We both giggled. This was great fun. We started talking to each other about this and that. He said he'd better not stay too long or someone might get suspicious. Grandad came as often as he could. One week it rained for three days non-stop. The next day after that the ground was soaking wet so I knew he wouldn't come, but it all dried up and we had sunshine again. The holes in the hedge had grown over and I dared not make them any bigger, so I called out:

"Are you there?"

"Yes, I'm here," he replied.

He was talking about the awful weather we had, and had brought an old newspaper to sit on because the grass was still wet. Then everything went quiet. I thought he couldn't have gone already. I waited a bit longer. Then I heard him say:

"Are you there?"

"Yes. What happened?" I asked.

"A couple passed and I didn't hear them coming until they were nearly on top of me, and they were giving me funny looks. They must have thought I was talking to myself. I'll have to be more careful in future."

I told him he should get a hearing aid.

"There's nothing wrong with my hearing," he said.

Another day I went and sat under the tree and I looked at the weeds. They had all grown over again, and there wasn't even a little hole left. I got brave and went over to the weeds and made more holes. I saw grandad coming—well, bits of him—and dashed back under the tree. And to my horror there was a nun halfway down the garden coming towards me. She was reading her prayer book.

"There's a nun coming!" I said to grandad. "Don't say anything. Can you hear me?"

There was no reply. My heart started thumping. Then he said:

"I heard you."

I let out a sigh of relief. I picked up my prayer book and opened it. The nun stopped and said, "Why are you sitting here in the shade? You should be up there in the sunshine."

"I like it here," I said, "its nice and peaceful."

I was hoping she wouldn't see the holes I'd made. She gave me a little smile and went on her way. That was a close one! I did not speak to grandad until she had reached the top of the garden. Then I said:

"I'll be glad when I go back to school and I can see you at the dinner hall."

I was going to start back at school that day and I was looking forward to it. The sun was shining and I went out on the swing for five minutes before I went to school. I couldn't wait to see grandad. The last time he came to the bottom of the garden he didn't stay long, and I said goodbye to him. I ran up the garden and went in the play yard, and spoke to some of the girls. The next thing a head popped up on top of the wall. It frightened a few of the girls, but I told them, its all right, it's only my grandad!

They all started giggling. He must have pulled himself up for a few seconds and it made my day. When I came out of the dinner hall that day, there he was with a big smile on his face.

"Look at the size of you!" he said. "You must have grown about four inches." He smiled. "Come on now, Link on!"

I put my arm through his and linked on. I was never embarrassed with linking onto him, and I never would be. He told me he had a letter from uncle

Bert that morning, that he was asking about me and that they were hoping I was doing well at school.

"I'm going to write back to them this afternoon," he said.

"Will you give them my love?" I asked. He said he would.

Mam had another brother called George who was in the army. He had got married and they had a baby girl called Patricia. So grandad said they were my uncle George and Auntie Mary, and Patricia was my cousin. I told him I knew. I had been to stay with them before he came to England. He said he didn't know that because they moved around a lot; it depended where they got posted to. He walked me back down to school and said, "The last time I went to the bottom of the garden, I tried to get a look at you in the play yard, but I couldn't see you; there were that many children there, and I could only hold onto the wall for a few seconds."

"I know; I saw you," I laughed. "It made my day!"

The rest of the week passed very quickly.

Ray was still coming to see me when he could. He came on Fridays about seven o'clock. They were always telling him off for coming so late and he was always telling them he couldn't help it, he had to work. But he always put something in the poor box before he left. He was telling me now he was going to the church hall to the square dancing. I asked him if he would take me sometime when I was older. He said he would. He gave me some pocket money and left, and I went back into the playroom. Sister Catherine was getting the boxes of sweets out. She would buy the sweets from the warehouse and we could buy them from her. We would buy one sweet for a halfpenny, or two for a penny, and so on. I gave her my pocket money. She put it in the cash box and she would write it down in her little book. Every time I got some sweets she would deduct it from my money. It was a good idea, as we weren't allowed to go to the shops.

The weekend passed and Monday came. I was wishing I could go to school every day. It wasn't because I liked school, but because I would see grandad every day. Grandad was there as usual; he said he had another letter from my uncle Bert that morning. They were coming down to Salisbury on Thursday evening, and they were staying in a hotel for the night and they were going home by Friday teatime. "They have written to your Mam to see if she can get the day off. I have to meet them at your mother's place at ten o'clock."

"Oh, do you think they will come to see me?" I said.

"I am sure they will," he said.

I was so pleased I told all the girls I was going to have visitors on Friday.

"You can't because you'll be at school," one said.

I hadn't thought about that.

"Well," I said, "they can come when I get back from school."

When I met grandad on Tuesday I said, "How can they come and see me? I'll be at school and they are going back at teatime."

"I'll work something out," he said.

I was down in the dumps again. Wednesday came and I met grandad.

"Don't I get a smile today?" he asked.

"I don't feel like smiling,"

"Oh well, you won't want to know my secret then."

I soon came round. "What secret?"

"Well, you are going to see your uncle and aunt after all, so now are you going to give me a smile?"

I gave him the biggest smile I could give and I was jumping all over the place with excitement. He told me to calm down and link on. He told me I wouldn't be going to school on Friday. When I met grandad next day I asked him what time they were coming to see me.

"I'll collect you about nine o'clock and take you to see them," he said.

"You mean I can come out for the day? Have you told Sister Catherine?"

"No, your Mam has to do that and you have to have her permission."

"And do you think she will give it?"

"Oh, I think she will. When I was up to see her yesterday she was knitting a jumper for you with odd balls of wool. She had the back and front done and was going on about not having enough wool and she made you a skirt out of a dress. Anyway, she wouldn't leave you in there when your uncle Bert was coming." Grandad left me at the school gate and said, "I'll see me tomorrow."

Oh, I was so happy I couldn't wait for morning! When I got back from school I was following Sister Catherine all over the place. Every time she looked round I was there. She said to me, "Is there anything wrong, child?"

"No, everything's fine," I said. I was hoping she was going to tell me that Mam had been and I was going out tomorrow for the day, but nothing was said so I gave up in the end. Sister Catherine got out her boxes of sweets and I got what I wanted from her, and was walking out the door to the play yard as another nun came in. She asked me if I knew where Sister Catherine was and I told her. I wondered what she wanted; she had a brown paper bag in her hand. I decided to go back in and see what the nun wanted to see Sister Catherine for. When I got up to them they were chatting away to each other. Then the nun said, "I have just come to let you know that Mrs Spencer has been. Muriel will be going out for the day tomorrow; her grandfather will pick her up at nine o'clock in the morning. Mrs Spencer said she was to wear these clothes."

She passed the brown paper bag to Sister Catherine. I thought, if Mam had been to the convent, why didn't she come and see me?

Sister Catherine came over to me and told me I was going out for the day tomorrow. She handed me the brown paper bag and said I was to put these clothes on in the morning. "I hope you have a lovely day," she smiled.

I went upstairs and took the clothes out of the bag. There was a vest, pants and a pair of white ankle socks. I looked at the jumper; it had pink, blue and white stripes with short sleeves. She must have run out of wool. I tried it on: it was a bit small but I loved the colours. I picked up the skirt and looked at it.

It took me back to our kitchen in Ennis, when Mam was twirling around in this dress she had made. She had asked me what I thought, and I had told her it was a bit long. She said it wasn't. This was the fashion now. It was called the 'new look'. Now she had cut the dress up and made me a skirt out of it! It still had the braid on the bottom of the skirt that she had got from my aunt Fanny in Ennis. It made me feel a bit sad, and I thought about them all over in Ireland.

I tried on the skirt. She had put elastic in the waist and I just had to pull it on. It was a bit long but that didn't matter. Then I thought about my shoes. They were in a bad state, so I went back downstairs and found Sister Catherine, and I told her about my shoes. She said, "If you go in the cupboard in the cloakroom there's a few bags of shoes just been handed in." She added, "I haven't had time to go through them yet, so they might be all summer shoes." So off I went to the cloakroom. I tipped out the first bag but there was nothing there to fit me. I tipped out the second bag and I saw these red sandals: they had a peep toe and a heel that was a couple of inches high. I was saying to myself, 'Please let them fit me,' and tried them on and they fitted me—well nearly! My toe didn't quite reach where it was supposed to, but they had an ankle strap on them—better that they were too big than too small! I picked all the other shoes up and put them back in the bags and put them back in the cupboard. I told Sister Catherine that I'd found some; I didn't want her to see them in case she wouldn't let me wear them because they had a bit of a heel on them. That was me, ready for morning!

By the time I got back downstairs Sister Catherine was telling us to tidy up. It was bedtime. We all went upstairs to get washed and ready for bed. She said she would be up shortly to read us a story. I think that was the longest night of my life. I was twisting and turning and couldn't get to sleep. I kept thinking to myself what would I say to Mam when I met her? Would she think I'd grown? She might come up to me and give me a big cuddle and say she was sorry. Or should I go up to her and give her a cuddle? At last sleep overcame me and I didn't have to think anymore.

When I got up next morning I felt excited and frightened at the same time, but I kept saying to myself it would be all right! Grandad would be there. I was sitting there, ready at quarter to nine, by which time all the girls had gone to school. Sister Catherine came over to me and asked if I was all right. I told her I was a bit nervous.

"You'll be fine," she said. "I'll say a little prayer for you"—and she went off to do something. I went to the cloakroom for my coat, which I hadn't worn for months. It was too warm for the summer. We had those see-through Mack's if it rained. I sat down again with my coat over my knee and Sister Catherine came back in.

"Come," she said, "I'll take you to the front hall now."

I got up and followed her. She told me to sit down, and I could hear the clock ticking. There was one minute to go. Dead on nine the doorbell rang. Sister Catherine went to open the door and there stood grandad! She said good morning to him and he lifted his cap and said good morning.

"Come along Muriel," she said, "your grandfather's here."

She knew my grandad quite well. Sometimes at lunchtime she would go to the shop, and if we were coming out of the dinner hall and she was coming back, she would walk back down to the school with us. We went out of the gate.

"You should put that coat on," grandad said. "It's chilly this morning, summer has gone."

I put the coat on.

"Grandad, you were right," I said, "I must have grown. Look at my coat."

He looked at me. "Oh dear, what are we going to do now?"

"I'll take it off and put it over my shoulders and then it will look better," I said.

Grandad said plans had been changed. "We are going to your mother's flat first and then we will walk into town and meet your uncle and aunt outside Marks and Spencer's."

When we got near Mam's flat I started to shake. Grandad stopped and he looked down at my arm that was linked to his.

"Now stop that shaking," he said. "You'll make yourself sick. None of this is your fault—always remember that. So pull yourself together."

We went up the three flights of stairs and grandad knocked at the door. Mam answered it and told us to come in. Grandad had hold of my hand and he led me across to the sofa and sat down. Mam sat on a chair opposite us. I so badly wanted her to come over and give me a cuddle, but she didn't, and I thought, should I go over and give her one? Better not, she might reject me, and then I would feel awful! Then she spoke, looking at me.

"How are you?"

"I'm all right thank you." It felt like a couple of strangers meeting for the first time and I wanted to cry. If only she would give me a hug! Cove came out of the bedroom; he said hello to grandad, but he didn't speak to me. Mam went into the bedroom to get ready. Grandad asked me if I needed to use the toilet.

"No," I said.

"Well, I had better before we go."

I was wishing I had said yes now, as I felt alone in the room with Cove. He looked at me.

"This is for one day only," he said. "Do you hear me, you little bitch?"

I nodded my head and said yes.

Everyone was ready. Mam told me to put my coat on. I told her it was too small, but I put it on anyway. Then she told me to take it off again.

"Surely you could have got a coat that fitted you from the convent?"

I told her I didn't realise it was too small until I was outside when grandad told me to put it on. I hadn't worn it all summer. So I put it back over my shoulders and we made our way up into the town and were outside Marks and Spencer's at ten o'clock. I was first to see them coming and ran up to them and my uncle put his arms out and I ran into them; then I got a hug from my aunt and my coat fell to the floor. My uncle picked it up and said, "Put it on, it's cold." I told him it was too small for me and that it looked better over my shoulders. They said they wanted to have a look in

Marks and Spencer's and walked over to Mam, and my uncle gave her a hug. Then he shook my grandad's hand.

"And this is Ernie, my husband," Mam was saying.

My uncle shook hands with him and so did my aunt. He held on to my aunt's hand and was patting it and was smiling a sickly smile up into her face.

"What a pleasure it is to meet you," he said.

They all made their way into the shop. Grandad didn't want to go in—he said he would have a walk around for a while and would meet us back there in an hour. He hated going into shops, especially in a big one like this. The rest of us went in. My aunt loved it. She was saying, "Oh, I like this," and, "This is lovely!" She was holding one thing after another up against her.

"Oh no, you don't want that colour; this colour suits you better," Cove was saying, and my aunt was beaming with pleasure.

My uncle bought her a twin set, so she was happy. Then he wandered over to the children's department and took me with him. He was looking at the coats and was trying one after another up against me.

"This is a nice one, let's try it on you." He asked me if I liked it. I said I did. "Right," he said, "we'll have that one."

Then he looked at the dresses and picked two. One had red and white stripes and the other was the same, only it had blue and white stripes.

"We'll show them to your aunt and see what she thinks," he said. "And then I'll go and pay for them."

"No," I said, "please don't buy them because you'll be wasting your money."

"What do you mean?" he asked.

"Well, I won't get to wear them because all the clothes are put together for the orphans, and you have to wear what you are given, so I would have to put the dresses among all the other clothes and wouldn't know when I would get a turn to wear them. So you see, you'll just waste your money."

He looked at me. "Well, I can still buy them and you can wear them when you go to your mother's at the weekends and holidays."

"I don't go to Mam's at the weekends or holidays," I said.

He asked me why not and I didn't know what to say. I just shrugged my shoulders. Then he asked me how many boarders there were in the convent.

"There are two," I replied, "but they go home every weekend and all the school holidays."

He seemed to realise I was getting upset and he didn't ask me any more questions, and went to show my aunt the coat and dresses. She approved, so he went to the counter to pay for them. He asked the woman if I could wear the coat now. She took the tickets off, and put it on me. I said thank you.

"Should I ask the lady to put the old one in the bin?" he asked.

"Oh no, it'll fit one of the other orphans," I replied. "I'll take it back to the convent."

He gave me a smile. "Let's go and find the others," he said.

We found them and they had all found what they wanted, and went outside to meet grandad. He looked at me and told me I looked very nice.

My uncle Bert was very much like my grandad in his ways. He was a quiet man and didn't like a fuss or crowds; he read a lot of books and liked music, especially Burl Ives singing 'There was an old woman who swallowed a fly, perhaps she'll die!' He didn't drink or go to pubs. We had a big picture of him on the wall of our kitchen in Ireland. My dad had knocked it down in one of his rages and all the glass got broken. Mam had it replaced once, but dad broke it again, so Mam gave up and it was put back on the wall without the glass. I used to show my friends the picture. He was dressed in his air force uniform, and wherever you stood in the kitchen his eyes seemed to follow you, and we used to play games with it; we would all stand in different places, and I would say, "He's looking at me," and someone else would say, "No he isn't, he is looking at me!" So my uncle Bert was my hero.

We were going to look around the market. Grandad didn't mind that, but I think he'd already been around it once while he was waiting for us. I linked on to him and he asked me if I was happy. I told him it was the happiest day of my life. The only thing was, uncle Bert had bought me two dresses and I didn't want him to waste his money.

"Oh, don't worry about them," grandad said, "you might get to wear them sooner than you think."

When we'd finished looking round the market, my uncle said we would find somewhere to have lunch. We found a place and we all went in and found a table for six. I had a tight hold of grandad.

"You're going to have the jacket off me in a minute, the way you're pulling at me," he smiled.

"I want to sit next to you," I said.

"Well, if you take your hands off my jacket, I'll get us a couple of chairs together."

He put me on a chair and he sat down himself. We were all asked what we'd like to eat. I asked if I could have sausage, egg and chips. We all tucked into our lunch and they talked about this and that. When we'd all finished, my uncle said he would like to go and see the Cathedral. Grandad told him it was a fine building and worth the visit. So we made our way towards the Cathedral, and uncle Bert was walking with grandad and talking all the time. I was walking with my aunt; Mam and Cove were in front of us. When we got near the school, I said, "That's where I go to school!" And when we got to the convent I said, "And that's where I live." My uncle didn't look very happy and I wondered what was wrong with him. We turned the corner and went down to the bottom of the road and turned right and there was a lovely view of the Cathedral. We went in and had a good look round. My uncle and aunt loved things like this and they were taking photos of everything. When we came out, he was taking photos of all of us on the steps outside. When he'd finished he put his camera away and spoke to Mam.

"I would like a word with you," he said, and she walked over to him.

He seemed to look very cross. Whatever they were talking about, she was looking down at the ground as though she was getting a telling off and looking ashamed of something. Then he was pointing to where she lived, and then up towards the convent. Then my uncle called to Cove.

"Ernie, can I have a word?" he said.

It seemed funny to hear him called Ernie! He went over and my uncle had raised his voice now and seemed to get even crosser. He was telling them it was a disgrace what they were doing to me—their voices were getting louder. I went over to my grandad and linked on to him. He had a little smile on his face all the time.

"We have been trying to get an extra room for the last ten months," Cove was saying.

"Did that stop you from going to see the child?" my uncle said.

They didn't know where to look.

"You're both working full time," my uncle continued, "so you could have looked for a bigger flat, and from what I hear there is a big living room with a sofa; she could have used that to sleep on until you found something else. I really am surprised with you—that child needs to be with her mother!"

She said she would sort it out.

"And don't blame the child for this," he said. "She didn't tell me anything—it was my father who told me."

They stared at grandad, but he still had that little smile on his face. Uncle Bert said it was time they were getting back; they had put their bags in the left luggage so they would have to collect them. Grandad said he would walk part of the way with them. I asked him if I could come and he said yes. I asked Mam for the red coat out of the bag and she gave it to me. Grandad said he would drop me off at the convent later. I couldn't wait to get going and said goodbye to Mam and Cove. I was a bit frightened by the way Cove was looking at me. If looks could kill, I would be dead. Grandad walked me back to the convent. I told him for once I was glad to be going back in—I didn't like the look on their faces, especially Cove's.

"That's my wee Ducksey," Grandad laughed.

I said goodbye to him and told him I'd had lovely day. He walked me to the door and rang the bell. The door opened and I happily went in with my red coat over my arm. The first one I saw was Sister Catherine. She asked if I'd had a nice day. I told her I had and that my uncle had bought me a new coat and that I had brought the red one back—it was too small for me, but it would fit one of the others. She took the coat from me and smiled.

When I went into the playroom all the girls wanted to know what I'd done all day, so the story of my day out had to be told and they said I wasn't to leave anything out. About half past seven, Sister Catherine came and told me I was to go to the front hall—Ray was there to see me. I thought to myself, all this in one day! I was over the moon. When I got to the hall Ray was talking to one of the nuns, the one that was always telling him off for coming late.

"It's just this once," Ray was saying to her. "I'm going away and I might not see her again for years."

"If I let one go they'll all want to go," the nun said.

"They have to be with an adult," Ray persisted, "and there are no adults here. Go on, just for an hour."

The nun gave in. "You have her back here for nine o'clock sharp."

Ray thanked her and went over to the orphan's box and put a ten-shilling note in. That was a lot of money. The nun told him to go and see Sister Catherine in the playroom. When we got to the back of the convent, I asked Ray what was going on.

"I'm taking you to the square dancing in the church hall," he said, "but just for an hour."

I couldn't believe what I was hearing! We went into the playroom and Ray was having a word with Sister Catherine. Then she came over to me.

"Come," she said, "I'll find you a blouse—that jumper's too small for you; every time you move your arms it rides up and you can see your vest." She found me a lovely white blouse that had a little stand up collar and short sleeves.

"There, that looks better." She told me to go and get my coat, and took me over to Ray. We went in the front hall and Sister Catherine let us out and closed the door after us. We walked up the road and I felt as though I was on cloud nine. When we got into the hall, the sound of the music made you want to tap your feet. Ray was teaching me to do some of the steps and would laugh when I did something wrong, and we'd try again. The hour passed very quickly and he had to take me back.

"Please don't go away," I said on the way back. "I couldn't bear it."

"Away where?" Ray asked.

"You told the nun you were going away."

"Oh that," he said. "I only said that to get you out, and you could come and see what the square dancing was like."

"But that means you won't be able to come and see me now!"

"Don't worry about that, I'll just tell them I didn't get the job after all; and the next time I come to see you I'll be on time. So what do you think of that?"

"Great!" I said.

When I got back into the convent, I went straight up and got washed and into my nightdress. I knelt down by the side of my bed and thanked God for the lovely day I'd had and then I said the rest of my prayers. When I woke up next morning I thought I must have dreamt it all, until one of the girls asked me what the square dancing was like. Then I knew I hadn't been dreaming.

A couple of days later, it was a Sunday afternoon. Sister Catherine told me my mam was here, and she was going to take me to live with her. She told me to go and get my things together. There wasn't very much to get together—my books and my box of hankies that were still unused and some bits and pieces I had collected along the way. Sister Catherine put them in a bag for me, and asked if I was all right.

"I thought you would be jumping about with excitement," she said.

I told her I was a bit frightened.

"If at any time you need someone to talk to I will be here for you," she replied.

We went down to the playroom and I said goodbye to the girls. They were all giving me a hugs and there were a few tears between us. Sister Catherine took me to the front hall, to Mam. I didn't know what to say to her because we were like strangers. I walked out the front door. (The door I was so frightened to walk in that seemed like a lifetime ago.) On the way to the flat, Mam was telling me to try and keep out of Cove's way as much as I could and I wasn't to be cheeky. This would be my seventh move since we came to England two years ago.

When we arrived at the flat, Cove was there. He didn't speak. It looked as though they had fallen out because he wasn't speaking to Mam either and she was banging things like the cupboard doors when she was putting the shopping away. She told me to come with her, and I went towards their bedroom, but she opened the other door that I had seen all that time ago and I'd wondered what was in there. Well, now I knew—it was a bedroom! I was very hurt because they must have had it all the time, as there was no other way into it. You would have to go through their sitting room to get in. They had lied to Uncle Bert about trying to get another flat with an extra room. I knew now that I wasn't wanted. If Uncle Bert hadn't come, I would still be in the convent. It's an awful feeling to know you're not 'Wanted'.

"There's your case," Mam said. "You'd better try your clothes on and see if they still fit you."

She went out and closed the door. I looked round the room; there was a wardrobe, a chest of drawers and a double bed. I lifted the case onto the bed and opened it. It was nice to see my clothes again, but most of them were too small; the pants and socks were all right as I was still very thin. And there were a couple of dresses that had a big hem, so I could let them down. The jumpers were far too small; the sleeves were halfway up my arms and they were short in length. The two nightdresses my uncle and aunt had bought me were all right: they didn't reach the floor any more and they were three quarter sleeves, but there was still plenty of room in them. I took the things that fitted me out to Mam.

"Is that all that fits you?" she said. "What about the jumpers?"

I told her they were way up my arms. She told me to unpick the hems of the dresses, which I did. I went back into the bedroom and I put my pants and socks in a drawer, and opened the wardrobe to hang my coat up, and the two dresses my uncle and aunt had bought me were hanging there. Then I went to bed. There would be no story from Sister Catherine tonight, but I soon fell asleep.

I went to school on Monday. I was pleased to see the girls from the convent, and they were asking me all sorts of questions about the flat and whether I had a room to myself. I wasn't feeling very well that day. I was getting cramps in my stomach all day and my grandad hadn't come to the dinner hall, and I was worried about him. I was glad when school was over.

I was the first one home so it was my job to fill the two coal buckets, clean out the ashes and light the fire. It was a lot harder work getting the coal here because you had to go down to the basement for it. I filled the two buckets but I could only carry one at a time up the three flights of stairs. I went down for the second bucket and halfway up the stairs I got stomach cramps, and dropped some of the coal. I got to the top and put the bucket down on the landing and ran back down the stairs to pick up the coal I'd dropped. When I got back in the room I flopped in a chair, and the cramps went away again. I cleaned the ashes out of the fireplace and I lit the fire. I looked at the ashes; I would have to take that down now, but the cramps started again, so I would have to wait a while. After a few minutes I got up again and laid the table for tea. Now I could take the ashes down and put them in the bin. Coming back up the stairs the cramps started again. I went and sat down and I was going to stay there until I heard footsteps coming up the stairs. Mam came in first. She said, "Hello," then said, "That's good, I don't have to clean the fire out."

I asked her if I could just have some bread and jam for my tea because I had a big dinner and pudding at school. She gave me some bread and jam and I ate it as quick as I could. I asked her if I could go and see grandad. She said I could and I was to be back for nine o'clock. So I made my way to grandad's and he was shocked to see me.

"Where have you come from?" he asked. "You haven't run away again?"

I told him the story about Mam coming to the orphanage and she had taken me home with her. He said it was about time. He didn't look well. I asked him what was wrong?

"I have a cold and a very bad headache, but I'll be better tomorrow," he said.

I told him not to bother coming to the dinner hall tomorrow. "I'll come and see you after school so you're not to go out." I told him I had been having awful cramps in my stomach all day.

"Have you told your mother?"

"I didn't want to tell her because she might think I was complaining and it's only my first day there."

He told me not to be silly. "You tell your Mam when you get back."

I looked in his cupboard. There was a tin of soup, and I asked him if he would have some. He said he would. I put some in a pan and heated it up for him. I looked in the coal bucket and it was nearly full.

"Do you want me to light the fire for you?"

He said no, he was warm enough. We sat and chatted for a while. Then it was time for me to go. I gave him a kiss and a hug. He said, "You're a good wee lassie," and I made my way back to the flat.

When I got in they were both sitting there but they still weren't speaking. I got a little bowl of water and took it into my bedroom and had a wash, and put my nightdress on and I was ready for bed. I took the bowl back in the living room and I said goodnight to them. Mam said goodnight but he didn't, and I got cramps in my stomach again but I didn't go and tell Mam. I said my prayers and was soon fast asleep.

When I woke up next morning my nightdress felt a bit wet. I thought I'd wet the bed! I was in a right state with myself. I looked at the bed and it was dry. I let out a sigh of relief, and took my nightdress off and had a look at it. There was a red stain on the back of it. I was bleeding! I opened my bedroom door a little bit and I shouted for Mam. She came into the room.

"What is it?" she asked.

I told her I was bleeding down below. She went out of the room, but she was back in a couple of minutes. She told me to wash myself and then she threw something on the bed.

"When you have washed, put that between your legs. I have to go or I'll be late; see you later."

I looked on the bed and my mind went back to Martin and me running up and down the road with one of those on our faces and looped around our ears. We had thought they were Doctors' masks, and I had never seen one since that day to this. I washed and put the thing on. But my pants were a bit loose and it kept sticking out at one end or the other. I was walking knock-kneed trying to stop it from moving. I got to school and I was praying that I wouldn't be called up to the front of the class. Playtime came and I was up the top end of the playground where they kept all the coke for the boilers. I went behind the pile of coke and I was trying to fix the thing so it wouldn't move about. Then I heard this voice:

"Are you all right?"

I nearly jumped out of my skin! It was one of the girls. I think she was a bit younger than me. I can't remember her name but she had lovely blonde hair way down her back. She said she had been watching me and I was walking funny. She asked if she could help. I burst into tears and told her what had happened from waking up this morning.

"That's your period," she explained, "didn't your mother tell you about it?"

"No," I replied, "but I've been in the convent and I only went home two days ago."

"Well, I will tell you," she said. "You will get a period every month for the rest of your life. It lasts four or five days and you will need a belt to keep the sanitary towel on and you better tell your mother you need a smaller size. The one you have on is huge."

I was horrified at hearing all this, but at the same time I was glad I didn't have to ask Mam about it. But I would have to ask her for a belt. I thanked the girl for telling me all about it. I felt better now. I thought about Martin and me running up and down the road with our Doctors' masks on and I understood now why we got a good hiding. I don't know how I got through the rest of the day, but I was glad when it was home time. When Mam came in she went in my room and put some smaller sanitary towels on my bed and one of them had a bit of elastic threaded through the loops. Ray was always saying I was the most naive person he knew and he was right.

The following Friday we were to break up from school for a week. They called it potato-picking week. We had to put our names in a book if we wanted to go. I told grandad about it and he said I was to put his name down. So I did. It came to Monday morning and we all met up outside the convent. There was a lorry coming to pick us up. Grandad was there first and we all went and stood with him. The lorry came and the man started calling names out of his book. There were a lot of names called out that hadn't turned up. We all got into the lorry and it set off for the farm. When we got there we had five minutes to get ready. It was a very dismal morning. We put our lunch bags and things against the wall. Then the tractors started going and it was digging up the soil and bringing the potatoes to the top. We followed and started putting the potatoes in the sack we had taken from a pile at the side of the field. Grandad was way ahead of us. He was doing the work of two or more children. We went on picking until the whistle went for lunchtime. By this time we were taking off some of our clothes because we were too warm. We sat on a wall at the end of the field and had our lunch. The whistle would go again. End of lunchtime and we would all start work again. By the end of the day we were all worn out. I looked at grandad; he didn't look well at all. I asked him if he was all right. He said he was fine. We queued up for our day's pay and we were allowed to take a few potatoes home with us. Grandad and I were last to get paid. The man gave me mine and when it was grandad's turn the man said to him, "Well done! I could do with a few more like you." Then he gave him his money. Grandad frowned as he looked at the money.

"What's this?" he asked

"That's your pay for a day's work," the man replied. "You were on the children's list and there is nothing I can do about it now. I am sent the money per child. I'm sorry."

Grandad had worked two or three times harder than any of us and he was given a Child's pay! He was angry. I pulled at his jacket and said, "Come on or we will miss the lorry home."

When we were seated on the lorry, I told him, "You're not coming back here tomorrow, it's too much for you." He looked worn out.

The lorry dropped a few others and myself outside the convent. Grandad stayed on until the next stop nearer the town. I had told him I would come and see him tomorrow after tea. I was glad to get home as my skin felt as though it was all dried up and I was longing to get a good wash down, but I got the coal up first and lit the fire; then I had a good wash and I felt a lot better. After tea Mam asked me if I was going to grandad's. I said no, I was too tired and I would go tomorrow after tea. She told me to ask him if I could stay with him on Saturday night as she was going out somewhere with Cove and they might not be back until Sunday morning.

After tea I was having a job trying to keep my eyes open. I would have to go to bed. I said goodnight to Mam and went in my bedroom, got undressed and said my prayers. I got into bed and I was out like a light.

It didn't seem like five minutes until it was morning. I ached all over, but I knew I would get used to it in a couple of days, and I did. I went to see grandad after tea and asked him about staying on Saturday night. He said that was fine.

"We'll have to do something special. I will let you choose."

I was glad when it was Friday and had finished with the potato picking. I brought some home every day, so Mam had a good stock of them. I didn't know what time she would be home that night—I forgot to ask her in the morning. She had changed her job again; she was now working in a mental hospital and she didn't like it very much. She said she was going to look for another job because she didn't like the shift work. Anyway, I got on with my jobs. I took the ashes out of the fireplace and put it in some newspaper, and put it in one of the empty coal buckets. I picked up the coal buckets and went down the stairs, and put the ashes in the bin and went on to get the coal. I put the kettle on to have a wash. Now the water bucket was empty. Cove usually filled them up but he wasn't home yet. I went back down and filled the water bucket and carried that back up. Then I noticed the slop bucket wanted emptying—so back down again! I only had to go down to the second floor to empty that. I got my wash at last, and stood in a bowl of water and it felt like heaven. I got washed and put some clean clothes on. I was going to see grandad but I thought I had better wait until Mam came home. I sat down and thought of what I was going to spend my potato picking money on. I had never had twenty-five shillings before and it was a fortune to me. I thought I would give Mam ten shillings and I could buy myself some new shoes for winter. I could get some in the market pretty cheap. The next thing I knew Mam was shaking me. I had fallen asleep. She was telling me it was time for bed.

It was Saturday and I was going to stay with grandad, and I was to choose where we were going to go. I wanted to go to the Salisbury fair but I didn't think grandad would want to go there, and the other suggestion was to go to the cinema. He would be wondering where I had got to last night. I got ready and told Mam I was going. She said she didn't know what time they would be back tomorrow. I told her it was all right, I would stay with grandad all day and so made my way to grandad's. When I got there he said, "Well hello, and where did you get to yesterday?"

I told him I had fallen asleep and it was too late when I woke up. He asked me where I would like to go. I asked if we could go to the fair.

"Well," he said, "you know I don't like things like that."

I must have looked very disappointed.

"Oh, all right then," he said. "Just this once, but I'm not staying long."

So I got to the fair. I don't know why I wanted to go because there was only one ride I would go on and that was the carousel with the horses going round and up and down. But I loved to watch other people going on the rides and the faces they were making. We walked around all the stalls—it was lovely to see all the coloured lights. We finished up at one stall where you had to throw a round ring and you had to get it over a square box and there were lots of different prizes you could win. I asked grandad to have a go.

"Which prize do you want me to go for?" he asked.

I said there was a lovely watch—would he try and win me that? He threw the rings and won the watch! I was very excited. He gave me the watch, and then he had another go and won himself a watch! The man gave him the watch but he didn't look too pleased. By this time there was a big crowd gathering round watching him. He had another go. He threw the first ring at a pound note and won it! He threw the second one and won a ten-shilling note, but he didn't get anything with the third one.

"I'll just have one more go and that's it," he said.

He threw the first ring and got a pound note. Then he threw the second ring and got another pound note! So he threw the third ring and he got a ten-shilling note. The man was looking very angry now! Grandad said to me that we were going now. When the man came over with the money he had won, he said, "I'll give you three pounds if you go away!" Grandad said "Fair enough!" and he took the three pounds. There were an awful lot of people around the stall now, and they were all having a go. Grandad had made it look so easy! He said he could have gone on a bit longer but it wasn't fair on the man and he could have saved himself three pounds because we were going anyway! We both started to laugh.

"Well," grandad said, "what do you want to do now?"

I asked if we could go to the cinema.

"We can go and look and see what's on."

There was a musical on with Nelson Eddy and Jeanette McDonald. I told grandad he would like this film. He gave me the money and told me to go and get the tickets. Grandad looked lost. I don't think he had been in a cinema before. The usherette showed us to our seats and the film was just starting. I was engrossed in the film, but after about five minutes, the woman behind me was tapping me on the shoulder. When I turned round, she asked me, "Are you with him?"

"Yes," I said, "He's my grandad."

"Well, will you tell him to sit down—my husband can't see a thing."

"He *is* sitting down," I replied.

I looked at him and he did seem a bit high up. I told him to stand up. He stood up and I could see he hadn't put his seat down! I put it down and sat him on it.

"Oh, that's better," he said, "I was beginning to get cramp."

The people behind us were telling us to be quiet. I turned round and said I was sorry, my grandad didn't know that you had to put the seat down. The next time I looked at him he was fast asleep and I thought I would just leave him; it was nice and warm in there and he looked very comfortable. After the film had finished I woke him up and told him it was time to go.

"I don't know what came over me, falling sleep like that," he said when we got outside.

We were passing the fish and chip shop and he asked me if I would like a bag of chips and I said I would. We got two bags of chips open and we ate them walking up the road. When we got back to grandad's it was very cold in the room. He made my bed up with the box and the bit of sponge. Then he lit the two little rings he used for cooking and put quite a bit of money in the meter.

"We can have as much heat as we want tonight," he said, "and tomorrow and the next day." He had a big smile on his face. "I didn't want to go to that fair, I was dreading it, but I'm glad I did—winning all that money!" The little room got lovely and warm, and we talked for a while about this and that. I told grandad I had a great time and thanked him.

"You're welcome, my wee ducksey, but it's time for bed now. You have to be up early for mass in the morning."

I was soon asleep.

Chapter 28
Reminiscing

RAY went to London to work. He wasn't there very long before he got called up for his national service. He had to parcel all his clothes up in brown paper tied with string, and then posted them to Mam to look after. A couple of weeks later Martin came home. Cove wouldn't let him stay with us so he had to stay with grandad. Grandad wasn't very pleased because he couldn't light his fire and Martin couldn't get a living-in job because it was winter, and to make things worse he started buying second-hand books from the market for a few pence each. I don't know why he bought so many, because he never read them. He had books piled in every nook and cranny in the little room. I went down to see them after my tea and could hear them before I went into the room. Grandad was shouting at Martin because he had come home with more books!

"You can get rid of half of these books! We haven't got room to walk past each other and you're bringing more books. Well, I've have had enough of it!"

I opened the door and went in and asked what was wrong. I tried to walk past grandad and he went to move and tripped over the books that Martin had just brought home. He fell on the bed and looked really angry. He picked himself up; grabbed his cap and was out the door. Martin kicked the books on the floor, and I looked at him.

"Martin," I said, "there isn't enough room in here for all those books. Can't you just have two or three?"

He started waving his arms about and pulling all the books down; they were hitting me on the head and then he started hitting me; I got away—this wasn't like Martin at all. I ran all the way home. Mam and Cove were just coming out the front door; they were going out. Mam asked me what had happened to my head. It was bleeding. I told her there was something wrong with Martin—he'd gone mad. I was told to go to the flat and wait there until they returned. They must have been gone an hour or so. When they came back they had Martin with them. His eyes were all swollen from crying but he looked more like himself now. He looked at me; his eyes were pleading as if to say, 'Don't hate me.' Cove went in the bedroom and slammed the door. Mam told Martin he was to go down to grandad's the next day and get rid of all the books.

"Can't I just keep a couple?"

"A couple and no more!" she said. "All this trouble you've caused—I'm sure none of you want me to be happy! Now you two get to bed and I don't want to hear another word out of the pair of you."

We said goodnight to her but she didn't answer. When we got in the bedroom I whispered to Martin:

"What was that all about? You scared me."

He said he was sorry and he came and gave me a cuddle.

"Everything was getting on top of me," he said. "That room was so small and there was nowhere to put anything; you couldn't light the fire and it was cold. I was buying the books for something to do."

"But that was making the room smaller. You must have seen that?"

"I do now, but at the time I felt as though I had nothing in my life; just a bag and a few clothes; the books made me feel secure as though I had something that was mine."

"But Martin, you don't read any of them!"

"I know, but when I get a house of my own I would have read them."

"Well," I said, "I should forget about that if I were you, and remember before we came to England, we talked about the big house with a lovely garden. Well, you ended up in a big hotel and I ended up in a convent. We both ended up in big houses, didn't we?"

"I wish I was back home in Ennis," he smiled. "We had bad times but we had lots of good times as well. Remember when Mam went up to meet her brothers in Northern Ireland, just before they got posted? When the war was on, and Mam had to stay overnight? Aunt Fanny was looking after us, and next day before Mam was home Aunt Fanny was washing our faces and combing our hair, she left you until last and put that lovely pink dress on you that Mam had made out of an old bridesmaid's dress, and a pink ribbon in your hair. She told us to sit on the front doorstep and wait for Mam coming. You went out the gate and they had just tarred the road and you sat on it! You were drawing pictures on the wet tar. Aunt fanny had a fit! She said, 'Oh mother of God, look at the state of her!' She dragged you in and washed you the best she could, and she had to put your dirty dress back on. Mam was coming up the road and we ran to meet her. She had three Hurley's in her hands; she gave one to Ray and me and then she handed you one and said, 'I couldn't find anything for a girl.' You burst into tears and said, 'Girls don't have Hurley's.' Ray took it out of your hand and said, 'I'll have it,' and we went into Auntie Fanny's and she explained about the tar on the new dress. We all ended up laughing! Do you remember?"

"I remember all that," I told Martin, "but we are stuck here and there's nothing we can do about it now; so you have the bottom of the bed and I'll have the top."

We lay there listening to Mam and Cove arguing until we fell asleep.

Next day I helped Martin to take the books to a charity shop. We had to do a couple of runs with them. Martin was a bit upset about it but I told him when he got a place of his own he could have as many books as he wanted. When we got back grandad was sitting in his armchair and had lit a fire. It looked a bit more like home now. Martin got his bag and packed his clothes. I told grandad I would come and see him tomorrow.

"Look," he said, "as I told your mother yesterday, she has three rooms up there so she should have plenty of room for Martin as well."

I told him it was Cove who wouldn't let him stay.

"When Ernie married your mother he knew she had three children, so he should see that they have a roof over their heads."

"I know it's not your fault, grandad, so calm down," I said. "You have always done your best for us and I don't know what I would do without you."

I gave him a kiss and we left. So Martin moved in with us and his life was hell. We were sitting at the table one night after tea having a game of Ludo. Mam was going out the door with a bucket of slops.

"Put that down," Cove said, "Ginger will take it."

"I have to go down anyway," she said, "I need the toilet."

When she had gone, Cove started making faces at us, putting his hands up to his ears and wiggling his fingers and sticking his tongue out at us.

"God," Martin said, "he looks a right idiot! Do the same back to him and he won't be so quick at doing it to us again. Go on, do it back!"

We did the same to him and we could hear Mam coming up the stairs. As soon as the door opened Cove said to her, "Do you see those two children of yours? They have been making faces at me and putting their tongues out!"

Mam stood in front of us. We were telling her he did it first and I said he was always doing it to me.

"Stop telling lies!" she said. "You know I hate lies; and what would a grown man be doing sticking his tongue out at you? Now tell him you're sorry!"

"But he started it!" Martin insisted.

That was it. Mam started slapping us and we thought she was never going to stop, and we were sent to bed. When we got in the bedroom I said to Martin, "I told you Mam won't believe a word we say, so it's better to let him make faces and don't take any notice of him."

"I don't know what's happened to Mam," Martin said. "She's not the same anymore."

Cove continued his spiteful ways.

We were both doing jigsaws on the table when Cove came over to look.

"You're doing very well with that," he said to me. I was so grateful for this bit of praise. Then he looked at Martin's.

"You're not doing so good, are you?" And he knocked Martin's jigsaw flying everywhere. I got hold of Martin's hand under the table. I was trying to tell him not to say anything.

Mam jumped up off the chair. "What's happened?" she asked.

"I was just having a look at their work and my arm slipped," Cove said.

"Oh, that's a shame," Mam said, "and he was doing so well."

Martin kept his mouth shut. And so it went on. Cove would pass Martin and he would pull his hair out. You could see the hairs on his hand and would wipe them down the front of his jumper to get the hairs off.

One day he went a bit too far and Mam saw him. He had got hold of Martin's ear and twisted it round. Mam asked him what he did that for, and he said Martin was cheeky to him. Martin hadn't even opened his mouth! We were sent to bed and there was a terrible row going on in the other room. I started to cry. Martin put his arms around me and told me he was all right.

I could feel the heat from his ear and that made me cry even more. The rows went on and in the end Mam wrote to Uncle George and Auntie Mary, and asked them if Martin could live with them for a while, and it was all arranged for him to go. Mam gave most of Ray's clothes to Martin to take with him. Uncle George had been posted to Aldershot; it wasn't that far away; or so I was told. That night, before he went, we were talking in our bedroom. Martin said he would miss me a lot and he would write to me; it was the best thing all round.

"I hate that man," he said. "I will always hate him."

I told Martin I would miss him too and that I would write to him.

"Just think, you're going to live with Auntie Mary and she's lovely," I said. "She's young and smiles a lot; and she has a lovely giggle. I love to hear her giggle."

Martin laughed. My auntie Mary had beautiful blonde hair and it wasn't out of a bottle. She hardly ever wore makeup—she didn't need to. My uncle George had fair hair and a big toothy smile, and Patricia with her lovely long blonde hair. Martin would love her. So that was Martin and I split up once more. I missed him a lot.

The rows between Mam and cove got fewer and I spent a lot of time with my grandad. I was told we were to move again; this was my eighth time moving. Mam had applied for another job and got it. She was to be a housekeeper in a big house, called Milford Hill Cottage, and it sat right on the top of a hill on its own. Mam was to get free accommodation for the three of us, which were two bedrooms and a sitting room. So I would have my own bedroom. It was a beautiful house. It was nearly all polished floors with mats here and there. There was carpet on the stairs and the landing at the top. Our two rooms and the sitting room had carpet on them but the rest of the house had all polished floors. We had to call the lady of the house 'Madam'. She lived there on her own and of course her little dog, a Pekinese called Nankie-poo. It was a lovely little dog and it seemed to take to me straight away, though I was frightened of it at first having been bitten by the Ryan's dog a few years ago.

So we settled down once more. There was a lovely garden at the back of the house and our sitting room looked out onto it. There were two big trees at the bottom and I just knew I would spend a lot of time up those trees. It was further to go to school now but it was nearer to grandad's. I didn't have any close friends. At school we all played and talked together, but I didn't have a special one like my friend Miss back in Ireland. I was a bit of a loner. Grandad was still meeting me at lunchtime and I told him not to come out in the cold. I told him I would be moving to the top class in a few months and then I wouldn't have to walk to the dinner hall as the older girls' classrooms were behind the dinner hall.

"Well, we'll wait until then," he said, "I'll stop coming."

I felt awful then. It sounded as though I didn't want him to come.

"I'll come and see you every day," I said. "I'm only thinking of you in this cold weather." But he still came.

Madam went away for Christmas. She said to Mam: "If you want to have any of your family to come and stay for Christmas, they will be welcome as long as you look after Nankie-poo and make sure he is brushed every day and took his vitamins that were to be put in his food."

My uncle and aunt came down from Harrogate for Christmas, and Martin came. Grandad was there and that made my day. Mam had made a lovely dinner and we all enjoyed it. Our visitors went and we were back to normal, getting the house ready for Madam's return. As soon as madam got in the door she picked up Nankie-poo and she was kissing him all over. She sat down with the dog on her lap, but the dog wasn't having any of it and was out the door like a shot into the kitchen and hid in the corner. She thought the dog was ill so the vet was sent for. The vet said the dog was fine but he needed exercise, not just a run around the garden. However, the dog didn't like walking much.

Chapter 29
Grandad Passes Away

IT was the 18th of February 1953. I was fourteen years old today, and I was getting on better with Mam now. She talked to me a lot more, even when Cove was there, and even he was better with me. Mam would say, "Do you want to come and look around the shops with me?" and that gave me a lovely warm feeling inside, because she wanted me to go with her. Even Cove didn't seem to mind. When we were down the town, Mam told me she was saving all her wages to help buy a motorbike for Cove; she said he'd always wanted one. Mam was earning three pounds a week but she worked from morning till night. Madam was always ringing the bell for her for one thing or another. The only time she got a rest was when she went to bed. There was a cleaner that came in a couple of times a week but she didn't do any heavy work; she just polished the furniture and did a bit of sweeping up. She told Mam she couldn't do this and she couldn't do that because she had a bad back. Mam said there was no point in her coming at all, but she had been with Madam for years.

Mam had a letter from Auntie Mary. It was to say that Uncle George was to be posted abroad, and she wanted to get their little girl Christine christened before uncle George went away. Madam was going away again in March so it was decided they would come up to us to get the baby christened. My Uncle Bert and aunt were going to come down from Harrogate. Ray couldn't come as he couldn't get leave from the army and Martin couldn't get time off from work.

The day before the christening Mam cooked a big meal for us all. Grandad came and he stayed all day until about ten o'clock that night. He was going to be a godfather to little Christine. Then they all started talking about what was going to happen tomorrow.

"Do you know what you have to do tomorrow, grandad?" I asked.

"Yes," he replied, "I know what I have to do. I'll meet you in the church." He added, "I'd better be getting down the road."

"I'll walk down the road with you," Uncle Bert said.

"No, " grandad replied, "I'll be fine, and it's a lovely night."

I saw him out the front door. He fumbled in his waistcoat pocket and he gave me a shilling to buy sweets. I told him I didn't want it.

"You keep it for me until tomorrow when the shops are open," I said.

"I want you to have it now," he insisted.

I took it out of his hand and gave him a kiss, and walked down the front steps with him. I watched him go down the road. He turned and waved and I waved back. I went back up the steps and in the front door. It had got a lot colder and I was thinking of grandad going into that cold room because he hadn't lit a fire today. He said it would be a waste of coal, but it was lovely having him all day.

Mam made a cup of tea and we all sat round the big kitchen table. Nankie-poo didn't know what was going on. If madam walked in now she would have had a fit with everyone feeding him tit-bits. Madam had bought me a bike for my birthday with a big basket on the front of it for the dog. I used to cycle down to the park with the dog in the basket. I would take him out of the basket and throw a ball as far away as I could so that he got some exercise. Uncle Bert said he was going to bed and we all followed.

It was the day of the christening and it was a very cold day, but the sun was trying to get out. It was 15th March so it wasn't going to get much warmer. We all arrived at the church but there was no grandad. All the grown-ups were looking very worried and they seemed to be trying to work something out. I was standing at the door watching for him, and I thought to myself, 'Grandad wouldn't let baby Christine down, he's her grandad.'

I knew he didn't like things like this, but I was sure he wouldn't let everyone down on purpose. They went ahead with the christening. I don't know who stood in for grandad. The christening was over and we all went back to the house. Mam put the kettle on.

"I can't believe he has done this!" she said. "You wait till I see him."

"Maybe he's gone to the wrong church? Or he might have got the time wrong."

"I told him where the church was last night;" she said, "and he said he knew where it was. You let him out the door last night—did he say anything to you?"

"No," I shook my head. "He gave me a shilling and said he would see me at the church."

We were all having tea and sandwiches and there was a lot of talking going on. After I had finished eating, I kept thinking about grandad. I couldn't settle and I told Mam I was going to look for him.

"I'll go on the bike and look around where he goes for walks and I'll go back to the church again—in case he got the wrong time."

I tried them all but there was no sign of him. I cycled up Albany road, and left the bike up against the wall and went in the house. The lady that lived downstairs was standing at the bottom of the stairs and I greeted her.

"I was getting a bit worried," she said. "Your grandad's light has been on since I got up this morning."

"He must have gone out and left it on or he's fallen asleep."

I went upstairs and opened his door. He never locked it. I went in, and there he was seated on his chair, his elbows on the arms of the chair reading the paper! All I could see of him was his cap.

"I've been looking everywhere for you!" I said and sat on his knee.

"God, you're cold!" I said and carried on with what I was saying. "They're not one bit happy with you up at the big house."

There was no reply from him.

"Grandad, are you *listening* to me?" I asked.

He still didn't answer me. I peeped over the top of the newspaper and he was looking straight at me! I got a bit frightened.

"Why are you looking at me like that?" I pulled the newspaper down a bit more. His face was blue and there was slaver coming out of his mouth. That's why he hadn't answered me—he was dead!

I was so shocked I got angry with him! I was shouting at him. I got hold of him and I was telling and begging him to wake up. "You can't leave me here on my own! What would I do without you? Please wake up! You said you would always be there for me! How can I go on without you?"

I stood there looking down at him, the newspaper still held in his hands in front of him. The woman from downstairs was talking to me from outside the door; the other tenants were there as well—they were trying to get me to come out of the room, but none of them came in. They were telling me to go and get my mother, but I didn't want to leave grandad. The tenants were talking to me again: they were saying if you go and get your mother there might be something she can do.

I made a move to go out, but then I went back to grandad. I wiped the slaver off his mouth and gave him a kiss and told him I would be back soon with help. I passed them all standing on the landing and the man that lived at the other side of the toilet said, "That light has been on all night; he must have died last night."

I ran down the stairs, got on my bike and cycled as fast as I could. Halfway up Milford Hill I threw the bike on the road and ran the rest of the way. When I got in the house I was screaming. Mam got hold of me.

"What's the matter?" she said. "Calm down! We don't know what you're saying."

"My grandad's dead!" I shouted at her.

They all gathered round me.

"What do you mean he is dead?" Mam said. "Where is he?"

"He's in his room! The other tenants are there but they won't go in his room. They told me to come and get you. There might be something you could do, but there isn't, is there, because he is dead?"

Mam asked me where my bike was. I told her I threw it on the road halfway up Milford Hill. One of my uncles went down and brought the bike back. They were getting ready to go to grandad's.

"I want to come with you," I said.

I was told I had to stay at home with Auntie Mary.

"But I didn't say goodbye to him!" I protested.

They told me there was plenty of time for that. I sat there numb with shock. I was trying to think straight. It must have happened last night when he left here. He still had the same clothes on; he hadn't even taken his cap off. He must have gone in, sat on his chair, put his glasses on and started reading the paper. I couldn't understand how the newspaper was still there in his hands, open as though he was reading it. I thought back to when I pulled the newspaper down a little bit, seeing two black staring eyes looking at me. They weren't my grandad's lovely blue eyes, and when I sat on his knee it was so cold. I should have known then that there was something wrong. I needed to see him again to tell him I was sorry for pulling and dragging him about, but I only wanted him to wake up. Oh God, what was I going to do without him? He would never say to me again, "Link-on." I can't describe the pain that was inside me; I don't think I'd ever had pain that hurt like this. I told grandad that I would be back, but they wouldn't let me. I thought about his best suit hanging on the hanger with his clean shirt ready to put on today for the christening, and his boots highly polished there on the floor. This was the day when most of my faith in God disappeared.

It must have been a couple of hours later when they came back from grandad's. They were all talking but it sounded as though it was miles away.

The next day they went down and cleared grandad's room out. He didn't have much for a lifetime's work. They gave his clothes, what there was of them, to charity and his boots that he must have polished every day of his life, the boots he had to hide up the chimney from my dad, were gone. The only thing they brought back was his suitcase. It looked like a Doctor's bag, only a lot bigger, and they gave that to me. It was very heavy and was all leather with brass catches on the top and a couple of side pockets on the outside and a date—I think the date on it was 1878—and that was the year my grandad was born. The case was highly polished like his boots were, and it took me all my time to carry it upstairs to my room, and that was the case empty. I put it on my bed and I looked in the side pockets, and there was his pension book. I put it up to my face and could smell him on it. I looked in it and he had got ten-shillings a week. I put it back in the case and put my arms around it. That brought a bit of comfort. But I didn't cry even though I needed to.

It was the day of the funeral and I still felt numb. Ray and Martin weren't here and I was wishing they were. I needed them today. I went in the kitchen to get a drink. The dog was at my heels all the time. It couldn't understand what was going on. I hadn't been playing with him or taking him in his basket on the bike. Mam and Cove were at the other end of the kitchen talking.

"Well, I don't think she should go to his funeral," he was saying.

"Oh come on, it's her grandad," Mam replied.

"Well," he said, "look what she was like the other day—you don't want a repeat performance of that, do you?"

The dog gave a little bark and they turned around and saw me.

"I want to go to the funeral, I want to say goodbye to grandad!"

"I think Cove is right," she said, "Look at the state you were in the other day."

They both walked out of the kitchen. I could hear Cove talking to Uncle Bert, telling him I would get too upset, and he was looking all concerned.

"Well, maybe you're right;" uncle Bert said, "it might be too much for her."

My uncle took me into Madam's lounge and gave me a jigsaw puzzle.

"See how much of that you can do while we're away," he said.

They were gone about an hour. I hadn't done any of the jigsaw puzzle. I just sat staring at it. I heard them come back in and they were all talking. They asked me if I was all right. I couldn't stand the pain in my head, which was throbbing. I asked Mam if I could go to bed. She gave me a couple of Aspro's and I went upstairs to my room with the dog at my heels. I put the dog in his basket in Madam's room and covered him up with his little blanket, and I went to my own room and got into bed. I wasn't in bed two minutes when there was a scraping at the door. I opened the door and Nankie-poo was standing there looking up at me. He gave a little whine.

"Oh, come on then," I said.

He shot straight past me and jumped up onto the bed. He always went in his basket when Madam went for her afternoon nap, and she wouldn't be very pleased if she saw him now, but the poor little dog didn't know what was going on. I cuddled him to me and fell asleep.

A couple of days after grandad's funeral we were to go to Newbridge hospital where Cove worked, to have tea with the old people. I was still in shock; my mind was just going over and over what had happened all the time. We were in a car. I don't remember who was driving, but I know Mam and my two aunts were in it. As we got near the convent, I could see Sister Catherine walking towards us. I remember shouting: "Stop the car!" It came to a sudden halt and I couldn't get out quick enough. I ran to Sister Catherine and put my arms around her and she cuddled me to her and the tears started to come.

"Can you leave Muriel for an hour or so?" Sister Catherine said to Mam.

Mam said they would come back for me. Sister Catherine took me into the playroom in the convent and we sat down. She had her arm around me and I let it all go—I just cried and cried, and she kept rocking me like a baby. This was what I needed—a cuddle, and some of the pain that was inside me started to come out.

"But he wasn't even ill," I said to her. "How could he die just like that?"

"Now, you wouldn't have liked it if he was ill and in a lot of pain, would you?" Sister Catherine said. "So God was good to him. He took him very quickly and your grandad didn't feel a thing. God rest his Soul, and he wouldn't want you to be upset like this." She gave me a hankie. "Now dry those eyes. I was on my way to the shop when you stopped, and I still have to go or the girls won't be getting any tea; are you going to come with me?"

"Yes," I said, and we were outside the convent again.

Sister Catherine wore a big black shawl over her habit. She put her arm out and I linked on. I was laughing and crying at the same time. When they came to pick me up from the convent, I felt as though a big weight had been lifted off my chest, and it was all down to a lovely nun who cared about me. When we got back in the house I saw Patricia and Christine for the first time in days. They were in the house but I must have been looking through them, and I thought to myself, "It was their grandad as well." I was glad they were young and didn't understand because I would have hated them to have to go through all that pain like I did.

"I forgot to tell you Ray is home," Mam said. "He's up at Newbridge hospital. He'll be here in half an hour."

When I saw Ray come in the back door I ran to meet him. He put his arms around me and I clung to him. I looked up at him.

"You didn't go to grandad's funeral," I said.

"I didn't know he'd died," he replied. "Mam didn't let me know until yesterday, and he had been buried by then so I have a couple of day's compassionate leave."

The house was full for the next couple of days so I didn't have time to sit and mope. Then it was time for them all to go and the house was silent again.

I would have to do something about this dog before Madam came home. He wouldn't go in his basket that was next to her bed. I would put him in and tell him to stay and close her door, but he would whine and scratch at the door until I let him out and he'd go straight into my room.

I dreaded dinnertime at school now. When I came out of the dinner hall I always looked to where my grandad stood and it made me feel sad. When I went to bed, I would get his pension book out of his case and I could smell him off it, which was a comfort to me.

Chapter 30
Prize Giving

LIFE went on. Cove got his motorbike sooner than he expected with Mam getting the insurance money for grandad.

My Mam & me on coves motorbike in Salisbury with Nankie-poo the dog

"Now with him getting the bike early I can start saving up for the deposit on a house, and we're going to have a week's holiday in May or June; we're going to Ireland on the motorbike."

I asked her who was going to look after Madam? She said she would find someone to do her job while she was away.

"You'll be here after school," she said, "so you can see to the dog and help out a bit with a few of the jobs." She continued: "I have a job for you. You could polish all the floors upstairs and do the stairs and the landing, and then I will give you three shillings a week. I'll save it up for you and you might be able to go to Ireland in the summer holidays."

I got very excited about this.

"I only said *might*," she added, "so off you go upstairs and let's see what you can do."

I went and got the polish and a load of rags and off I went upstairs to start polishing. I started polishing in Madam's bedroom. She had a little room to the right as you walked into the main bedroom. She kept all her clothes and shoes in this little room, and there was a dressing room with a door on the far left of the bedroom where she went to get changed; all her hatboxes were kept in here, and more shoes. I thought, 'I've never seen so many hats and shoes in my life!' All her clothes seemed to be black or grey. She was an elderly lady; I wondered how she could walk on the polished floors in high-heel shoes. I pulled all the shoes out of the little room and polished it, then put them back in, all standing in pairs side by side. Then I started on the big bedroom. I lifted the chairs and Nankie-poo's bed up off the floor. I thought, 'Oh God, I'm never going to get to the end of this room, it's huge!' But I got on with it. I was wishing I had the big buffer from the convent to take the polish off, but it was no good wishing. At last I came to the end of the room. Now I had to start on the dressing room, I seemed to be hours at the polishing. I hoovered the corridor and swept down the stairs with the hand brush. It was all done at last. The cleaner with the bad back would come and do the dusting. I told Mam I'd finished.

"You have earned your first three shillings," she smiled. "I'll put it in this tin box for you and you can save it up."

Since Cove had got his motorbike he could now come home at lunchtime if he wanted to. He was treating Mam like a princess because she had bought him a motorbike. He would put his arms around her and tell her how much he loved her and Mam was lapping all this up. He never seemed to have any money and I couldn't understand this, so I asked Mam.

"He had to send money home to his mother," she said.

I thought it very strange that his mother still didn't know he was married; but I dare not ask because Mam would go mad if I started asking questions about his mother. I thought, "Well, she will soon find out when they go on holiday."

The next Saturday came and it was time for the floors to be polished again. I was glad it was only once a week. I was going upstairs when Mam shouted to me that she was going down the shops and she wouldn't be long. She had only just gone when I heard Cove's motorbike stop outside.

"Is there anyone home?" he shouted.

"Mam's gone down to the shops!" I shouted back, and carried on polishing the floor. I put the cloth in the big tin of polish and got on with what I was doing. I was on my hands and knees and I thought I could feel my dress moving at the back of my legs. I stopped for a few seconds and put my hand at the back of my legs. I thought I must have imagined it, and started polishing again and I felt something going up my dress. Next thing my pants were being pulled down and I jumped up, and tried to turn round, but I was tripping over my pants. They were down to my knees!

When I did turn round it was Cove—and he was touching my private parts and trying to put his fingers up me. I screamed my head off! I was trying to pull my pants up and screaming at the same time. I was trapped in the corner of the small room. I could hear the dog barking so I screamed all the more. Next thing I heard was Madam shouting: "Muriel, where are you?"

Cove put his hand over my mouth and said, "If you say a word, you'll end up back in the convent, and you won't be seeing your Mam for a long time."

He took his hand away from my mouth. I was crying and my body was shaking, but I said to him, "I'm going to tell my Mam!"

"She won't believe you, she'll say you're telling lies," he hissed. "She'll believe me because she loves me." He added: "Shout down to her."

I shouted down: "I'm upstairs Madam."

"I don't know what's the matter with Nankie-poo! He was going mad to get out of the room."

Cove passed me on the top of the stairs and started walking down. He said to madam, "It was my fault, I forgot something; the dog will have heard me going up to the bedroom for it."

Nankie-poo was wriggling to get out of her arms. She let him go and he flew up the stairs to me.

"Well," Madam said to Cove, "he must be a very good guard dog if he heard you come in."

She walked back down the long hall looking very pleased with herself. I walked back down to Madam's bedroom with the dog close to my heels; I went in and closed the door. I sat down in front of it and cried my eyes out. The dog was licking my face and whimpering. I put my arms around the dog and told him he was a good boy, and he put his head on my chest and I cried all over him. I sat there for a while thinking, 'Why is this happening to me?' I was just a skinny teenager; it must be my fault, otherwise why would men do this to me? If Cove loved Mam, why would he do things like this? He was supposed to come from a very religious family. I just couldn't understand it. I couldn't tell Mam and even if she did believe me, it would hurt her too much because he was her life; so I would have to keep quiet about it. He wouldn't have done this awful thing if my grandad were here. He's only been dead about six weeks and I was still trying to get over his death. I had lost a chunk of my religion when he died, and now I had lost another chunk of it. If a religious man, like he was supposed to be, could do something like that, then I didn't want to be in that religion anymore.

I heard Mam come in. I would have to pull myself together, and I wiped my face and got down on my hands and knees and started polishing the floor again. Mam came into the bedroom and looked in the little room.

"Is that all you have done since I went out?" she said. "I knew you would get sick of it sooner or later! Well, you are not going to get paid for it until it's all done."

I wanted to scream at her to shut up, but I didn't dare. Then she asked me had Cove been home, and I told her he had. She asked if he had left a message, and I said, "No." I didn't lift my head up once during the conversation. She left the room and went downstairs and I was glad I didn't have to look at her. I would have to try and keep out of Cove's way from now on; I would have to have somewhere to hide.

I was playing in the garden with Nankie-poo, as the weather was getting warmer. The dog ran into the bushes and I followed him. When I got nearer I could see there was a little makeshift table and a stool. It looked like someone came here to eat; maybe it was the gardener. He came a few times a week in the summer, but only once a week in the winter. There was a big tree next to the den. And I started to climb it; this was one thing I was good at. It would be a good place to hide myself from everyone when I wanted to. I was glad I had found a place. I called the dog and took him back to Madam.

About two weeks later it happened again. I didn't know what to do or who to tell. I was thinking of telling Sister Catherine, but she was a nun—how could I tell a nun something like that? I asked Mam if she would buy me some jeans.

"No, they're scruffy looking things," she said.

I begged her to get me some. "You're always telling me off for tearing my dresses," I said, "and jeans are very strong and they won't tear."

She gave in and I got some. When she tried them on me, the waist was too big.

"They're miles too big for you," she said, "they'll have to go back."

"It's all right," I said, "I can wear a belt."

She gave in and I was over the moon. Cove wouldn't be able to put his hands up me now! I had them that tight I could hardly breath. Mam would come along and tell me to loosen the belt or I'd cut myself in half. As soon as she turned her back I would tighten it again.

Halfway through May, I had to go into hospital to have my tonsils out. I didn't mind going. At least he wouldn't be able to do anything to me there—I would have peace. I was home again after about ten days.

Today was the third of June 1953. The queen was to be crowned today, and there were celebrations going on everywhere. I walked down our back lane to see what was going on. Everyone seemed to be laughing and singing. I walked back up to the front of Milford Hill. There was a walkway on the left-hand side of the road and it had a hedge all the way up to the top. I looked through the hedge. I could see all the people who lived there. They had tables out along the street, and there were sandwiches, cakes, orange juice and lots more. In fact, the tables were full of food and drinks. They all had paper hats on, streamers and little flags. It all looked very nice and colourful, and everyone was happy. I got back up to Madam's house. She had a big flag and a couple of small ones on her house. All of a sudden I felt very lonely and I wished my grandad were here.

June was a lovely month. The nights were lighter and I spent a lot of time up in the big tree reading my books. It came to the time for Mam and Cove to go on their holidays. All I could think of was Cove going away and I would have peace. He was still trying to touch me, but the belt on the jeans was that tight you couldn't get a finger down them, never mind a hand; but he was still putting his hand in between my legs, trying to feel me. He would lift up my top; I don't know what for, because there was nothing there. I think he liked to see the fear on my face.

A couple of days later the doorbell rang. I answered it. It was one of the girls that worked in the mental hospital.

"I have come to see your Mam," she said.

I asked her to come in.

"Mam is with Madam at the moment; but you can wait in the sitting room."

She came in and I sat down with her. I asked her if she had come about the job.

"No," she said, "I have come about the accommodation for your mother in Limerick. I wrote to my Mam and I have just had a reply. She said she can put your mother up for her holiday."

"What do you mean?" I asked. "They're both going on holiday."

"I know," she said, "but he is going to Ennis to stay with his Mam and your mother is going to stay in Limerick with my Mam. Don't ask me why."

I had no need to ask her why. I knew my Mam wasn't good enough for him to take home to his mother's, even though her name was Spencer now. And us Burns children were never good enough; we were trash in his eyes. Oh, I was so mad! I couldn't believe she would let him treat her like this.

Mam got a woman to stay while they went on holiday. She was a young woman and she had a little girl and all went well while they were away.

They got back about teatime and I asked Mam, "Did you enjoy your holiday?"

She said it was all right. "We called in to see Sue and Willie in Ballyglass, but it was a short stay; and then I stayed in Limerick."

I asked if she had been to see my aunt May and Uncle Mickey.

She said "No"—she hadn't seen any of them. She looked a bit fed up with herself, so I didn't ask any more questions.

The first of July came and Mam said I was definitely going to Ireland. She said I was to go with a couple she knew. They would put me on a train at Waterford and it would take me to Westport, and I was to stay with Sue and Willie for a week and then I was to make my way down to Ennis to stay with my aunt Fanny. I was over the moon about it but I had better calm myself down as there was still four weeks before I could go.

I went to school the next day with my head in the clouds. One of the girls at school asked me if I would like to come and stay at her house for the weekend. She said she lived out on Salisbury plain. I said I would ask my Mam when I got home from school. But I had my polishing to do on the Saturday to get my pocket money. I asked Mam when I got home.

"What about the polishing?" she asked.

She must have seen my face drop.

"Oh, all right then, just this once, but on Thursday after school you can get the dry mop and go over all the floors."

I said I would. So I was going to Salisbury plain.

After school on Friday we got on the bus, and it seemed to take ages. The bus stopped and we got out in the middle of nowhere.

"There aren't any houses!" I said.

"My house is there," my friend said, "it's hidden by the trees."

We walked towards the trees and there was the house, in the middle of them. We went in and her Mam and dad said "Hello" to me and then we went upstairs. About ten minutes later we were called down to tea. After tea was finished, we went out to play. There seemed to be miles of flat land with nothing on it apart from these big high stones. We made our way across the field to where they were and looked up at them. I had never seen stones that tall in my life! The stones were going in a big circle and there were other stones laid flat on top of the tall stones. There wasn't a soul about, only us children. We stayed there for a couple of hours just playing games.

Next morning I couldn't wait to get back to the stones. We were playing tag and hide and seek, but when you were standing in the middle of the stones on your own, counting up to fifty while they all hid, it was a weird feeling. The wind started to get up and it was making weird sounds, so we decided to go back to the house. We were just coming to the road. There was a man standing there waving his hands about. He asked us what we had been up to. We told him we were just playing.

"That isn't a playground and don't let me see you in there again," he said.

The man seemed to appear from nowhere. I will never forget that visit to the stones. I found out later that it was called Stonehenge and it was a prehistoric ruin. As I stood waiting for the bus next day, I thought, 'I'm glad I don't live out here.' The bus came and I got on it; there was only another woman and myself on the bus, and for once I was glad to be going home.

The day before we broke up for the summer holidays there was to be a prize given for the best work that had been done all year. The priest had told everyone at mass to make an effort to go, and we were told to remind our mothers and fathers to come. I told Mam about it. She said she would do her best as long as she was back for four o'clock to get Madam's tea.

"You'll have plenty of time," I said. "It starts at two o'clock and it will be all over by three."

After dinner we moved all the tables down to the back of the church hall, and we brought all the benches to the top of the hall for people to sit on. Dead on two o'clock all the nuns were sitting up on the platform. The hall was full, so they would be pleased at the turnout.

The prize-giving had started and Mam hadn't come. Every time the door opened I would look to see if it was Mam, but she never arrived. All of a sudden I heard my name called out. My legs were shaking. Some of the children were pushing me up towards the platform. I was getting a prize for the best needlework. I'd made a nightdress. It was pale green with little pink flowers on it. I remember cutting it out. I had watched Mam for years cutting things out and pinning the pattern to the material. The material had to be the right way on, so I had no problem with that. It all had to be stitched by hand and it had to be done with French seams. It had taken the whole term to make it. Everyone was clapping and I was so proud. I wished Mam had been there to see me. I think I was still wearing that nightdress three years later.

Chapter 31
My Holidays in Ennis

IT was near the end of July 1953 and at last the time had come for me to go to Ireland. I was all packed and ready. Mam took me to Salisbury railway station and we met her friend Mrs Quinn there. She had a couple of children and her brother travelling with her. Mam was telling me again I was to be good and to do as I was told. My spending money was put in a little purse and I was to make it last, doling it out so much a day. We said our goodbyes and the train moved out of the station at last. I had no fear of getting on the boat this time as I was looking forward to the journey. This time the sea was nice and calm, not rough and windy like it was three years ago on our way to England.

When we arrived at Waterford in Ireland, Mrs Quinn and family put me on the train to Westport and arranged to meet me at the boat on the return journey back to England. I seemed to be sitting on the train for hours. Every time we pulled into a station I was looking to see if it was Westport. I was all excited when I eventually saw the sign. I had arrived and could see Willie standing on the platform. He hadn't changed a bit! As I stepped off the train he was walking towards me with a big smile on his face.

"Well, hello there, lovely legs!" he said. "How are you? Look at the size of you!"

He gave me a big hug and I was so pleased to be back. I couldn't wait to get to Ballyglass. I wondered if everything would be the same as it used to be. And it was! The boreen was still overgrown and the bramble bushes were still hitting against the car as we drove up, and as we turned into the farmyard, everything was just the same, as though time had stood still. Sue came out of the little cottage door and I ran to her. She put her arm around me and we walked into the cottage together. It looked just the same—the big square fireplace with the black hooks hanging down from the chimney and the kettle on one of them boiling away. The flour box was still in the same place with the gramophone perched on top. The room looked a bit smaller than I remember it, but I suppose that was because I had grown. I had a lovely warm feeling inside me—it was great to be back! Sue and I sat up quite late talking about old times and all the things we used to get up to. I was asking Sue about Harry and Emily Clinton and the girls. Emily had another baby since I left. It was another girl and her name was. Joan. That was five girls they had now. Sue said they were all fine and we would be going to see them the next day.

"But you will have to go to early mass so that you will be back in time for us to go to church," she said. "Then we can all go into Westport together."

I told her I didn't want to go to mass, and she looked at me surprised.

"Now what's all this about?" she said. "Is it because you lost your grandad? I know you're very upset about him, but time is a great healer."

I told her that was part of it. "There's a lot more to it than that," I said. "I just don't want to go."

"Well," she said, "I can't force you to go and you will get over your grandad's death in time."

This was my opportunity to tell her what was going on at home with Cove, but then I thought, Sue would write to Mam and tell her about it, and Cove would tell Mam I was telling lies and she would believe him and she would hate me. Sue asked about Ray and Martin and what they were doing. I told her Ray was in the army and that Martin worked away a lot. She asked if Mam liked her job. She was always a great cook when she had the stuff to cook with. I told Sue she worked very hard and that she started early in the morning; it was very late at night when she finished.

"A bit like farming then," Sue said, and we both laughed. "And how is Ernie (Cove) getting on?" she asked.

"He's all right," I said dismissively.

"No more about him, thank God." She asked how I was doing at school and what I wanted to do when I left. I told her I was doing fine and that I would be leaving in about six months and that I wanted to be a dressmaker. I said I had won first prize at school for sewing.

"Well done," she said. "You must take after your Mam. She's great at sewing. Well, young lady, I think it's time we went to bed. We've got a new mattress since you were last here. I've given it a good shake. It's made of duck down so it will be a lot more comfortable than the straw one we had."

I said goodnight to Sue and went through to their bedroom, where Willie was fast asleep, and into the little room and got into bed. It was lovely and soft! I was thinking about the times when Mam and my brothers were all in the bed with me, and I felt a bit sad then. All was quiet for a few minutes and then a cricket started making a noise. I didn't mind as it always sent me to sleep.

"One of these days I am going to get that cricket!" Willie used to say, but I don't think he ever did.

I was woken up next morning with the cock crowing *cock-a-doodle-doo*; I sat up in bed and remembered I was at Sue's, which was a lovely feeling. I got dressed and went into the kitchen. Sue was there, humming away to herself as she was doing her jobs.

"Oh, you're a biddy early this morning!" she said when she saw me. "I thought you would be having a lie in?"

I told her I wasn't tired and that I didn't want to miss anything.

"I don't think you'll miss anything around here," she smiled. "Sit down and I'll put a couple of eggs on the boil and make a cup of tea. Willie will be in shortly for his breakfast." Sue was cutting the homemade bread that she had made this morning. She always put a cross on top of the bread so that she could cut a quarter off at a time and slice it up ready for the table. I put some on my plate and buttered it. Sue put the eggs into eggcups and placed them in front of me. I broke the tops off with a knife, making a mess—all the egg yoke was running down the sides. So I took a piece of bread and wiped it up and dipped into the egg. It tasted lovely! I can still taste it today.

"Hello," Willie said as he came in. "You're up early! I thought with all the travelling you would be in bed until lunchtime."

"She thought she might miss something," Sue smiled.

"Sure," Willie grinned. "What would she miss around here?"

Sue and I laughed.

"Did I say something funny?" Willie raised his eyebrows.

I watched him as he started to take the tops off his eggs. I remembered he used to do it very slowly and the eggs would be perfect. I thought, it's funny how things stick in your mind.

After breakfast I helped Sue with the dishes. She said she was going to the well for water.

"Are you coming?" she said.

I was, and picked up a bucket outside the cottage door. Sue also picked up two buckets and a long piece of wood and we walked down the boreen, past the duck pond to the well that was about a quarter of a mile away. We filled our buckets and Sue put one on each end of the wood and with a bucket on each side of her, got hold of the wood with both hands. She bent down and put her head under the wood and stood up so that the wood rested on her shoulders and started walking. I followed and it was taking me all my time to carry one. I got in front of her to open the gate and let her though. She was an amazing woman. She wasn't much taller than me and very slim, but she was very strong.

We got ready and went to Westport. Sue and Willie went into church and I was having a look around the town. I found a shop open and got myself an ice cream and went and sat on the wall near the hump back bridge and watched the water. I was feeling very guilty now because I hadn't gone to mass. I was waiting for something awful to happen to me. Then I thought of all the bad things that had happened to me and they couldn't get much worse!

Sue and Willie came out of the church. They were talking to some people, and I went over to them. They said goodbye to their friends and went to the car and made for the Clintons' house. It was only a mile from the town. They were all pleased to see us. Harry and Emily were saying how much I had grown. Hilda wasn't there but Olive, Georgie, and the two younger ones were. Olive had grown and she had her haircut. It made her look different; more grown up. Georgie had grown a bit as well. Olga was little and she had lovely fair hair down her back. Joan, the baby of the family, had dark hair and lovely eyes. It was great to see them all again. It was hard to believe it was three years since I last saw them. We stayed a couple of hours at the Clintons and then we went back to Ballyglass. As soon as we got in the cottage, Sue and Willie got changed into their working clothes and started work again.

The next morning I put my jeans and a zip-up jerkin on. It felt good not to pull the belt so tight like I had to at home. I tied a chiffon scarf around my head like an Alice band and walked into the kitchen at the same time as Willie was coming in for his breakfast.

"What have we here?" Willie said. "You look like one of those cowgirls you see in the film with those trousers on!"

I told him they weren't trousers, they were jeans; they were a lot stronger and they were better for climbing trees. He asked Sue if there was any film left in the camera. Sue said she thought there was enough film left for a couple of pictures in the camera and went and got it. Willie told me to come and sit on Neddy's back. I got up on Neddy but I was scared stiff he was going to make a bolt for it, but he didn't! Those things only happen to Martin.

Me sitting on Neddys back at Sue & Willies in Ballyglass, Wesport

Next day Hilda and Olive came to see us. They had cycled over. I couldn't believe it when I saw Hilda—she looked like a woman! She seemed very quiet and it wasn't like Hilda. She came round after a while and we all had a good afternoon talking about the old times.

The following day I borrowed Sue's bike and cycled to their house. I had forgotten what the hills were like. I had to get off the bike and walk up some of them. We went to Castlebar one day to see Willie's brother and have a look around. My week was nearly up and it had passed so quickly.

Saturday came. I was very sad leaving Sue. She gave me a big hug and I got in the car with Willie and made our way to Westport, stopping at the Clintons to say goodbye to them all. Then Willie took me to the station and put me on the train for Ennis.

As I sat on the train all sorts of things were going through my mind. Would Ennis be the same? I hoped it would; what if no one knew me? Then I thought, I remember them all so they were bound to know me. As I got nearer to Ennis my heart was thumping and I had butterflies in my tummy; I was saying under my breath, I'm coming home at last! I got off the train. Mam had said I was to go straight to aunt Fanny's. I had to pass my nanna's house to get to my aunts, and as I passed I had an urge to go in but I thought better of it. When I got to my aunts the front door was open and I went into the little hall and opened the door into the living room.

"Hello!" I shouted. "Is there anyone in?"

My aunt came through from the kitchen.

"Oh, it's you Muriel!" she said. "Come and let me have a look at you, child."

I put my case down and went over to her and she gave me a big hug.

"Will you look at the size of you!" she exclaimed. "I can't believe you have grown so much."

I was so happy to see her. She had always been very good to me and now she was making me feel so welcome! She told me to sit down and she'd make me a cup of tea.

"That's what I was doing in the kitchen before you came in," she said. "I was making you some sandwiches for when you arrived!"

We talked for a while and then she told me to take my suitcase upstairs. Two minutes later I was back down in the living room. I asked my aunt if it was all right to go and see my nanna and granda. She asked me to sit down again.

"I have something to tell you," she said. "I'm afraid your nanna died a while ago, God rest her Soul. Your granda is still there. Maureen and Billy had moved down there and they were looking after him."

I started to cry.

"Maureen was ironing and she got pains in her chest," she continued. "She went upstairs to bed and the pains got worse. The Doctor was sent for and there was nothing the Doctor could do to help her and she died, God rest her soul."

I couldn't take in what she was telling me at first; then I just burst into tears again, it was such a shock. My nanna was old so I could accept that in a way, but Maureen was only young and she had three young children, one of them only a few months old. I thought about Maureen's husband Billy— what must he be going through? Losing his wife and the mother of his children! And Maureen was my Aunt Fanny's daughter. I was crying on my aunt's shoulder. "I'm so sorry," I said.

"That's enough now, stop that crying," she said gently. "You're here for a holiday, and are you going down to see your granda now?"

"I'll go later," I said. "I was going for a walk first."

She understood I needed to be on my own. I walked up St Flannan's terrace; it was very quiet for a Saturday and there wasn't a soul about. When I got to what used to be our house I stopped for a couple of minutes and looked at it and Mrs Reidy's. They looked the same as when I left. Across the road the two little houses were still there. Mrs O'Donoghue's house was empty and looked neglected. I wondered where they had gone? This house was where my friend Brian lived with his parents and his twin brothers and a sister. His cousins Joe and Liam lived with them as well. Joe was the little boy who got Patrick's red coat when he died all those years ago. I think Mrs Ryan was still living in the other one because it looked cared for. And it had net curtains on the windows. I walked on up towards Captain Mack's corner. When I got to my friend's house I decided to call and see if she was in. I went up the steps and knocked on the door. It was her little sister Angela that answered. I asked if Miss was in.

"No, and I don't know when she'll be back."

She came out of the house, closing the door behind her.

"I'll call back later," I said.

She followed me down the steps. "You're Muriel, aren't you?" Then she asked, "What's England like?"

"Much the same as over here," I said.

"I bet you're rich?" Angela said.

"No, I'm not."

"Do you live in a big house in England?"

"Yes," I laughed. "I do, as a matter of fact, but the house isn't ours. My Mam is the housekeeper."

Before she could say anything else I said, "Goodbye. See you later."

She shouted after me: "I'll tell Miss you called for her!"

I walked back down to my aunt's. She asked me if I was all right and I told her I was, and that I was going down to see my granda. I walked down towards his house. I wasn't looking forward to this. What if he just nods his head when I go in, like he used to do? What will I say to him? When I got to the gate I could see he was sitting on his bench under the window, and went up to him.

"Hello granda," I smiled. "It's Muriel—how are you?"

"I'm all right," he said. The smile spread on his face as he looked at me. "My, you have grown a lot! Nearly a young woman now! But you need to put a bit of meat on you; you're too thin. Well, tell me all the news—how are the boys?"

I told him they were both well. Ray was in the army and Martin was working away, but comes home every now and again.

"And have you left school?"

"Not yet," I said. "I have another six months to go."

"And what do you want to do when you leave?"

"I want to be a dressmaker."

"That will be a good job. You will make plenty of money at that. And how is your Mother? Did she marry again?"

"Yes, she did."

I couldn't tell him a lie, and thankfully he didn't ask who she married. That was a relief.

"And how is your grandad?"

I told him he had died in March.

"I'm sorry to hear that. Did you hear about Maureen?"

I said I had. I held his hand and said I was sorry.

"Why couldn't God have taken me?" he said. "I'm an old man and I have lived my life. Why did he take a young woman like that? She had three young children."

I didn't answer him because I couldn't understand it myself. All I could do was pat his hand. This was the first time in my life I had a conversation with my granda and it would have to be this very sad occasion. I stayed with him for a while longer and then I got up to go. He asked me if I would come and see him again. I said I'd come and see him tomorrow. He lifted his hand like he always did when I was leaving. I went out the gate and looked back at him. I will always remember him sitting on that bench under the front room window.

I walked back up the road towards my aunt's house. I saw Maureen's husband Billy coming down the road towards me. He had a baby in his arms. He was just going in his mother's house as I was crossing the road. I called to him and he stopped.

"Oh, it's you, young Muriel!" he said. "How are you?"

I told him I was fine. I said I was sorry about Maureen. I asked if I could look at the baby. He bent down and said, "This is Oliver."

He was the most beautiful baby I had ever seen! I told Billy the baby was lovely. He stood back up. He looked down at Oliver and said, "That's your second cousin Muriel!" Then he asked how my Mam was. I told him she was fine and working hard.

"That's good. I'll see you later. I have to go." He went into his mother's house with the baby and I continued up the road to my aunt's. When I went back in the house my uncle Pappy and Joan was there. My uncle looked just the same, but Joan had changed; she was a woman now. Her hair was cut short and she looked different. We gave each other a hug. I said I was sorry about Maureen. They both nodded their heads. I asked them where Margie was. My aunt told me she had got married. "Joan will take you to see her in a day or two," my aunt said. This was my first day home in Ennis and there was so much sadness.

I went to mass with Joan next morning, but it wasn't the same anymore. Too much had happened to me. When we came out of mass I saw my friend Miss and went over to say hello. It was a bit awkward at first, as we didn't know what to say to each other; it had been three years. We arranged to meet the next day. I said I would call for her. We said goodbye to each other, and I went back to Joan who was talking to someone; when she had finished talking we set off for home. Joan said she would take me to see Margie later. I was looking forward to that. I wondered if she had changed. We talked about this one and that one all the way home as we were catching up on the last three years.

After dinner Joan and I went to see Margie. She hadn't moved far. She had got a flat in a house about four doors from her mother's. We went in, and Margie was in the kitchen. She looked a lot more grown up. She was wearing an apron tied at the back in a bow. She looked a proper little housewife. She asked how my brothers were and how my Mam was. She didn't ask if Mam had married again and I was glad about that. I didn't want to tell her a lie. She made us a cup of tea and we talked about Maureen and the three children she had left behind.

We left Margie's and went up the Clare Road to see uncle Miko, and aunt Chris and the two boys, Ernie and Oliver. Ernie wasn't there; he had gone to work in Dublin. And his brother Oliver was going to be a Priest. They asked us if we would like a drink. We said no thanks, we had just had one at Margie's. We left there and went down to my Granda's house, and he was in his usual place, on the bench outside the front window. Joan and I sat with him. He was happy to see us. I asked where my uncle Jackie was. He said he was away for a bit of a holiday. "I think he has gone to stay with your aunt May in Limerick," he said. He had just finished speaking when my uncle Rafe walked up the path. So I saw three of my dad's brothers on the same day! Uncle Rafe was a great Hurley player and had won many trophies. My brother Ray idolised him. I asked him how my aunt Annie and the children were. I used to go to school with Carmela. She was about a year older than me, but we saw each other in the playground. Uncle Rafe said they were all fine. "You'll have to go up and see them," he said. I said I would go up before I went home.

Billy Pigott came in the gate with Anthony and Finbar and Joan asked where Oliver was.

"I left him with your Mam," he said. "She's just fed him."

"We'll go now and take Oliver for a walk in the pram," Joan said.

Anthony and Finbar asked if they could come.

"You can if you behave yourselves," Joan said.

Grandad Burns, with Auntie Maureen in the background & his 3 grandchildren Anthony, Finbar, & Oliver & relative John Marsh

We went and picked up Oliver and went for our walk. We were out for about an hour. Anthony never stopped talking all the time we were out and every wall he saw he would climb up it; then he would say, "Muriel, look at me! I'm going to jump. Will you catch me?"

I would put my arms out to catch him and then there would be squeals of delight. Finbar was much more serious. He kept at Joan's side until we were about halfway home. Then I felt his hand clasp onto mine. I kept swinging their arms up and down and pulling them together. Now they were both having a great time. When we got to my aunt's house I left Joan and took the two boys back to granda's house, to their dad, and said goodbye to them.

"Will you come and play with us tomorrow?" they were shouting after me.

I told then I couldn't because I was going out, but I would come and see them the day after. As I was walking back to my aunts, I thought how awful it was going to be for them without a mother. I wished I could take them back to England with me.

The next day I called for my friend Miss and we walked up the Clare Road towards the town; she was asking me, was it great in England and were we rich now? I answered no to each question, saying Mam works hard. "She is the housekeeper in a big house," I said. I told her most of what had happened since I left Ennis and went to Harrogate and Mam having to come back for me. I told her about going to Salisbury and the little room where we had to live.

Then I said, "I could tell you something else but you would have to cross your heart and hope to die." We stopped walking and she crossed her heart.

"Remember that grocer man that Mam used to talk to up there outside the shop?" I said.

"Yes," she nodded.

"When I got to Salisbury he was there; and do you know something else? She married him! He has made Martin's and my life a misery. He is the most horrible man I have ever met! Mam is besotted with him and she won't believe a word Martin and I say when we try to tell her the things he has done, and she calls him Cove. If they knew that I had told you they would go mad."

Miss asked me why they didn't want anyone to know they were married. I told her it was because Cove didn't want his mother to find out as she still lived here. Miss asked why he didn't want his mother to know.

"It's because the Burns family aren't good enough," I said. "I'm not even aloud to mention her name in front of him."

"There must be something wrong with him," Miss said. "He needs to see a doctor. I'm sorry you're so unhappy." Then she said, "Would you rather be living here then?"

"Miss," I said, "you don't know how many times I have wanted to be back home, especially since my grandad died. It got worse after he died. He knew there was no one to stop him." I was going to tell her about the sexual abuse I had to put up with but I felt too ashamed and I kept thinking maybe it was my fault but I couldn't see how. Miss and I walked up O'Connell Street and down Parnell Street. There were little narrow streets you could walk through that brought you into the market place and another little street that would take you back to O'Connell Street. These little streets were all over. Ennis is a lovely town and I wished I could stay there. We seemed to have been out for hours. Miss said she had better be going. We walked back down the Clare Road. She asked me what I was doing tomorrow. I told her I would go and see Anthony and Finbar in the morning and if it were a nice day, I would walk over to Corrovorrin to see my family's grave. Miss said she had to go somewhere tomorrow.

"But if you wait until Wednesday I will come with you—if it's a nice day." So it was arranged we would go on Wednesday. We came to the second gate on the Clare Road and Miss went through; it led to her back door. I walked down Saint Flannans Terrace until I got to my aunts. I'd had a lovely day and it was great having someone my own age to talk to and I was glad she was going to Corrovorrin with me.

I went down to see the boys the next day. I was just crossing the road when I heard Anthony's voice behind me. I looked round and both boys were beckoning to me; they were at their nanna Pigott's today.

"Can we come out to play?" Anthony asked.

I told him to go and ask his nanna first. Mrs Pigott was a plump woman with snow-white hair, which she wore in a bun. She didn't come out but the boys came running out the door.

"Yes!" they shouted. "We can come out!"

I played with them outside the house for a while. I was clasping their hands in mine and then I would swing them round and round one at a time and they would get dizzy; there would be screams of laughter and they would say, "Again please, do it again!" After a while I was that dizzy myself I could hardly stand.

"That's enough now," I said, "We'll go for a walk."

I took them down around Ard-Na-Greine. We came out on Station Road and back up to Connolly's Villas, where my granda lived. When I was little it was a long walk for me. I hoped it would be the same for the boys. We called in to see granda for a while; after that I took them back to Mrs Pigott's house. I told them I wouldn't see them tomorrow because I was going out, but I would see them the day after.

Miss called for me on Wednesday. It was a dull, damp day but it wasn't raining. My aunt had given me a few roses for the grave. We set off for Corrovorrin. As we passed my granda's house, Anthony was standing inside the gate. He was asking if he could come.

"No, not today," I said. "I'll come for you tomorrow." His face dropped and I nearly changed my mind, but then I thought, it's too far for him to walk and a graveyard was the last place he would want to be. Miss and I walked on. It started to drizzle, so when we got to the graveyard I put the roses down on the grave, I said a prayer and then we left. We walked up towards town, but the weather was that miserable we decided to go home. After I left Miss I called in to see my godmother, Florrie. She looked a bit upset.

"I thought I wasn't good enough for you anymore," she said. "I heard you had been here three or four days and you didn't come to see me."

I said I was sorry. I told her she would always be good enough for me and that I often thought about her and I always would. How could anyone forget 'Florrie'? She gave me a hug and said it was lovely to see me. She started talking about things we had done a few years back.

"Remember, Lahinch?" she said, "and the great times we had there? And the time you and Martin milked my goat to make your Mam goodie when she was ill?"

I nodded. Then she burst out laughing. It was great to hear her.

She talked on for about half an hour about this and that.

"Did you know where the O'Donoghues had gone?" I asked. "I saw the house was empty."

"They haven't gone far," she said. "You know your granda's house? Well, straight across from there, they have been building new houses, and the O'Donoghues have got one of those." Then she laughed. "It's down the road you used to call Scabby Lane."

I told her I would have to be going. My aunt would be wondering where I was. She stood up and gave me a hug.

"Sure it's been great seeing you again. Call again before you go back!"

I left Florrie's and walked down the road. Time was getting on and Joan would be home soon. As I got to my aunt's gate I saw Maudie Riedy coming up the road. She must have just finished work. When she got up to me I greeted her.

She looked at me first. Then she realised who I was.

"Oh, look at the size of you!" she gushed. "How are you and how is your Mam and the boys?"

I said everyone was fine.

"When you go back," she said, "tell them all I was asking after them."

I had grown but she was still way above me. I looked at her feet! They were still as big as I remember them. I thought about Mam saying years ago, "If your feet grow any more, you'll end up with feet like Maudie Riedy!"

It was great to see her. I remember how good she had been to us. She went on her way up the road and I went into my aunt's. I was talking to Joan later that evening.

She said she was going to a dance in Limerick on Friday night and I could come with her if I wanted to. There was a bus laid on to the dance hall and it would bring us home when the dance had finished.

"They won't let me in," I said. "I'm too young."

"Don't worry," she said, "I'll make you look older."

Friday came and Joan got to work on me. She put some powder on my face and lipstick on my lips; she finished off with a bit of rouge. She combed my hair back at one side and put hairgrips in; she left the other side hanging loose around my face.

"There, you look older now!" she said, admiring her work.

We got on the bus—it was leaving from outside the Old Ground Hotel. When we got to Limerick I started to get nervous.

"You'll be fine," Joan said. "Let me look at you."

I stood there and she looked me up and down.

"You'll have to take those ankle socks off and put them in you're bag."

I did as she said. We paid our money and went into the dance hall. It was packed with people—they must have been six deep in front of us! The music started up and it thinned out a good bit.

"Oh look," Joan said, "there's Gabriel and Kevin—they're your cousins. You remember them, don't you?"

I said I did. They were my Auntie Jo's boys, and they lived in Limerick. It was their house that Ray had run away to years ago. They shook my hand and told me how big I'd got. They asked me how Ray and Martin were. I told them they were fine. I felt very grown up because no one had ever shaken my hand before. We were talking for a while, then Kevin asked someone to dance. Then Gabriel asked Joan.

"Will you be all right?" she asked.

"Yes," I said.

They went on the dance floor and I was watching them dance when this fellow came over and asked me to dance.

"I'm sorry," I said, "I can't dance." And I ran into the darkest corner I could find. When the dance finished I could see Joan looking for me. I went over to her and told her what had happened.

"That fellow must think I'm mad," I said.

Joan laughed at me. I told Joan I would stand with her and when someone asked her to dance I would go over to that corner over there. She had a couple more dances and I went into my corner. Joan got me up a couple of times, trying to teach me to dance but it was no good; my shoes had crêpe soles and they kept sticking to the floor. We had a good laugh about it. The dance finished and it was time to get back on the bus for home. This had been my first grown up adventure and I had enjoyed every minute of it.

We slept late on Saturday. We were woken up with the boys downstairs. When I came down, Anthony said, "You never came to play with us yesterday. You said you would."

"I am sorry," I said, "I had a lot to do but I'm here today. We'll go up and see if Miss wants to go for a walk, shall we?" That cheered him up. "Just let me get a cup of tea and something to eat first."

They were running in and out saying, "Are you finished yet?" I gulped the rest of my tea down. I was taking the dishes into the kitchen and my aunt took them out of my hands.

"You get going or they will never leave you alone," she said.

We walked up the road to Miss's house and knocked on the door. Angela answered. I asked if Miss was in.

"I'll go and get her," she said.

Miss came to the door. I asked her if she wanted to go for a walk. "I have the boys with me!" I said.

"I might as well," she said.

We walked up the Clare Road. When we got to the shop I got us all ice creams and a few sweets for the boys. When I got my purse out to pay for them I got a bit of a shock. My money was nearly all gone. I hadn't doled it out at so much a day, like Mam told me to. I paid for the ice cream and the sweets. I only had a few shillings left and I would have to make it last until Thursday, which was the day I was going to stay in Limerick with my aunt May for the last couple of days. My uncle Mickey worked in the cigarette factory and Mam had given me some money for him to get two hundred Gold Flake and I was to bring them back with me, so I daren't touch any of that money—I would just have to make it last. And this was only Saturday! We walked past the church and down Station road eating our ice creams.

"If it's a nice day tomorrow," Miss said, "we could go for a walk up the Rocky Road."

"Yes," I said, "That would be great. I'd love that."

"So would I," Anthony said.

I told him it would be just Miss and myself tomorrow; we wanted a day on our own. "I will come and see you two on Monday." When we got to my granda's house I asked them whose house they were in today.

"We'll just come with you," Anthony said.

"I'm going to aunt Fanny's," I said, so we made our way to aunt Fanny's. I said goodbye to Miss and that I would see her tomorrow.

It was raining when I got up on Sunday morning. Joan and I went to mass; I didn't see Miss there! So I would go up after dinner to see her, as we couldn't go up the Rocky Road in this weather. It stopped raining just before dinner. About half an hour later, the sun was shinning and it was very warm. I went up for Miss and we decided to go.

"I don't know if I should put my coat on or not." I told her it was very warm; I had this little jerkin on but I had to take it off it was that hot.

She picked up a short jacket and said, "I'm ready."

On the way I was telling her about the dance in Limerick and how Joan had made me up and did my hair different and after all that I spent most of the night hiding in a dark corner, but it was lovely to watch everyone dancing. Joan had got me up a couple of times to show me how to do it but my crêpe soles shoes kept sticking on the floor. Then Joan would say, "Slide your feet along the floor." I couldn't so I had to lift them up. I must have looked a right sight and I was so embarrassed, but we had a good laugh about it. Miss and I were laughing about it now.

"I wish I had been there to see you!" she said.

We walked along linking arms until we came to the little cottage on the corner. We went down to the gates; one was very big and the other was small, which we called the kissing gate—because you had to push the gate halfway going in and then push it back to get out the other side. There didn't seem to be many people about today; usually it was packed on a Sunday. I suppose it was because of the rain this morning. As we walked further in, we were slipping and sliding all over the place. With so many people coming here in the summer, the grass between the stones would get worn away and that made it harder to walk on when they were wet. We laughed and screamed as we tried to walk on the stones, holding on to each other. We met some people coming towards us and they were the same, laughing and squealing. They told us, if you go further up it gets a lot worse. We thought we had better turn around and go back. We made it to the gate and went over to the little stream and sat on a rock. We took our shoes and socks off and went in the stream to wash the mud off our legs and clean our shoes the best we could. Then we got back on the big rock until they were dry. We put our shoes and socks back on but stayed on the rock as it was very warm now. There were a good few people coming through the gate and we were trying to see if we knew any of them, but we didn't. We sat there for a while talking about the times we came here picking hazel nuts and you would find a cluster of them and get very excited, and Martin would tell us it was better to pick the ones in twos and threes because those big clusters hardly had anything inside them. We both had a good laugh.

"The nuts will be ripe and ready for picking in a couple of months," I said to her, "and I won't be here." I felt a great sadness inside me, and I didn't want to go home.

"I wish you could stay," Miss said.

We got up off the rock and walked out the kissing gate, linked arms and walked home slowly.

The next three days passed very quickly and I was going around the houses saying my goodbyes to everyone, and I left my granda until last. When I got to his house he was sitting on his bench. He was wearing his trilby hat and had both his hands clasping the top of his walking stick with his chin resting on top. He seemed to be miles away. Anthony and Finbar were in the garden, and I played about with them for a while, then took them to the shop across the road. We went down the steps to the door and checked my purse before going in. I had two shillings left. We went in and I spent the lot on sweets. I took them back to granda's.

"Those two will get bad teeth with all those sweets you keep giving them," he said.

I told him that would be the last as I was going tomorrow. "I'm here to say goodbye." I gave him a kiss on the cheek, something I had never done before. I could swear he had tears in his eyes. I said goodbye to the boys and gave them a hug, but they were more interested in eating their sweets. I walked up the path and out the gate. When I got well past the house I burst into tears. I got to my aunts and went straight upstairs. My case was just about packed. Just a few odds and end's to go in. I would leave them until morning. I put my handbag on top of the case and looked in it. There was only the envelope Mam gave me to give to Uncle Mickey when I got to Limerick. I looked in my purse again; that was empty. Then I thought, 'Oh no!' I hadn't kept the bus fare to Limerick. I got myself in a state about that. I would have to ask my aunt if she would lend me some money. I went down stairs and explained to her what had happened.

"Calm down now," she said, "it's all right." She went in her purse and gave me a pound.

"I won't need all that," I said.

She insisted and I took it. I told her I would send it back to her as soon as I got home. I hardly slept a wink that night; I kept thinking about the three little boys and how I would love to take them with me, and I thought about my granda who I might never see again.

Morning came and I had some breakfast. I didn't feel like eating, but my aunt insisted I ate something. I had said all my goodbyes by now. I clung to my aunt. She said the same words she had said three years ago:

"Don't get upset now, sure you'll be back to see us again."

Uncle Pappy picked up my case and took me to the bus. I was leaving Ennis again and it was breaking my heart. When I got to Limerick my cousin Thomas met me off the bus. We made our way to Ellan Street where he lived. It was a terraced house. It always looked very narrow to me, but it was very tall. I think it had three storeys; we went down the hall to the kitchen, and my aunt was sitting on a stool with her back against the wall. She didn't look well at all. When I got to her she gave me a hug.

"Look at the size of you, a young lady now."

"Aren't you feeling very well?" I asked. She said she had been feeling off for a couple of days.

"But don't worry, Thomas will look after you and take you out. Michael is at work and so is your uncle Mickey. You'll see them later."

Aunt May only had the two children, Michael and Thomas. Michael walked with a limp; I think he got Polio when he was young. I told her I had a letter for Uncle Mickey. I took it out of my bag and put it on the table. Thomas took my case upstairs. When he came back down he asked me if I wanted to go out for a while.

"Yes," I said, "but what about your Mam?"

My aunt said she would be fine. I asked her if she would go and lie down for a while.

"Yes," she acquiesced. "I'll feel better after a rest."

Thomas and I went for a walk around the town. We went in and out of the shops. We had no money but I enjoyed the window-shopping. I was telling him I didn't want to go back home.

"Well," he said, "why don't you stay?"

"My Mam would kill me if I didn't go back," I said.

"Well," he said, "go back home and ask her if you could live in Ireland."

"I think the answer would be 'no'. She wouldn't let me."

When we got back to the house aunt May was up. She had prepared a salad for tea. My uncle Mickey came home and Michael just after him, and they both made a big fuss of me. I told my uncle Mam had sent him a letter, and it was on the table. He picked it up and opened it. He looked at aunt May.

"Muriel wants me to get her two hundred Gold Flake," he said. "She has sent the money. I'll need to remember tomorrow." He handed the letter to aunt May to read. We all sat down to our tea. When we finished, I washed the dishes. Uncle Mickey and Michael went out, and my aunt said she was going to lie down again. There was just Thomas and I. I asked him if he would play the Piano Accordion for me. He looked a bit embarrassed.

"Go on, please play it," I said.

He got it out and it made a few odd sounds first. Then he started to play music on it. It was so beautiful I could have cried! He continued playing for about half an hour; then he stopped playing.

"That's enough for one night," he said.

I thanked him and asked if he would play it again tomorrow, as it was my last day. He said he would.

The next day we did all the things we had done the day before. My aunt had given us a shilling each to spend but we didn't need money as we were enjoying ourselves. When Uncle Mickey came home at teatime he gave me the cigarettes and told me to put them at the bottom of my case. Later that evening

Thomas played the Piano Accordion and I will always remember how beautiful it sounded.

Next day Thomas took me to the train station. I didn't want to go.

"You'll have to go!" he said. "You can ask your Mam if she will let you come back."

He then threw my case into the guard's van and gave me a little push and I was on the train. I don't remember much about the journey. I was upset and all I could think about was the people I had left behind. I remember seeing the boat and the gangplank up to it. There wasn't a soul about. I went up the gangplank and when I got on the boat, there stood Mrs Quinn. She gave me a good telling off for being late. It wasn't long before the boat sailed.

I was leaving Ireland and I didn't know if I would ever see it again.

Chapter 32
A Nice Christmas

WE arrived back in Salisbury on the Saturday evening. When we came out of the station there was a car there to meet us; I don't know if it was a taxi or one of Mrs Quinn's friends, but they dropped me off at Milford Hill Cottage and carried onto where they lived which was further on.

I picked up my case and went round the back of the house. Mam was in the kitchen, and she looked up as I came in the back door.

"Oh, you're back, did you have a nice time?"

I told her I had a lovely time but it was a very sad time as well. I couldn't get the words out quick enough to tell her all that had happened.

"My nanna died last year," I said, "and Maureen died about four weeks ago; she left three children, all boys. I wanted to bring them back with me; please Mam, can they come and live with us? They wouldn't be any trouble; Oliver hardly ever cries; I have taken him for lots of walks in his pram and he's always gurgling and smiling. The other two, Anthony and Finbar, are big enough to wash and dress themselves." She stopped me before I could say anything else.

"You're talking through your hat," she said. "Where in heaven's name would I put three children? I'm the housekeeper here; I don't own the place."

I hadn't thought about that, but I didn't give up.

"Can I go back to live in Ennis then? And I'll be able to look after them; I could live with Aunt Fanny?"

"That's enough," she said. "I don't want to hear another word about it. When you're eighteen you can do what you like, but until then you will do as you are told, and when Cove comes in you are not to say a word about all this, do you hear me?"

"Yes," I said, "but there's something else; I ran out of money so I had to ask aunt Fanny to lend me some. She gave me a pound. I told her I would send it back to her as soon as I got back home. If you could lend me a pound you could take it out of my polishing money at so much a week."

She said she'd do it that way. "The polishing wants starting tomorrow," she said. "I know it's Sunday but Madam is going to church and then she's going to have afternoon tea with a friend. You'll have plenty of time to get it all done; that means you'll have to go to early mass, then you can start the polishing when you get back."

I told her I'd start as soon as I got in from mass. I asked her if she had some writing paper and an envelope.

"You don't have to do it this minute," she said. "You can't get a stamp until Monday, and you should have made your money last you."

I could hear Madam's voice out in the hall: "Is young Muriel back? Because this dog is going mad!" The next thing I heard her say was, "Ho, you bad dog!"

It must have got out of her arms: I could hear it scampering up the corridor. Nankie-poo was jumping all over me! It took me all my time to stay on my feet. I bent down and picked him up. He was licking my face and whining. I calmed him down eventually. Madam came into the kitchen.

"It's nice to see you back," she said. "Nankie-poo has been missing you so much; he needs to go in his basket on the bicycle; he hasn't had a long walk for weeks."

It was funny because the dog wasn't getting any exercise sitting in the basket, but Madam thought he was getting plenty of fresh air and it would do him good. I told her I'd take him tomorrow.

"That's good," she said, "he misses you; I don't think you should go away for such long periods of time!" She trotted back down the corridor, the dog staying with me.

Mam told me to take all my washing out before I took my case upstairs. I did as she asked and put it in the wash bin, and gave her the 200 Gold Flake; that seemed to cheer her up. I went upstairs to my room with the dog at my heels. I felt a stronger person somehow; maybe it was because I had been to Ireland on my own and felt more grownup.

Mam came into my room next morning to get me up for mass. The dog started barking as soon as she shook me. She told me to shut him up as Cove was asleep. I got ready for mass and picked the dog up and carried him down the stairs so he wouldn't bark. Mam said she would have something ready for me when I got back. I couldn't eat anything as I was having Holy Communion.

"Cove and I will be going to late mass," she said, "because I have to get Madam off to church first."

I went out the back door but when I got outside the gate I decided I wasn't going to mass. I walked down the back road and made for where my grandad used to live. I stood outside the house and was saying to myself, 'I've come to say goodbye to you.' It was the first time I'd been there since I found him dead. Mam wouldn't tell me where he was buried; she said it was better I didn't know.

A strange thing happened in that house about a week after grandad died. There was a fire in the room he lived in and they couldn't find out how it had started. There was no one living in it at the time, so thank goodness no one was hurt. Mam saw a write-up in the paper about it. I looked at the house again and I said goodbye to him. I left and walked down to the church. I didn't go in. I continued walking past the school and the Convent, then down the little road by the side of the Convent until I came to the iron bars where grandad used to come and talk to me. I was on the outside now trying to look in but it was all overgrown and I couldn't see anything. I sat down on the grass for a while and felt at peace there. After a while I thought mass must be nearly finished now so I got up and walked back the same way as I'd came. I'd just got past the church when the people started to come out, so I walked back home thinking if Mam finds out I hadn't gone to mass she would kill me. I went in the house and there were sandwiches on the table for me. I sat down and ate them; I could hear Mam saying to Madam, that the car was here to take her to church. After a few minutes she came back in the kitchen.

"Good, you're back," she said. "I'm just going to get washed and changed for mass; will you make a cup of tea for Cove? He is in the sitting room."

I made the tea and took it into him. He was reading the Sunday paper. He looked round the side of it when he heard me come in.

"I heard you were back," he said. "I hope you didn't say anything you weren't supposed to while you were away?"

I told him I hadn't; and put his tea down and got out of the room as quick as I could. Mam came downstairs about ten minutes later all ready to go to mass. She called to Cove and he came out of the sitting room. They went out the front way; she said they would go for a walk after mass as Madam was out. I picked up the basket with the polish and rags in and made my way upstairs with the dog following me. Mam and Cove came back about two and a half hours later. I could hear them laughing and carrying on in the kitchen. I'd finished my work and put everything back in the basket. The dog had gone downstairs as soon as he heard them come in. I walked down the corridor and had just reached the top of the stairs when Cove started to come up them. I froze, but then I thought he won't start anything because Mam was in the kitchen, so I continued to go down. We met in the middle; he put his left arm out to stop me and put his right hand up my dress! He was touching me—I couldn't believe he was doing this to me and he had just come from mass! Mam was in the kitchen getting the dinner ready and the door was slightly opened. I was trying to pull his hand away and put the basket down at the same time.

"I'm going to tell…"

He didn't let me finish what I was saying, and put his face right up to mine and said, "She won't believe you because she loves me, he, he, he!"

I could feel his spittle against my face. I felt sick. I got some strength from somewhere and I pushed him back against the side of the staircase. I looked at him and said, "I know Mam won't believe me, but I'm going down to see the priest and tell *him* what you have been doing to me all this time!"

His face went white and now I could see the fear in his eyes.

"If you ever touch me again I'll go to the priest, *Do You Hear Me?*"

I must have been shouting because he told me to calm down. He went down the stairs, through the kitchen and out the back door, and what was left of my religion went with him. I picked up the basket from the stairs and went down to the kitchen.

"What's the matter with Cove?" she asked. "You haven't been upsetting him, have you? He looked very angry."

I said I hadn't. "I've just come downstairs."

Cove never touched me again after that. He was more frightened of the priest than he was of Mam. But he could hurt me in other ways, and he did. If I wanted to do something or go somewhere, he would tell Mam she wasn't to let me. I didn't care as long as he wasn't touching me.

Weeks went by. Cove kept away from me. If we passed on the stairs he'd never say a word or try to touch me. It was a wonderful feeling, being able to walk around the house without being frightened.

I'd sent my aunt Fanny the pound I'd borrowed from her. I was very worried because it was an English pound note, but Mam said she'd be able to change it at the bank. My polishing money for the next six weeks was stopped altogether; I thought she was going to take a shilling a week or one and sixpence at the most, but I thought wrong. When it got to the sixth week I'd paid back eighteen shillings, and she said she'd let me off with the last two shillings this time; she said she hoped that would teach me a lesson. "If you borrow, you have to pay it back; if you want something, you have to save up for it; and a roof over your head and food in your belly are the most important things in life; and they come first." I thought I had been badly treated, but years later I was grateful my Mam had shown me how to manage money.

It was good to get my polishing money again; I could buy odd balls of wool very cheap from the market and I was buying the wool to knit socks for Christmas presents. I was taught to knit socks when I was in the convent. I didn't think I would ever master knitting with four needles, but I did.

My uncle and aunt were coming from Harrogate to spend Christmas with us and Martin was coming as well, so I got a good few balls of wool in different colours and when I got home I picked out a nice beige colour for Martin and started knitting his socks. I was on the second sock and had knitted about five inches under the heel when the wool ran out. I couldn't understand what had happened at first, then I realised the wool was thicker than the wool I had used in the convent. I asked Mam about it.

"Thicker wool doesn't go as far," she said.

"What will I do now?" I asked.

"All you can do is to unpick it all and start again," she said. "You'll have to put stripes around the top of each sock in a different colour of wool; that way you will have enough wool for two socks." It was heartbreaking having to unravel all my hard work, especially when I'd got down below the heel of the second one and I'd made such a good job of turning the heels. I could have cried! I started all over again, and this time I ended up with a pair. I knitted Uncle Bert grey ones with navy blue stripes around the tops. Mam asked me what colour I was going to knit for Cove? I wasn't going to knit any for him but I thought better of it. I didn't want to start a row so I told her his would be dark green with brown tops. When I'd finished the socks I knitted some mittens for Mam and my aunt. I put stripes on the cuffs, just in case I ran out of wool again. I'd a couple of balls left in light blue and half a ball of white; I put them back in the bag and thought I would knit myself some socks after Christmas.

It was the day before Christmas Eve. I asked Mam if she had any wrapping paper so I could wrap up the socks.

"No," she replied, "I've used it all."

I asked if she had any brown paper. She said, "No", and went in the sitting room. I started searching through all the drawers in the kitchen and found some. It was greaseproof paper; Mam used it to line the cake tins when she was making cakes. I took it up to my room and got the socks and mittens out of the drawer and wrapped them up, and tied them with bits of wool and they didn't look too bad.

Christmas Eve came and Martin arrived first. It was lovely to see him and we talked for ages. I was telling him all about Ireland and all the things that had happened since he had left there and how I didn't want to come back here. I told Martin about Cove and what he had been doing to me. It felt good being able to tell someone about it, but I said, "It's no good me telling Mam because she wouldn't believe me, so I told him if he touched me again I would tell the priest, and he hasn't touched me since."

"The dirty bastard!" Martin exclaimed. "You *should* have told the priest! He should be put in jail for that!"

"But what about Mam?" I said. "She would blame me and throw me out! Anyway, he is more frightened of the priest than he is of Mam, so don't say anything because it will make things worse for me."

That was one thing about Martin—I could tell him all my troubles. We were very close and we stayed that way all through our lives. I asked Martin why he wasn't in the army doing his national service like Ray. He said he hadn't passed his medical; there was something wrong with his heart but it was nothing to worry about.

My uncle and aunt arrived. Mam made them a cup of tea in the kitchen, and when they'd finished Mam took them into Madam's sitting room. It was a big room with a lot more chairs in it than ours. Madam told her she could use it while she was away. They all sat there for hours talking about this and that, and Martin kept giving Cove dirty looks and I was sure he noticed. When it was time for bed I said goodnight to everyone and Martin said he was going too. He said goodnight and as he left the room he gave Cove the dirtiest look I have ever seen.

I went upstairs to my room and sat on the bed thinking about my grandad and wishing he were here. I missed him so much. I went over to grandad's case and got his pension book out. I got undressed and into bed with Nankie-poo at one side of me and grandad's pension book at the other. I could smell him off the book and that gave me a lot of comfort.

We all gathered in Madam's sitting room next morning and the presents were handed out. My uncle made a big fuss when he opened the one I gave him, and tried the socks on straight away—he said he'd never had such a lovely pair of socks! Martin said he liked his. Mam was opening hers, and said, "Is this my greaseproof paper?" She had a little smile on her face. My uncle said, "We'll save the paper and it can be used again." They all laughed; my uncle took some photos of us all and we all had a lovely Christmas day.

Christmas and New Year had gone and it was now 1954. I started back at school and it was good to see them all again; especially Valerie—she was the girl that lent me all the books; she was very pretty with a lovely smile and long hair that she wore in plaits down her back. I had been to her house a few times. She told me at school she'd got the latest Enid Blyton book from The Famous Five adventures, and had read it; and if I wanted to borrow it I could. I said, "I'd love to!" She said, "Well, if you walk home with me after school I'll get it for you." After school we walked home together. When we got to where she lived you had to go through a shop; there wasn't much in it. I think her father was an antique dealer. He was standing in the shop when we went in. He smiled and said "Hello" to us. We went to the back and there was a door that led into their living room. Her mother was there and her two older sisters. Valerie went to her bedroom to get the book. Her mother asked me to sit down and gave me a glass of orange juice and some biscuits.

"It won't be long now until you leave school," she said. "Do you know what you want to do?" I told her I wanted to be a dressmaker; I liked sewing.

"That would be a good trade to be in," she said.

There was a mirror over the fireplace. Valerie's sister was standing in front of it brushing her hair. The other sister came up next to her and they started pushing each other playfully to look in the mirror. They were laughing and their mother told them to behave, but she had a smile on her face when she said it. I thought to myself, this house is full of love; you could feel it—this is how families should be.

Valerie came back into the room with the book and I thought how lucky she was to have such a nice family. I wished she could be my best friend, but she already had one at school called Janet. I'll always remember Janet because she told us her granny had choked on a fish bone and died. I wouldn't eat fish for years after that; even now I go through my fish with a fine toothcomb and always think of Janet's granny when I see fish!

Valerie gave me the book. I said thank you to her mother for the drink and biscuits and set off walking home to Milford Hill. I couldn't ask any of the girls back to my house because Madam wouldn't like it.

Chapter 33
My New Job

THE beginning of February came along. I'd be fifteen soon but I couldn't leave school until Easter. As I was coming out of school one day, sister Agnes stopped me and handed me a letter and said I was to give it to my mother when I got home.

"Now what have you been up to?" she said when I handed her the letter.

"I haven't been up to anything," I said defensively as she opened the letter.

"Sister Agnes wants to see me on Wednesday," she said, reading the letter. "She wants to talk about you leaving school."

"She'll want to see all the children's parents about getting jobs," I said.

When Mam arrived at school on the Wednesday I was called out of my class and we went into a little office and sat down. Sister Agnes came in and sat opposite us. She asked Mam what she had in mind for me when I left school. Mam said she hadn't thought about it, but there were plenty of shops looking for school leavers. Sister Agnes looked at me.

"Is that what you want to do?" she asked. "Work in a shop?"

"No," I replied, "I want to be a dressmaker."

The nun turned to Mam. "Your daughter is a beautiful sewer and I know a tailor's that would take her on," she smiled. "The only thing is she'd only get a few shillings a week because she'd be in an apprenticeship. I think she would do well and it's a good trade. Anyway, Mrs Spencer, think about it. Sleep on it tonight, but you will let me know tomorrow, won't you?"

Mam said goodbye to Sister Agnes and went home. I went back to my class with my head full of it. I was going to train to be a tailor! I would be able to make suites, coats, and anything; it was all I could think of for the rest of the day. When Cove came in from work I could hear their raised voices; Mam was telling him it was a good chance in life for me, but he wouldn't hear of it.

"She should be out there earning her keep!" he insisted.

So that was it. I wouldn't be able to be a tailor—I hated him! I knew he would get back at me in other ways. You would think it was him that was keeping me and it wasn't—it was my Mam. I started to rebel after that and I would take half days off school to go to the cinema. I spent my dinner money on cigarettes and a gang of us shared them in the toilets. A nun came in and caught us one day—we could hardly see her for all the smoke! She took all our names and said she'd be in touch with our parents. I told her my Mam knew that I smoked.

"We'll see about that," I said to the other girls. "When she gives us the letters to take home we'll all tear them up!"

She didn't give any of us any letters to take home that day or the day after, and I thought we'd got away with it; but when I got home from school Mam was standing there with her arms folded.

"Upstairs!" she ordered.

When I got to my room she was behind me; she closed the door and took her shoe off. She gave me a good hiding with it. I was sore—very sore! The nun must have posted the letters. None of us looked too well when we arrived at school the next day.

Eventually it was my last day at school. All the girls were saying they would keep in touch with one another. I don't know if any of them ever did.

I went for an interview at a grocer's shop called Harry Heads. As I stood in the shop waiting to be interviewed, this big tall man in a long white apron kept rushing past me. He had white hair and wore dark horn-rimmed glasses; he seemed to be rushing from one counter to another, and there was a strong smell of coffee to my left. I looked across; there was a woman putting coffee beans into a machine and you could see it coming out as coffee powder. At the right-hand side there was a cooked meats counter and they sold bacon, sausages, and all sorts of funny looking things I'd never seen before. Next to that was tea, sugar, tins of soup and packets of currants and sultanas with other packets that I'd never heard of. At the top end of the shop there was washing powders, soap, toothpaste and all sorts of cleaning things. Before long the tall man in the white apron came over to me.

"Muriel Burns?" he asked.

"Yes?"

He told me to follow him. We went into a little office and told me to sit down. My knees were knocking and my hands were shaking. I hoped he couldn't see how nervous I was. He sat opposite me.

"I'm Mr Head," he said. He smiled at me and handed me a piece of paper with sums on.

"Now let's see if you can add up and subtract," he said.

There were ten sums on the paper, five for adding and five for subtracting. I was good at this subject at school and it didn't take me long to do them. I handed the piece of paper back to him.

"That was quick." He checked them and said, "Very good, you've got them all right." Then he told me about the customers that came in his shop. "You must remember the customer is always right; whether they are or not, you must be polite and smile at them. The wage will be Two-Pounds-Twelve and Sixpence a week. You can start on Monday. Be here for nine o'clock."

"Thank you," I said and went out of the shop. That was it—I'd got a job! I'd have liked it better if I could have got one at Woolworth's but they didn't want any staff.

I settled into my job the best I could, and at the end of the first week I took my wage packet home and gave it to Mam. She took the two pounds out of the packet and gave me what was left. It must have been six months before I got to serve anyone; I spent my days filling the shelves up, and going up a wooden ladder to an attic where all the washing powders, soaps, and that sort of things were kept. I would take an empty box with a list of all the things that were needed for the shop, and would carry them down to the shop and fill the shelves up. I hated going up into that attic because there were loads of spiders and I was terrified of them.

The weather was getting very warm now and you could feel it more in the attic. Sometimes I thought I was going to pass out, it was that warm. At lunchtime I started to take my sandwiches outside and sit on a bench to eat them; then I would walk down the street, window-shopping.

One day I noticed a little café called Toni's. I thought I'd go in and have a cup of tea as it was quiet. The man behind the counter was very friendly; he was Italian but he spoke very good English. He asked me where I worked and if I liked it there and the hours I worked. I felt good when I came out of there, and this became a regular thing—going to the little café.

One Saturday at lunchtime I went to Toni's and there were lots of motorbikes parked outside. The café was just about full so I decided I wouldn't go in today, but Toni looked up and saw me through the window;

and he held a cup and saucer up and smiled. So I went in and sat on the only stool left up near the window. All the boys were seated along the front of the counter with their motorbike gear on and their helmets down at their feet. Toni was laughing and joking with them. He kept bringing me into the conversation; then a couple of the boys that were sitting next to me started talking to me; then other boys joined in, telling me not to believe a word they were saying. I was enjoying myself that much I was nearly late back to work.

I had been going to the café for about a month on a Saturday lunchtime and I got to know the boys a lot better. They were telling me they came to the café about three nights a week. It was a sort of meeting place for them and I should come down; they always had a good laugh. I started going a couple of nights a week, and met a girl in there called Rosemary. We became good friends; we got on well together.

It was near the end of September before I got my chance to go behind the counter in the shop. For the first couple of weeks I was grinding coffee beans; and in between doing that I was filling shelves. I got to serve my first customer in October with one of the other women standing behind me to make sure I was doing everything right, and then she would check my adding up. After a week of that it was a great feeling to be able to serve on my own. I felt very grown up and of course with filling shelves for so long I knew where everything was kept. That made it a lot easier.

I was still going to the café a couple of nights a week and got a big crush on one of the boys. I think he was older than the others; every time I saw him my heart would start thumping. I would feel my face going red, and it wasn't long before the rest of them noticed my red face every time he came in; so they started teasing me about it; they must have told him I'd a crush on him and he changed; he used to talk to me all the time and often gave me a lift home, but now he started to go down the other end of the counter away from me. I was broken hearted; I would go home and cry my eyes out all night. Poor Nankie-poo had more baths with my tears than he ever had in the sink and this went on for a month. I still went to the café but it wasn't the same. I couldn't even tell Rosemary what was wrong or how I felt. I thought she would laugh at me. I seemed to have a permanent pain in my heart; I'd never felt like this before.

One night I went to the café and sat with Rosemary. Some of the boys came in and sat along the front of the counter. She was talking to them and having a laugh. She turned back to me and said, "You know that Stuart? He hardly ever comes in now and he was ever so nice; he was in one night last week but it was the night you didn't come down. He must be working overtime because he was always in here." I could feel my face going redder and redder. I got down off the stool as fast as I could and went outside. Rosemary followed. I got away from the café window to a dark place, and she was asking me what was wrong. I told her I felt sick and would have to go home. I was glad she couldn't see my red face in the dark. She wanted to go and get one of the boys to take me home, and I asked her not to; it would be better for me to walk and get some fresh air. I might be sick on the motorbike, I said, and that would make things worse. When I got in the house I gave myself a good talking to; all this would have to stop when his name was mentioned! I'd have to pull myself together.

December was a very busy month in the shop and I was glad; it would take my mind off other things. I still went to the café at lunchtime and sometimes on a night but I didn't go on a Saturday lunchtime; I would pass by on the other side of the road and if Stuart's bike were there I would just go on my way.

We did a couple of nights' overtime for the next two weeks. I didn't bother going out at night at all. I met Rosemary on the street one day and she asked me what was wrong. I told her I was too tired to go out at night after I'd finished work, but there was only a week until Christmas. "I will meet you at the café on Christmas Eve and we'll find something to do," I said.

We were having the family again this year for Christmas. My aunt and uncle Bert were coming from Harrogate and uncle George and aunt Mary from Aldershot with their two children, Patricia and Christine; my brother Martin would be with them. I was glad Martin was coming; it would take my mind off Stuart and my broken heart. I'd be able to talk and tell him all about it.

Christmas eve came and we were rushed off our feet all day in the shop; I was glad when it was closing time. Mr Head called all us women together and asked us to sit down anywhere we could find a box on the shop floor. Mr Head came over to us with a tray of glasses and a bottle of gin.

"I want to thank you all for the hard work you've put in over the year, and especially for the last few weeks," he smiled. "I would like you all to have a drink with me." One of the women started pouring out the drinks. Then she said to Mr Head, "What about Muriel?"

"Just put a small amount in a glass and fill it up with orange," he said. Then he added: "I want to wish you all a Merry Christmas and a Happy New

Year!" All the women lifted their glasses. I did the same and we all wished Mr Head a Happy Christmas. The women were talking and laughing among themselves; then Mr Head put some more gin in their glasses; he didn't put any in mine and I was glad because it didn't taste very nice. The women seemed to be talking a lot louder and they all looked a bit flushed. I'd never seen them like this before—they all looked so happy! I took a big drink out of my glass to try and get rid of it as quickly as I could; then another big drink and the glass was empty. I sat there watching the women for about five minutes, then I seemed to lose my focus. I was seeing double and felt very dizzy. All of a sudden I started laughing. I didn't know what I was laughing at—it sounded far away. I could hear one of the women in the distance. She was saying, "But she's always so quiet she hardly ever opens her mouth." Mr Head was looking at me; he seemed to have two heads, and I started laughing again and could hear myself saying, "Mr Head has two heads—now that's funny, isn't it?"

He looked at the woman and asked how much gin she had put in my glass. I could hear the woman saying; "Just a small amount."

"Well," he said, "she's drunk."

I heard him ask two of the women if they would take me home. He said he'd order a taxi, and said, "When you get to the house, would you explain to her mother that we had a Christmas drink and that she only had a small drop in the bottom of her glass." He went on: "Tell the taxi driver to wait until you get her in the house."

Two women stood me up and put my coat on; my legs felt like jelly, and they took me outside and waited for the taxi. When we got to my house the women walked me up the steps to the front door and knocked. Mam answered. She asked the women what was wrong with me, and they explained all that had happened and added, "She only had a small drop of gin in the bottom of her glass and it was filled up with orange juice."

"Thank you for bringing her home," Mam said, and added, "but she shouldn't have been given alcohol at all, should she?"

Mam pulled me into the hallway and shut the front door. She dragged me down the corridor and up the stairs to my room and threw me on the bed. She started walloping me with her slipper. I felt the pain but it was a dull pain. I knew everything she was saying but it seemed to be far away in the distance. Now she was shaking me by the shoulders, saying, "You have spoilt Christmas for us all!"

I told her I felt sick. She rushed out and got a bowl and just made it back in time. The horrible taste of that drink came up and that was all. I hadn't eaten that day—I had worked through my lunch hour and the sandwiches were still in my bag. I started to come back to normal and I felt very tired, and just wanted to go to sleep. I curled up in a little ball and I didn't hear another thing until morning.

I was woken up on Christmas morning with the dog barking outside my door. I was trying to remember why the dog wasn't in the room with me because he always slept in my room. Then I started to have hazy memories about the night before. I had the most horrible taste in my mouth and dashed out to the bathroom. I must have cleaned my teeth three or four times until all I could taste was toothpaste. Then I had a good wash and went back to my room and got changed. Martin came down the corridor towards my room. He had that slow smile on his face; I was so pleased to see him! He came in and put his arms around me and burst out laughing.

"Did you have a good time last night?" he grinned.

"No, I didn't, it was horrible!" And I meant it!

He cuddled me to him and said, "I think they have all seen the funny side of it now. Apart from Mam and Cove. We'll go to mass now and when we get back it'll all be forgotten."

When we arrived back from mass they were all in Madam's sitting room. There was a lovely Christmas tree against the wall on the left near the window. They must have put it up yesterday when I was at work; it had lovely coloured baubles and silver tinsel all over and presents underneath. Martin pushed me further into the room and everyone wished us a Happy Christmas, and the presents were handed out. Mam gave me mine. She said, "You don't really deserve this with all that carry on yesterday!"

"Thank you," I said, and opened it. She had got me a pair of soft leather gloves and they were orange tan in colour. I wondered why she'd picked that colour, since I didn't have anything to go with them. I thought I should be grateful; after all, I didn't deserve anything.

It was wonderful to see my little cousin's faces, especially Patricia's. She was older and knew what was going on, but Christine was happy just playing with the wrapping paper. Martin and I took the girls out to the park while Mam and my aunts got on with the Christmas dinner.

I had a long talk with Martin while we were out. I told him all about my broken heart. I could talk to him about anything; he was always there for me.

He told me it was just a crush I had. "You wait and see," he said, "in a month or two you'll wonder what you saw in him." I thought a month or two was a very long time to put up with a broken heart!

We took the girls back to Auntie Mary. Patricia was feeling the cold.

We had a lovely Christmas dinner and pulled the crackers between us. We all got paper hats. Everyone was happy.

Chapter 34
Learning to Dance

It was January 1955. I'd started back at work a week before and had to take a lot of teasing about Christmas Eve. The first day back was the worst but now they were beginning to drop it, thank goodness.

Mam told me I'd have to look for another job and it had to be somewhere that didn't sell alcohol. She also told me I wasn't permitted to go out at night for two weeks and that would teach me a lesson, and I was to keep away from the café at lunchtime.

One day at lunchtime I met my friend Rosemary. She thought I had fallen out with her because I hadn't turned up at the café on Christmas Eve. I told her all that had happened; she laughed at first, then she said, "But it wasn't your fault! It was just a Christmas drink. Come on, we'll go in the café and have a cup of tea."

"I'm sorry," I said, "I can't. I've to stay away from the café for two weeks as well."

"Well," she frowned, "I wouldn't put up with that! I'd soon tell my mother where to get off!" She walked away; down towards the café and called back to me: "I'll see you in two weeks then?"

The two weeks seemed to drag by and I was fed up with my own company.

At last, it came to an end and I was free again. On the first night of my freedom I went down to the café, and when I got there the place was empty. The girl behind the counter was Italian. Her name was Roberta, but she couldn't speak a word of English. She was the nanny to Toni's children.

I wondered what she was doing there. I asked her for a cup of tea; she seemed to know what tea was. I gave her the right money and she smiled at me. She stood there and kept smiling at me. I was beginning to feel uncomfortable; I tried to ask her where everyone was, pointing to all the empty seats. She just shrugged her shoulders and carried on smiling. I'd nearly finished my tea and thought I might as well go back home. I was about to get off the stool when Toni came in. He came straight across to me.

"Hello!" he smiled, "It is very nice to see you! How are you? I heard you were in a bit of trouble with the Christmas drink."

I said I was all right and that I'd just finished my punishment for having that drink. He laughed and went behind the counter and started talking to Roberta in Italian. I couldn't understand a word they were saying, but she went through the door into the kitchen at the back of the café. Toni came over and started talking to me. He said he had to go out for half an hour and had to leave Roberta in charge of the shop. He was asking me if she had been all right. I said there hadn't been anyone in but me. He said it was always very quiet for a couple of months after Christmas; people stay home and keep warm. It was the same everywhere, he said. I thought if this were true I'd have no chance of getting another job. Toni gave me another cup of tea and said it was on the house.

The door opened and Stuart came in! My heart started thumping and I could feel my face going red. I put my elbows on the counter with my hands on my cheeks, pretending to be looking out the window. I could hear Toni talking to him and hoped they would carry on until my face stopped burning. Stuart sat on the next stool to me and said, "Hello." Toni asked if I was all right. I told him I was fine. My face had cooled down so I took my hands away as a few more people come in. Toni was now talking to them. Stuart turned to me and started talking, mostly about motorbikes and the places he could go with having a bike.

"It must be nice to go anywhere you like when you want to," I said. "I'd love to go on a motorbike."

"Well," he said, "I'll take you if you want, but not tonight—it's getting a bit late. I'll pick you up at half past seven tomorrow night at your house, if you want to; we can call in the café when we get back." I was trying to keep my voice calm and said, "Okay then, I'll be ready." He told me to put a warm coat on—it would be cold. He got up and went out the door, saying goodnight to everyone. I started to shake, and couldn't stop. Toni was still talking to some people, so I got off the stool and made for the door. But he saw me.

"Are you going so soon?" he asked. "You're not well, I can tell."

I told him I was a bit off colour and said goodnight.

When I got home I asked Mam if it was all right to go for a ride on a motorbike tomorrow night with one of the boys. She knew that one of them always brought me home at night, but this was different. She must have felt sorry for me after keeping me in for two weeks, and said I could go! But, she said, I'll have to put plenty of clothes on—she'd look out hers for me. I went to bed the happiest person alive!

When I went to work next day the hours seemed to drag. I was looking at the clock every five minutes. It had been raining all day and didn't stop until about three o'clock. I was so glad because I was afraid he wouldn't come if it were still raining. At last it was time to go home. Mam had my tea ready when I got there. I told her I wasn't very hungry.

"Well," she said, "if you don't eat your tea you're not going outside that door tonight."

That was it—I sat down and ate the lot! About quarter past seven, mam said, "Come and get this suit on." She had it laid out in front of the fire to air because she hadn't had it on since she came back from Ireland. It looked creased and didn't smell too good either.

"Do I have to put that on?" I said. "It looks huge! Can't I just wear my coat?"

"No, it's far too cold," she said.

She started putting it on me. It was far too big! She started to zip and button me up and made me put on her little brown suede ankle boots with zips up the side. That was the last straw—I was boiling inside this suit! She pulled up the collar and zipped that up too, followed with a crash helmet on my head and a pair of gloves that nearly reached my armpits. I could hear the horn sounding outside. Oh my God, he was early! I couldn't go out the front door in case Madam came out of her room and the dog was barking with the sound of the horn.

I went out the back door and took a short cut across Madam's little garden to the front of the house. It was mostly a rockery with a little bit of garden. I tripped over a loose stone on the path and landed headlong among the rose bushes. It was all muddy with the rain! I picked myself up and with the light shining from the lamppost I could see I was covered in mud. I climbed over a small wall and made my way over to the steps from the cottage. I could see Stuart at the bottom of the steps parked at the kerbside. He sounded the horn again and I missed my footing and slid down the rest of the steps. He was looking at me as though I had come from outer space! I don't think he could believe his eyes when he saw me standing there in front of him. I thought for a minute he wasn't going to let me get on the bike! But he did. We went along a road that was near the back of our house with a wooded area on the left-hand side. As we were driving along I could see a motorbike parked at the side of the road near the trees; as we came closer I could see it was Cove's bike—and there he was at the side of a tree with a woman! Their hands were all over each other and they were just about eating one another! All I could think of was poor Mam. If she got to know about this it would break her heart, so I decided to keep it to myself. The night was ruined now anyway. I knew Stuart wouldn't stay out for long; he would be glad to get rid of me and I felt I was the ugliest person that had ever been born. I was right! He dropped me off a short while after and said, "See you." So I didn't get to the café like he said last night. I walked round the back of the house and through the back gate. When I got in the kitchen Mam looked at me in horror.

"Oh my god, what's happened to you?"

"Its all right," I said, "I fell in the garden on my way out; its just mud—it'll come off."

"I didn't expect you back for another hour or so!"

I took all the gear off and hung the suit up in a cupboard. I told her I'd brush it down when the mud dried.

"I don't know where Cove has got too," she said. "He's never this late. I hope he's all right."

"Don't worry," I said, "he's maybe broken down somewhere." I felt like saying I know where he is—he's down the road snogging with a woman! But I didn't say it—I couldn't hurt her like that. I was hurting too. I wished Mam would put her arms around me and give me a big hug and make the pain go away.

February came and it was going to be my sixteenth birthday on the eighteenth. It was in a week's time. Mam told me Madam was going away for three or four days.

"You can ask a few of your friends to come to the house on your birthday if you like," Mam said. "You can use Madam's sitting room and have a little party. You seem to have been right down lately."

I didn't think I was hearing right. "You mean girls?" I asked.

"Well," she said, "you can have some of your motorbike friends as long as there is ten of you and no more."

I was over the moon! I started to plan things. I would be able to ask Stuart, dress up nice and do my hair in a different way. I was going to put a bit more makeup on. The things I was going to do was nobody's business. Mam bought me a black straight skirt with a slit up the back and a white polo neck jumper. I'd asked a few friends from the café to come but Stuart hadn't been in. A couple of days before my birthday his mother came into the shop; one of the girls had told me who she was, so I wrote a note on a scrappy piece of paper. I got brave and went to her and asked if she would give it to Stuart. She looked at me and I could tell she wasn't very pleased; she took the note out of my hand without saying a word and went out the door. I was happy now he'd come to the party when he got the note.

Mam had made sausage rolls, cakes, jam tarts; and a load of sandwiches; she put a bottle of ginger beer and a bottle of fizzy orange on the table with glasses, and had pulled the rug back so we could dance on the polished floor. I was very grateful to her for doing this for me. All my friends arrived together; there were four boys and four girls, but there was no sign of Stuart. I kept going to the window looking out for him; after about half an hour of this, one of the boys came to me; he put his arm around my shoulder and said, "Muriel, he isn't coming."

"Maybe his mother didn't give him the note," I said.

"She did," he confirmed, "because he told us. I'm sorry, don't let it spoil your party."

I thought they all knew, but they didn't want to tell me because they didn't want to hurt me and I wasn't going to let them down. As for now—we we're going to have a party! We put a record on; it was the laughing policeman, and it got us all going. It ended up a great party after all, and I no longer had a crush on Stuart; after all, he didn't even have the decency to come and tell me himself!

Martin came to stay for the weekend in March. He was going dancing to the Salisbury Pally on Saturday night. He asked me if I'd go with him.

"You'll have to ask Mam if I can go," he said.

He asked her and she said, "Yes, but you're not to let her out of your sight."

When we arrived at the dance hall Martin paid for us both to go in. Then we went upstairs and he told me to put my coat in the cloakroom. When I came out he was waiting for me.

"What do you think of it?" he asked.

I told him it was like the dance hall in Limerick, only a lot smaller. We moved to the back of the hall. There was a group of girls standing there. Martin started talking to them; they seemed to know him. He introduced me to them.

"This is my little sister, Muriel," he said. Then he told me, "The girls work up the road at the mental hospital and they're all Irish."

"Hello," I said. They seemed very friendly; one of them was asking Martin to save a dance for her. The music started up and Martin pulled me onto the dance floor.

"I don't know how to do it!" I said.

"Well, listen to what I'm saying," he said, "and at the same time look down at my feet and follow them."

I stood on his toes a few times, and was just getting the hang of it when he started to dance quicker. He started twirling me round and round. I was going dizzy, and asked him to slow down: "Martin, slow down!"

"Muriel, it's a quickstep!" he said.

"I know, but you're bumping into everyone!"

"I'm not," he said. "It's *them*—they don't know how to do it."

I was glad when the dance finished. We went back to the girls, and they were saying to me, "Isn't he great at the quickstep?"

"He was dancing too fast for me," I said. "The others weren't dancing like that."

"Well," one girl said, "they aren't Irish, are they?"

I thought to myself, they must have a different quickstep in Ireland than they do in England!

The night wore on and there was a group of boys now mingled in with the girls. They were in the forces. The night was nearly at an end, and Martin was having his last quickstep with one of the Irish girls and she was enjoying ever minute of it. Then it was the last waltz, and he got me up to the lovely sound of Glen Miller. When it had finished I went to get my coat. Martin was waiting for me and was talking to one of the boys that was in the forces.

"Muriel, we've been offered a lift home," he said.

I was glad—I was tired out. When we got to the house, Martin got out straight away; and went up the steps and I could see him with his back leaning against the front door. The car door was open and I had one leg hanging out, but the boy kept talking to me. I kept saying I would have to go. He was away from home and I think he was homesick. I looked up at

Martin—he seemed to have fallen asleep standing up! I said to the boy I must go; then the front door to the house flew open and Martin disappeared and Mam came running down the steps. She grabbed me by the hair with one hand and dragged me up the steps and was hitting me with the other hand! When we got to the front door Martin was halfway up looking shocked. She closed the front door and let go of me; then she started hitting Martin! She was shouting at him: "You're drunk!"

"I'm not," he protested. "I haven't touched a drink."

"Well, why did you fall in the door?"

"I was leaning against it!"

"I told you not to let her out of your sight!"

"I didn't," he said. "That boy gave us a lift home and she was just talking to him."

With that she burst into tears and went to bed. Martin and I stood there looking at each other in shock. I couldn't believe she had been hitting Martin like that; he was nearly twenty years old!

"That's it!" Martin said. "I'm not coming here anymore. I'm not putting up with this."

We went off to bed but our night had been spoilt.

When we came down next morning we heard Mam and Cove arguing. He was on about her drunken son and her drunken whore of a daughter.

"Come on," Martin said, "lets go to mass."

After Martin went back I was looking for another job. I got one in a shoe shop and hated every minute of it. I was so used to being on the go all the time. It was only the weekends we were busy. I was standing there bored most of the time. I started smoking then and when I tried to stop I couldn't— I was hooked; it was the worst thing I had ever done. I went in the café one day at lunchtime. Toni asked me if I knew anyone who was looking for a job—he needed help in the café.

"Can I have it?" I said.

"Yes." His face lit up. "It would be nice to have someone I know."

So that was me, working in Toni's café. I loved working there; it was the first time I was really happy since I left school over a year ago. As I got to know the customers, they started talking to me about this and that and sometimes they would tell me their problems. I felt like an agony aunt! Roberta did a bit of cooking in the kitchen and when we were quiet I would try to teach her a few words of English. We laughed a lot as she was trying to pronounce them; she learned quite a few but she couldn't manage the name 'Muriel'; so I got her to say 'Mu', and she was happy with that!

I had a lovely summer and went all over the place with the boys on their bikes. We went to Redcar, Bournemouth, and to Southampton to see Johnny Dankworth and his band, and the lovely Clio Lane who was singing with the band. I always went on Johnny's bike. He was one of the boys from the café. We were sort of going out together because we went everywhere with the group. On a Saturday night we always went dancing; sometimes to the Salisbury Pally one week and maybe the dance hall in Wilton the next week, which was a couple of miles away; it is where the famous carpets are made. Every time I see the name or a carpet I think of that dance hall!

When I had to work a couple of nights at the café all the boys and girls would come in to see me and have a good laugh and a good time. It wasn't really work! I was very happy there and got paid as well.

One day Roberta beckoned me to come down to the other end of the café where she was standing. She looked very sad and kept saying, "I go one week." I couldn't understand what she was trying to tell me. She kept pointing at her finger. I looked at it and couldn't see anything wrong. Toni came out of the kitchen and said something to her in Italian and she went through to the kitchen.

"I think she has hurt her finger," I said to Toni. "She told me 'she go in one week'—I don't know what she means.

Tony laughed. "She was trying to tell you she is going back to Italy next week. She is going to be married. She will be staying there with her new husband."

"I'm sorry to hear she's leaving," I said. "I'm going to miss her."

Roberta came back and I gave her a hug; I then got a pen and paper and said, "When you get home to Italy you write to me." I started scribbling on the paper and pointed to her. Then I scribbled again and pointed to myself. She smiled at me. I printed my name and address in big letters and gave it to her. I didn't know if she understood or not—I would have to wait and see.

On Roberta's last night all the boys and girls came to the café. Outside there were bikes parked everywhere. We had a bit of a party for her and she was so pleased she started to cry. We would all miss her lovely smile.

Mam and Cove seemed to argue a lot these days. It was always about him coming in late from work. His excuses were he had to stay late at the hospital because someone hadn't turned up for work or the bike had broken down and he had to push it home. I saw him a couple of times in the country lanes with his woman and once in a café out in the middle of nowhere. We'd stopped to get some sweets and snacks; I was looking in the window and there was Cove sitting at a table with this woman; she had her back to me so I couldn't see what she looked like, but her hair was dark and shoulder length. He was touching her hand; then he lifted both their hands and placed their elbows on the table; I was sure she had a wedding ring on. The boys came out with the snacks and we left for home with Cove and this woman still in the café. When I got home that night Mam was worried sick about Cove. She said, "I'm going to ring the hospital where he works." She went along to Madam's door, knocked and walked in and asked if she could use the phone. Madam said she could. She phoned his work, and they told her he had left ages ago. When he did come home she said, "Where have you been? I rang the hospital; they told me you left ages ago!" I watched his face. He looked shocked. I could see his mind ticking over.

"I was on my way home," he said, "and this dog came out of nowhere and ran right in front of me; I swerved to avoid it and I came off the bike. When I got up and pulled myself together the bike wouldn't start. I had to push it all the way home."

Mam went over to him, concerned. "Oh my God, are you all right? Have you hurt yourself?"

"No," he said, "I think I'm all right, just a bit sore on my back."

"Take your jacket off," she said, "and sit down, or maybe you would be better lying down?" She was helping him take his jacket off. "I'll make you a cup of tea." There wasn't a mark on him or even a bit of dirt.

"I think I'll go and lie down," he said.

Mam was helping him up the stairs. "Will I phone the hospital and tell them you won't be in to work tomorrow?"

"No, no," he replied quickly, "I'll be fine in the morning. It's shock more than anything."

She came back down and said, "I've propped him up with pillows. He says his back is a bit sore."

I thought, poor Mam! She will never see the lying bastard for what he is. Couldn't she see that if he had pushed that bike home on a hot night like tonight that the sweat would be pouring out of him? And as for hurting his back—well, he didn't hurt it falling off his bike! Now she was saying, "I'll just make Cove a cup of hot sweet tea; it's good for shock." I wanted to scream at her: "He has just had a cup of tea in a café with his girlfriend!" But I couldn't do that to her. I wanted to shake her to make her see. She made the tea and took it up to him. When she came back down she said, "I'm going to make Madam her cocoa and when she's finished I'll get her settled down. I'm going to bed myself." After seeing to Madam she came back and poured herself a cup of tea and said, "I'm taking mine up to bed and sit with Cove."

A few minutes later I heard my name being called. I ran upstairs with the dog at my heels. She was in my room. I went in and it was slap, bang, wallop! Now it was me who was in shock! She had my cigarettes and matches in her hand. "I came in here to get one of your pillows as Cove has mine; I lifted up the top pillow to get the one underneath and look what I found! What have I told you about smoking, time and time again? If I ever see you with cigarettes again I'll skin you alive, do you hear me!"

"Yes," I said meekly.

"Now you know where these are going, don't you? In the fire! I'm not going to tell you again." She was going back downstairs when Cove called to her: "What's all the noise about?"

"Nothing," she called back. "I was shouting at Muriel to get her bedroom tidied up. I'm just going to see to Madam."

Well, at least she didn't tell Cove I'd been smoking.

Mam took me shopping and bought me a green short jacket. She said it was called a Swagger jacket; it hung loose and was made with lots of material in it. She also got me a pair of black suede high-heeled shoes. On Sunday afternoon I got all dressed up in my straight black skirt, white polo-necked jumper, new jacket and shoes. I thought I was the bee's knees! I met Rosemary and went for a walk round the town. It was a very warm day and I was sweltering in the jumper and jacket, but in no way was I going to take the jacket off! I wanted to show them off. My feet were killing me trying to walk in high heels. My ankles kept wobbling every now and then; I suppose I should have tried walking in the house before venturing outside in them. We went into the market place and saw this boy Rosemary knew; she went over to talk to him with me trailing behind her. When I got up to them I could see the boy had a suit on and the jacket was down to his knees and a bootlace tied around the neck of his shirt and big thick crêpe soled shoes; his trousers were so tight down to his ankle I wondered how he got his feet in! Rosemary was laughing at him. He didn't look pleased! Then she said, "I'm only kidding, you look great!"

"Thanks," he said, and smiled. With that two off his mates called him over to them; they were dressed in the same suits, only in different colours. I watched them walk away. I'd never seen such narrow trousers!

"They look good, don't they?" Rosemary said.

"Yes—is that a new fashion?"

"Yes," she said, "they're called Teddy Boys, and there will be a lot more of them in weeks to come."

I told her I'd have to go home because my shoes were hurting me. I'd big blisters on both heels. She left me at the bottom of Milford Hill, saying, "See you later." I got to the walkway at the side of the hill and took my jacket and shoes off and walked in my stocking feet. Oh, what a relief!

The following week Rosemary and I went to the Pally on our own. I was wearing my high heel shoes with big plasters over my heels; just in case, we put our coats in the cloakroom and went into the dance hall, and stood at the back.

"Rosemary," I said, "there's lots of girls wearing flat shoes."

"It's the fashion," she said.

The music started and a few girls got up with their partners. They were wearing black flat shoes and were hardly moving at all.

"What's up with them?" I asked.

"It's the new dance called the creep!" a girl behind me said. "And when the fast music comes on, it's jiving."

"Here's me," I said to Rosemary, "just got my first pair of high heels that I've waited for all this time and now the fashion is flat shoes! I can't win!"

"Well," she said, "I'm not wearing flat shoes; I think they look awful, but we'll have to learn to do the creep and the jive." It was a good job Martin wasn't there—he would be knocking everyone down with his Irish quickstep!

I received a letter from Roberta at the beginning of July, if you could call it a letter. It said, "I very happy you happy, love Roberta"—and there was a photo of her in the envelope. I was so glad to get one; at least she tried! There was no point in writing back because she wouldn't understand a word I wrote. I showed it to everyone in the café; they were all pleased to hear she was happy.

Later that week Mam said she wanted a word with me. I asked her what was wrong. She seemed to be in a bad mood all the time lately. She said she wanted to go away for a few days on her own. "I have discussed it with

Cove," she said. "He'll cover the first two days and if you could do the third, I'll be able to go. I need to have cover for Madam, someone here all the time with her. Cove is going to get his two days off together; so if you ask for the third day, then that's it covered."

I said I'd get it off. "Where are you going?" I asked.

"I'm off to Harrogate to see my brother," she replied.

I asked if Uncle Bert was ill or something wrong. She said no, it was just a break. This wasn't like Mam, going away without Cove. I wondered what was wrong.

Mam set off on the Friday morning. Cove took her to the station. I was on the late shift at the café so I was able to get Madam her breakfast and lunch. Cove came back about twelve; I wondered where he'd been all this time.

"When I dropped your mother at the station," he said, "I went to see a friend. I was there longer than I thought."

I went to work and retuned home about ten o'clock. Cove said he'd given Madam her cocoa and he was going to bed. I went into Madam's bedroom to see if she was all right, then to my own room, which is next door to hers, and got ready for bed; but I was scared stiff, being in the house with Cove. I got into bed with the dog next to me and kept listening; I could hear creaking floorboards but I told myself they were always creaking. I couldn't settle so I got out of bed and put a chair under the knob of the door. I eventually dropped off to sleep.

Next day I was home early from work. Mam had made a couple of steak pies before she left and said they would last us two days. Cove had peeled some potatoes, carrots, and opened a tin of peas.

"Its all ready for you to cook," he said. He was being extra nice, I thought! What's he up to?

"Mam said I could have Johnny up for a couple of hours," I said, "but we will stay in the kitchen."

He said that would be all right. Just before Johnny arrived Cove came in the kitchen and said, "You can go in the sitting room if you want—I'm going out for an hour or so."

Johnny came and we talked about this and that, and played a few card games. I wasn't very good at it so we decided to chat instead. He stayed a couple of hours and it was gone nine when he left. There was no sign of Cove so I tided round a bit and washed the cups up. It got to quarter to ten so I made Madam's cocoa; after she had finished she brought her cup into the kitchen and said, "I'm going to bed now." I gave her ten minutes, then went to see if she was all right. I went back downstairs. I thought I had better lock the doors. I didn't like sitting by myself with them unlocked; when Cove came he would have to knock. I sat on a chair in the kitchen, put my arms on the table and fell asleep.

I was woken up by the dog barking; he was at the back door. I looked at the clock; it was half past twelve. I went over and picked the dog up to stop him barking and opened the door. Cove came in.

"The bike broke down," Cove said, "and I had to push it all the way home." He put his hand on my shoulder; it made me cringe. "Now, it would be better if you didn't say anything to your Mam about this; you know how much she worries and you don't want to upset her, do you?"

I shrugged his hand off my shoulder. He made me feel sick! How Mam couldn't see through this man I'll never know. The collar of his shirt was covered in lipstick. I left the kitchen without saying a word and went to my room. I just left him standing there—I'd make him sweat for a while.

He went to work the next day and I was glad to see the back of him. I did notice his shirt hanging on the washing line outside the back door; he'd been scrubbing the collar and that's all; the rest of the shirt was dry. I bet he was wondering if I'd seen the lipstick?

I looked after Madam all that day and I managed all right.

"I'll be glad to see your mother," she said.

"So will I," I said. "She'll be home tonight."

Mam came back from Harrogate a lot happier than when she went. She didn't say very much to me when she arrived home. All she said was, "I'm very tired; all I want to do is go to bed. I'll tell you all about it tomorrow."

I went to work next day. When I'd finished, Johnny gave me a lift back home, and it was just after five. I went into the kitchen and sat at the table. Then Mam dropped her bombshell.

"We're going to live in Harrogate in a few weeks' time," she said. "I'm fed up with this job. I never get any time to myself and never get to spend much time with Cove. As you know I've been saving up for a deposit on a house and I think I've just about enough now. I'll get a job up there during the day and I'll be able to go to bed when I like; and I won't have to sit up to make Madam's cocoa and see her to bed. It'll be hard at first, we'll all have to pull our belts in, but it'll be worth it in the end."

I couldn't believe what I was hearing! I had lost count of the times I'd moved since I left Ireland five years ago. The last thing I wanted to do was move again.

"I don't want to go!" I said. "All my friends are here and I've a job that I like. I'm happy here. Why don't you buy a house here and you can get a day job; it's the same thing."

"Less of your cheek!" she said. "I want to go and live in Harrogate and you are coming with me. When you're eighteen you can do as you want, but until then you do as I say. Anyway, your friends can come and visit you—they have motorbikes." She was going on as if it was a few miles down the road instead of three hundred! I decided that what I'd do was go and look at some bed-sits, to see how much it was to rent one. So off I went, and looked at three different ones. They were asking more than I was getting in wages. So that was it—I'd have to go to Harrogate! I told Toni I would have to leave because I didn't have anywhere to live.

Me aged 16 Years old

"I very sorry you have to go," he said. "At anytime in the future you need job and I have vacancy, I take you back!"

I told all my friends I was moving to Harrogate. They were all teasing me at first: "That's in Yorkshire, you know! They don't make a pot of tea up there; it's called a brew! And the kids are called bairns!" I wished they would stop; it was making me worse, but they all said they were sorry I was going.

Time flew by and it got to the night before we were leaving. Cove wasn't coming with us—he was to follow in a week or so later. I thought to myself; he's going to have a great time when we're gone. We didn't have a lot of packing to do as we only had our clothes; I packed mine in my grandad's case and Mam came in to see how I was doing.

"You're not dragging that old case with you!" she said.

"All my clothes are in it and I'm not leaving without it," I said firmly. "You can't take it off me; it's mine."

"Well," she said, "you better not be moaning when you have to carry it!"

"I won't," I said.

All the packing was finished and we were ready for morning. Cove must be staying at the hospital until it's time for him to join us in Harrogate. Mam took Madam's cocoa in for the last time. She was in an awful state because Mam was leaving: she would come into the kitchen trying to get her to stay; she was offering to put up her wages by half again, but Mam had made her mind up and no one was going to change it. It was heart breaking next day having to leave Nankie-poo; I picked him up and gave him a cuddle and told him to be a good dog. He'd been my best friend since I moved to Milford Hill. I wished I could take him with me. I shed a few tears and the dog was licking them off my face, whimpering, knowing something was wrong. I said goodbye to Madam; she wished me luck in my new life.

"I don't know what Nankie-poo is going to do without you," she said. Poor Madam looked so unhappy; I felt really sorry for her. I went back in the kitchen where Mam was having a cup of tea.

"I'll meet you at the train station," I said. "I'm going to see Toni before I go."

"You'd better not try anything," she warned, "like running away, because I'll get the police if you're not at the station—so be told!"

I made my way down Milford Hill. When I got to the bottom I stopped at the shop and went in and bought ten cigarettes, a box of matches and a few sweets; then I made my way to Toni's. When I went in, there was a new girl behind the counter. I asked for a cup of tea; she gave me one and took the money; there was no please or thank-you from her. Toni came in and went behind the counter. They were getting busy.

"What you do here?" Toni asked when he saw me.

"I've just popped in to say goodbye," I said. "I'm meeting my mother at the train station."

"I wish you lots of luck," he said. "Don't forget what I say about job; I go now—it's busy."

I sat and drank my tea and lit a cigarette. I knew I wouldn't be able to have one on the train or Mam would skin me alive. When I'd finished I made my way to the station. I'd waited about five minutes when Mam and Cove arrived in a taxi. They got the cases out of the car and put mine down in front of me. Cove paid the taxi driver and we went into the station. The train was on the platform and I was having a job trying to lift grandad's case onto the train—it was that heavy.

Cove brought Mam's two cases onto the train and placed them on the luggage rack. I kept mine down at my feet. Mam went into the corridor to an open window and was talking to Cove. I stayed where I was and the train started moving.

We were leaving Salisbury.

Chapter 35
Moving Again

MAM came back to the compartment. We had it all to ourselves. I sat next to the window facing the engine. Mam didn't sit at the side or opposite me; she went to the other end of my seat so we were apart from each other. I could see she had been crying. I thought it was best to say nothing. I stared out of the window. I listened to the sound of wheels on the track and the rhythm of the train with all the scenery flying past. It made me think of all sorts of things, like the journey down from Harrogate five years before and all the awful things that had happened to me since then; it was no wonder I had lost my faith. Mam brought me out of my daydream. She was shaking her handbag and turning it upside down emptying all the contents on the seat next to her; then she put them back in again; then she stood up and was searching through her coat pockets. She looked in a very bad mood and sat down again.

"Is there anything wrong?" I asked.

"I have bloody well forgotten my cigarettes and matches, haven't I?" she said crossly. "They were on the kitchen table; I thought I'd picked them up but I can't have done."

I said nothing. She sat there for another ten minutes or so. I just carried on looking out the window. I was thinking about Martin. He had never been back to see us since the time he fell in the door and now we were moving further away from him. I didn't know when I would see him again. I was brought back with Mam saying my name.

"Muriel," she said, "have you got any cigarettes?"

"No," I said, "you told me I wasn't to smoke."

She sat there a bit longer. Then she said, "Are you sure you haven't got any?"

"Yes, I'm sure," I said.

"Well, if you have any and give me one, I'll let you smoke."

I went in my handbag and took the cigarettes and matches out and gave them to her. She couldn't get one out quick enough; she lit it and let out a big sigh of relief.

"You made me suffer all this time," she said.

I reached over for the cigarettes and matches. "I can smoke now, can't I?" She never answered.

When we got to Harrogate Mam got a taxi to my aunt and uncle Bert's. We were going to stay with them for a little while until she and Cove found the house they wanted to buy. She would have to wait until Cove came. When he did arrive they went looking at houses. I could tell my uncle didn't like Cove, and Cove didn't like my uncle. Mam was stuck in the middle of it all. In the end there was a bit of a row and Mam said she would look for a house to rent. I don't know what they had rowed about but there wasn't a very good atmosphere in the house. The next thing I was told to pack my clothes—we were on the move again.

We went to live three streets away. It was vary basic—not a lot of furniture at all and it smelt awful. We were facing the side of a slaughterhouse. I didn't know if it was still in use or not, but it smelt very bad. We were there three or four weeks before they found a house they wanted to buy. It was very big and had a hallway with a great big window on the right with the staircase directly in front of you. On the left were two doors; the first led to a big sitting room with a very big bay window and a door on the right that took you into the dining room which had four doors and French windows; the first door on the right went back into the hall and the second into a kitchen. A door on the left led you down to the cellar. The French windows led to a conservatory and another door on the right took you into the kitchen again. Also, there was a door in the conservatory to the back yard. At the top of the stairs there was a bathroom and a separate toilet, two bedrooms and another small staircase, which led to a box room and another bedroom. I thought, what do they want a house this size for? I didn't like it much—it gave me the creeps.

This is the house we moved to in Harrogate from Salisbury

They had been to look at other houses like my aunt and uncle's; they were selling for about five hundred pounds, but they didn't seem to like any of them. Although this one was twelve hundred pounds, I wondered where they were going to get enough furniture to fill the place. Anyway, they bought it, so it was cases packed again and we moved into the house. Mam and I got a job in Farnham, about five miles away. There was a bus that the company arranged that picked us up in the morning and brought us back at night. We worked in an ammunitions factory inspecting bullets for scratches or dents. I hated the job. I couldn't stand anything to do with violence and I knew that the bullets would be put into guns and used for killing people.

Cove got a job as a labourer; it was strange to see him coming home from work all dirty. Ray came out of the army at the end of October and came to stay with us; and he got a job in a steel factory so we were all working. The only person missing was Martin; he wouldn't come near the house while Cove was there. Ray didn't like Cove either—he called him 'a slimy git'.

The winter set in and it was freezing at the ammunitions factory. We were never warm. Even when we got home the house was cold. We had to light a fire but it took hours to warm the place.

Christmas eve came and I went to a dance with Ray and a few others; it was the first time I'd been dancing with Ray as a grown up and I loved every minute off it. It was after twelve when we arrived home. Mam and Cove were in bed so we didn't see them. Then it was New Year's Eve and a crowd of us went to a dance in Knarsborough. It was a good night and when the clock struck twelve they let loads of balloons down from the ceiling and everyone was kissing each other. It was now 1956 and I was having the time off my life.

In mid-January Cove came home from work early. He had been paid off for winter and he told Mam he wasn't feeling well. He ended up getting the 'flu and was in bed for a week. He couldn't go to work anyway as he didn't have a job, but when he got on his feet Mam said, "You'll have to do the cooking, see to the fire and the house."

At least now it was warm in the house when we got home and our tea was ready; but Mam said all that doesn't pay the mortgage! She put in as much overtime as she could. If she could get a Saturday morning she would take it.

On the eighteenth of February I turned seventeen. On that day I received a parcel from my auntie Mary and uncle George. I opened it, and there was a lovely blouse, a couple of waist slips and some pants. I was jumping around the room with excitement! The blouse was my style—white with black dots, a stand-up collar that was piped with plain black, and long sleeves with the cuffs done the same as the collar. "I'm going to wear this tonight at the youth club," I said.

"Will you stop jumping about?" Mam said. "Cove's not well. You should be thinking about him. But no, all you think about is yourself! You're a selfish little bitch! You could stay in for once and help me."

I didn't deserve what she had just said to me. I burst into tears and went upstairs and didn't come back down. She had spoiled my birthday.

The blouse that auntie Mary sent me I wore until it almost fell off my back. Ray had been to the youth club to teach ballroom dancing. I was very proud of him. So it was my brother that taught me to dance, and I was able to dance with anyone, and follow them. I made friends with a girl called Kathleen at the youth club, and we went everywhere together; we even dressed alike and learnt to jive together. It was good to have a friend.

Cove got ill again near the end of February and had a nosebleed that wouldn't stop. He was taken into the Harrogate hospital and stayed there for two weeks, but he got worse and was moved to a hospital in Leeds. I felt sorry for Mam; she was working all day and going from Harrogate to Leeds to visit him. It was twenty-two miles each way. I had left the ammunitions factory and got a job in a chemist just around the corner from where we lived. Mam had put in for another job at a different ammunitions factory in Thorp Arch near Wetherby. The money was a lot better and she was waiting to hear from them.

"I'll have to take a week off work," she said, "I'm worn out with all the coming and going, and it's costing me a bomb in bus fares; I don't know where its all going to end." For the first couple of days she went during the day to see Cove; on the third day when I got home from work she wasn't there, so I laid the table for tea and lit the fire. Ray had been in and gone out again. It was just after seven when Mam came in; she looked frozen solid and was as white as a ghost and sat by the fire. I went into the kitchen and made her a cup of tea. When I took it to her she was still sitting with her coat, scarf and gloves on. I took the scarf and gloves off her.

"Come on," I said, "drink this tea; it'll warm you up."

She was staring into space; then she let out the most horrible screams out of her mouth. I tried to hold her hands but she pulled them away and started screaming again. I got very frightened and started crying. I was doing everything I could to calm her down.

"Mam," I said, "what's wrong?"

She started making awful noises in her throat, and started shouting, "My Cove is dead!"

Eventually I got her to lie down on the sofa, but she was still making those awful noises.

"I'm going to get help," I said. "You're to lie there until I get back."

The tears were running down my face. I could hardly see and I was thinking, it isn't my fault he's dead. I hadn't prayed to Blessed Martin for over two years; in fact; I didn't pray to anyone anymore. I got to my uncle Bert's house and hammered on the front door. My uncle let me in and I was trying to tell him about Mam, but I couldn't get it out. Uncle George and auntie Mary were there. Aunt Mary came and cuddled me to her,

"Now, now, stop that crying and tell us what's wrong?" she said.

"I think my Mam has gone mad," I said. "She's making the most awful noises. Cove has died; she got back from Leeds over half an hour ago—she's in a bad way."

My two uncles went out the door and I stayed with my aunts.

Cove died on the twentieth of March, 1956. He was 38 years old. His two brothers came over from Ireland for his funeral, but his mother didn't come and I'm not sure to this day if she ever knew he had got married to my Mam. Mam was in a bad way after the funeral; she seemed to hold herself together while Cove's brothers were there, and that must have been hard because one of them looked like Cove; but as soon as they left she just went to pieces. Ray went out that night; he told me he was going to the White Swan.

"I need to get out of the house for a while or I'll go mad," he said. "I'll see you later."

I stayed with Mam. She was crying all the time and letting out some awful noises from her throat. I didn't know what to do or say to help mend her broken heart. I tried to cuddle her to me but she pushed me away. I thought if Martin had been there he would know what to do, but he didn't come to the funeral either. Mam went quiet for a couple of minutes; then she said, "Where's Ray?"

"He's gone to the pub for a while," I said.

Now she started on about Ray drinking alcohol. "It's disgusting, and your brother has no respect for the dead! He's just like your father. He should be here with his family. Go and get him! Tell him to come home."

I went and put my coat, scarf and gloves on. I didn't fancy the long walk to the White Swan. It was about a mile away, but at the same time I was glad to get out of the house. I was thinking what I was going to say to him when I got there. He's a grown man, twenty-two years old, and I had to tell him to come home! When I went in the pub the heat hit me; it was lovely and warm. I found Ray standing at the bar talking to some of his friends, and when I went over to him he said, "What are you doing here? Is there something wrong?"

I told him Mam had sent me to tell him to come home. "She says you have no respect for the dead," I said.

"Cove was nothing to do with me," Ray said angrily. "Why should I have to come home and mourn him?"

"Please, Ray," I pleaded, "Mam will just go on at me."

"You go back home and tell her you couldn't find me," he said. "I'll be home later." As I left the pub the cold air hit me and I thought about the long walk home. When I got in the house I told Mam I couldn't find him, and she seemed to accept that.

A few days after the funeral Ray had gone to work; Mam was still in bed and I was just going out the door to work when the mail arrived. I was about to put it on the windowsill in the hall when I noticed there was a letter for Cove and it had a Salisbury post mark stamped on it. I thought this is going to upset her again, seeing his name on the envelope, but it might be important so I left it there with the others. When I got home from work Mam was sitting in the dining room crying with the letter in her hand. She looked up at me.

"That bastard has been cheating on me!" she raved. "He's been having an affair with a woman in Salisbury for a good while! They have been writing to each other; all the time he was off work letters have been coming to my house while I was out there slogging my guts out to keep him and the house going!" She was getting more and more angry, shouting about all the lies he had told her. "And they must have been having a good laugh at me in Salisbury! I gave up everything for that man, and look where it's got me!"

Mam threw the letter at me and said, "Read it!"

"I don't want to read it," I said. "I knew about his affair. I have known for a good while, but I didn't think it was still going on."

Mam's eyes were blazing. "You *knew* about it and you didn't tell me?!"

I was getting angry now. I shouted at her: "Because you wouldn't have believed me! He could do no wrong in your eyes! Martin and I tried to tell you things lots of times, but you would always take his side! And I'll tell you another thing; after my grandad died he was sexually abusing me until I came back from Ireland, and then I told him I was going to tell you. He laughed in my face and said, 'She won't believe you because she loves me!' You were in the kitchen in Salisbury when he tried it on again. I was halfway down the stairs, but I knocked the smile off his face when I told him I was going to tell the Priest! He was more frightened of the Priest than he was of you! That man ruined all our lives and I will *never* forgive him!"

I ran upstairs and lay on my bed and cried my eyes out. Ray came home and I met him at the top of the stairs.

"Look at the state of you," he said. "What were you crying for?"

I told him about the letter.

"I know," he said, "I read it earlier on; he was a bastard, wasn't he? You should have heard Mam! She was coming out with swear words that even I had never heard. She's in a terrible state. She's angry now because she's hurt, but she'll calm down—just give her time."

I wished I'd told her now about the affair in Salisbury, but I didn't want to hurt her. It was awful trying to live with Mam now; she seemed to be angry all the time, and I couldn't do anything right. I was glad to get to work, to be out of the way. I liked working in the chemist. The manager and his wife were very nice, and so were the rest of the shop assistants. I was shown where everything was kept and under the counter there were drawers marked with a letter. I was told that if someone asked for, say, soap, I would look in the drawer with S on it and so on.

I was in the shop one Saturday. It was almost lunchtime and very busy with lots of people queuing up at the counters. They all seemed happy chatting away to each other whilst waiting to be served. They were mostly women and a couple of men; one man was with his wife and the other on his own. He was in my queue. It came to his turn to be served.

"Can I help you Sir?" I said.

He put his hand up to the side of his face and said in a whisper, "A packet of Durex, please."

I thought, Durex—that would be in the drawer marked D. I couldn't see anything by that name, so I went through it all again, just to make sure. I could see the man was getting agitated. The other assistants were busy at their counters on the other side. Just at that moment the manager came out with a lady's Prescription, and handed it to her. I shouted up to him from my end of the counter: "Do we sell, Durex?"

Everyone in the shop stopped talking and were looking at me. The man I was serving went Bright Red. The manager beckoned me to come up to where he was.

"I'll see to the gentleman," he said. "You stand there, and don't move." He put something in a bag and served the man. The man couldn't get out of the shop quick enough. The manager took me into the back and was trying to explain what they were, but gave up and called his wife. She explained what they were and took one out to show me. Now it was my turn to have a Red Face! The manager was locking the shop door and the two assistants went into kinks of laughter; the tears were running down their faces and it was a long time before they forgot that one.

Ray was still teaching the ballroom dancing at the youth club. I didn't go as often because Mam would be on her own, and I hated being on my own with her; she would moan all evening about bills, and how she was supposed to pay them. Ray and I helped all we could but we didn't get big wages. Ray was lucky—he could go out whenever he wanted. I had to stay in and listen to Mam going on about bills. She never smiled anymore and she was as hard as nails. This went on for a couple of months. I wished I could get her back—the one I had in Ireland, the one that would do anything for her children; I had lost her six years ago and wondered if I would ever get her back.

It came to the end of May. I was in the kitchen with Mam and she said, "Will you go and call Ray? He's still in bed." I went up to his room but he wasn't there. His bed hadn't been slept in. Then I saw a note on his pillow. I picked it up and looked at it. Ray was gone; he had left in the middle of the night. Oh my God, how was I going to tell her this? I went back downstairs and said, "Ray's gone."

"Gone where?" she asked.

I handed her the note. She looked at it and started calling him all the names under the sun.

"He couldn't tell me to my face!" she screamed. "He goes sneaking off in the middle of the night! Now, how am I going to manage?" She went on and on. I wanted to put my hands over my ears, like Patrick used to do, but I thought better of it. I didn't want to get a good slapping. Eventually Mam took in a woman lodger to help pay the bills; it was someone that worked with her so she wasn't a stranger.

I went out one night to meet some friends. One of the girls had just turned eighteen, and we were going to Knarsborough for a couple of hours. We all went into a pub; three of the girls had beer and they were going on at me to have one, but I said, "No," I just wanted an orange juice and that's all I drank. We got the bus home and I arrived at the house just after half past ten. I thought I would go straight upstairs as the house was in darkness. I got up the first few steps when the dining room door flew open and the light went on. Mam was standing there with the sweeping brush in her hand.

"I thought you were in bed," I said.

"You've been drinking!" She stood there glaring at me.

"I haven't," I said. "I've been in a pub, but I didn't have a drink."

"Don't you lie to me!" she shouted. "I can smell it off you!" She started hitting me with the sweeping brush. I turned and ran upstairs with her after me. I must have been hit three or four times on the back. I ran up the second flight of stairs and into my bedroom, shut the door and put a chair under the knob. I could hear her crying on the stairs but I daren't go out to her. I might just as well have had a drink. I'd got punished for it anyway. I sat on the bed and thought, 'I can't take anymore of this—tomorrow I'm going to write to Toni, in Salisbury, and ask him if he has any jobs.' I would phone Madam and ask her if I could stay with her until I found somewhere to live. I wrote the letter next day and posted it first thing Monday morning. I waited all week but there was no reply. I came downstairs on Sunday morning and went into the sitting room. Mam was standing near the fireplace.

"Put it back!" she said.

"Put what back?" I asked.

"The money you stole off the mantelpiece."

"I haven't touched any money," I said.

"There was One and Sixpence on the mantelpiece last night when I went to bed! You were still up and it's not there now. You are the only one who could have taken it."

"I never touched your money," I said. But she went on and on about it all day.

Teatime came and she told me to lay the table. As I'd just finished, the lodger popped her head in the door.

"Hello," she said. "By the way; I borrowed that One and Sixpence this morning; I had no change for the bus. I'll be down in a minute and sort it out."

"Oh," mam said, "I wondered where it went." I just wanted to scream at her!

Later that night when we were on our own, I plucked up the courage to tell her I'd had enough. I was going to tell her I'd written to Toni, but she didn't give me a chance.

"I know what you've been up to!" she said. "I think you're going to leave me as well—you're going to have to think again because Toni has no job for you; he's no jobs vacant at the moment, but he will let you know when there is one." She took a letter out of her apron pocket. I could see it was addressed to me! It was from Toni. She had opened my letter!

I was furious and started shouting at her: "You have no right to open my letters! I have had enough of all this carry on! First of all you put me in an orphanage while you lived just around the corner; you never came to see me once; you ignored me at the garden fête. Do you have any idea how much that hurt me? Why did you do that to me?"

"It was *him*," she said. "He didn't want you."

"But you are my *mother*! You didn't have to do as he said!"

"But I loved him, and look what he's done to me."

"And look what he's still doing to me!" I said. "He's dead—and you're still hitting and blaming me for things I haven't done. All the heartache he has caused you is being taken out on me. It's not my fault you got a rotten husband; nor is it Ray's, or Martin's. It's your own fault! You should have seen through him years ago."

I thought she was going to hit me but she didn't. She sat down and burst into tears—and I did the same.

Mam started to soften up as the days went by. We got a letter from Martin; he was getting married and wanted us to go down to Aldershot for the wedding. Mam said she couldn't get the time off work so I went on my own. I stayed with uncle George and auntie Mary. It was lovely to see them both again and the two girls. My aunt came to the wedding and my uncle stayed home to look after the girls. I couldn't believe Martin was getting married; he looked far too young but in another few months he would be twenty-one. He and his new wife, Ann, looked a lovely couple and I was very happy for them.

The next day I travelled back home and my Mam was very pleased to see me. I think she had it in her head that I wouldn't come back.

Mam came home from work one day and said a man that worked with her had asked her out for the day on Sunday. I told her she should go—it would do her good. She thought about it for a while and decided to go. But when it came to

Saturday night she got cold feet and said she wouldn't go unless I went with her. He was going to call at the house for her in the morning and she had no way of getting in touch with him to tell him not to come. I gave in; I thought I'd go with her—it would get her out of the house. The man's name was Ron—and there he was, next morning, to pick her up. She went out to meet him.

"You don't mind if my daughter comes with us, do you?" she said.

"Not at all," he replied.

I think he got a shock when he saw the size of me!

He took us to York, about twenty miles away, and took us up this very narrow cobbled street and said it was called The Shambles—and there was Mam and I trying to walk in high heeled shoes! Then he took us to York Minster and said we'd go up the steps to the top for the sake of the lovely view. So we started going up these very narrow steps that went on forever! Eventually we reached the top and I was glad of the rest. Then we had to go back down; that was ten times harder than going up! I was so glad to be down; my feet were killing me and I wished I were home. Then he said, "We'll have to walk around the Bar Walls," so off he went with us trailing behind him. We didn't know the Walls went almost round the city! All I can remember was the throbbing of my feet and the blisters on my heels. Indeed, I was so glad to see home! I left Mam talking to Ron outside; the first thing I did was get a bowl of water and put my feet in—stockings and all! Mam came in and I said to her, "I'm never ever going on one of your dates again!"

"Don't worry," she said, "I won't be seeing him again, and hurry up with that bowl!"

We both had a good laugh about it all.

Mam was getting better all the time. I could see a big difference in her. She went out a few times with some women from work and enjoyed herself. It was getting near to Christmas and she put up a tree and got some decorations, not the ones you had to stick together, but proper ones. She got crêpe paper in different colours and made fans. She'd already made the Christmas cake a few weeks before. Everything was lovely. I'd got my mother back—the one I had in Ireland!

Happier days, my Mam & Bill on the left, Martin back left, Ray back right, me in the middle & Rays wife Pauline on the right

    I couldn't have wished for anything more; and to top it all, she had met the gentlest giant of a man called Bill Higgin. They got on like a house on fire. He'd never been married and had no children, but he was the best dad I could ever hope for and he and Mam were the best grandparents any child could wish for. They were always there for me and they had twenty-eight years of marriage together and were very happy.

I was eighteen now; an adult, and I hoped to go Beyond the Rocky Road and start my own life.

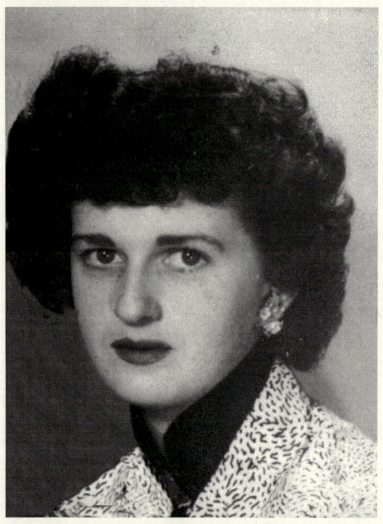

Me aged 18 Years old

I have forgiven my Mam and dad for what they put me through when I was a child, but I'll never be able to forgive those two men who sexually abused me in my young life.

Chapter 36
Meeting Arthur

IT was a few months before my eighteenth Birthday. I was getting on a bit better with my Mam and I was glad about that. Mam had lost her husband in March and on top of that she had found out he'd been having an affair for a long time.

There were three of us left in the house—Mam, a girl lodger and myself.

I'd had a terrible life and I was hoping now that this was going to be the end of my rocky road; but alas, it wasn't to be.

I met the man I was going to marry in Woolworth's. At the time I couldn't stand him; I thought he was a big show off.

A few weeks later it was my birthday and some of my friends and I went to a youth club where we had a good time, but it closed at ten o'clock! One of the boys who wasn't with us invited us all to his house for a party. And when we got there the man I'd met in Woolworth's was standing by the fireplace talking to some other boys. I later found out his name was Arthur. The girl who was our lodger was also there. The party was going fine for a while; then one of the boys come over to me and asked if I'd like a glass of orange. I said "Yes please" and smiled. He returned a few minutes later with the orange and I thanked him, and off he went back to his friends. I stood there on my own for a while drinking the orange and by the time I'd finished it I was getting more confidence in myself, so I joined all the others and was enjoying myself. Then another boy took the glass out of my hand and said, "I'll get you a refill—its orange you drink, isn't it?"

"Yes," I smiled. "Thank you."

He came back and handed me the drink and stayed with me for a while, talking about this and that. Then he went back to his friends. They were all looking across at me and laughing amongst themselves. I had no idea what it was all about. I went and sat on a chair among some of the other people, which included our lodger and the man called Arthur.

After a while I began to feel sick! But then it seemed to wear off. I finished my drink and before I knew it, there was another one put in my hand. I started to drink it but I was starting to feel funny; my speech was slurring and the noise started to sound far away. I could hear our lodger shouting: "They've spiked her drink with Vodka!"

The man called Arthur started shouting at them as well. He was telling them that they could have killed me. Then they started shouting and fighting broke out. In the end they told Arthur to get out and to take "her" (meaning me!) with him. I can remember putting my foot outside the door and the fresh air hitting me. The next I knew we were outside the toilets in Devonshire Place. Arthur had been carrying me on his shoulder. I told him I needed the toilet; there were a lot of steps to go down and he helped me all the way to the bottom and sat me on a toilet and went back up the steps—and that was the last I saw of him.

I kept being sick and my arms and legs seemed to be flopping all over the place. I must have passed out after that. The next time I opened my eyes I was frozen stiff and I thought my head was going to burst. I tried to stand up but my legs were numb and had no feeling in them with the cold. I sat down again and put my hands inside my coat, trying to warm them the best I could. After a while I tried rubbing my legs until I could feel them and stood up and tried walking with pins and needles in my legs. I was stumbling all over the place. I managed as far as the steps and had to crawl on my hands and knees until I reached the top. The streetlights were on and I could see my coat covered with vomit and my stockings torn to bits. I felt and smelt terrible!

I suppose I was lucky to be alive. It was a freezing cold February night with a heavy frost and I'd no idea of the time! I started walking home. I knew it was about a mile from where I was because I'd been there before looking for my brother, Ray, when my stepfather (Cove) had died—and that had been another freezing night last March. As I was walking along the walkway they call Harrogate Stray, I kept bumping into the wall on my left. It was only a few feet high. I tried to keep to my right but my luck was out and I kept banging my legs against the wall and they were starting to bleed. I had to sit down and rest for a while and was crying my eyes out at the sight of the blood streaming out of my legs. I didn't sit for long as I could feel the cold oozing up into my body. At last I came to the end of the Stray and turned left down the very long road home, stopping every now and again for a rest.

At last I saw the level crossing and kept telling myself 'I haven't got far to go now'. I arrived at our front door only to find it locked! This started me off crying again. I felt as though I'd no energy left in my body to make it round the house to the back door. I opened the gate quietly and made my way round only to find that door locked as well. It had small window pains in the top half; I looked around and found a lump of rock by the house and used it to break the window close to the lock, praying all the time that the key would be on the inside of the lock and that Mam wouldn't hear me. I put my hand through and let out a sigh of relief when I felt the key!

I was so happy to get into the house. I went as quietly as I could until I reached my bedroom, which was in the attic, and went straight to bed. The next I knew was my mother standing over me with a broom in her hand. She brought it down as hard as she could and hit me in the stomach and one of the buttons on my coat came off and I could see it flying across the room and smashing against the back wall. She was lifting the broom again ready to hit me when the lodger came running through the door. She was trying to get the broom off my Mam and shouting, "It wasn't her fault! We had gone to a party after the youth club and a couple of fellows had been spiking her drinks!" She continued: "I'd told them to stop it and so did another man called Arthur. There was a bit of a fight going on and they told Arthur to get out and take her with him, so I assumed he'd taken her home."

My mother was fuming!

"Why didn't she come home with you?" she demanded.

"Because Arthur was supposed to bring her home!"

My mother told me to get out of bed. I was trying to lift my head off the pillow. I thought it was going to explode with the pain and dizziness. She grabbed the shoulder of my coat and pulled me out of bed. I could hardly stand up straight. Then she started going on about the sick on my clothes and the blood on my legs, then pointed to the mud and bloodstains on the sheets.

"And where have you been all night?" she demanded.

I told her I'd been in the toilets at Devonshire Place; I must have passed out and when I woke up I was freezing cold and didn't know what time it was. I explained that I eventually managed to stand up, saying it took me a long time to walk home—I had to break the glass in the back door to get in. "I'm so sorry," I said, "I'll pay for the glass to be replaced."

"You'll do more than pay for the glass!" she was fuming. "You can strip the bed and get all the bedding washed; but go and have a bath first—you stink!" And she stormed out of the room, slamming the door behind her.

I thought my head was going to split in two. I felt sick again. She'd gone back downstairs and I was glad I didn't have to listen to any more shouting.

After I'd had a bath I was beginning to feel a bit better so I collected all the washing together and made my way down to the kitchen. It was a good job we had a big sink with all the bedding and clothes. I got busy with the scrubbing board and soap and after putting them through the old mangle to squeeze out the water, I hung them on the clotheshorse in the conservatory to dry, then cleaned up the broken glass at the back door.

Then I went back upstairs to get clean bedding and make up my bed. I was longing to lie down and go to sleep, but I daren't.

When I went back down the stairs Mam was in the dining room banging things about and giving me awful looks. Just then the doorbell rang and she went to answer it. It was Bill, the man she was going out with.

Bill was a lovely man—she was lucky to have met him.

He came in and said "Hello, Hinny" to me, and I said "Hello" back.

Mam's face changed. It was all smiles now, and I thought; this is my chance to go upstairs and have a lie down. My head was still thumping.

As I lay there I started thinking about getting my own flat. I knew Mam would be all right now, because she was going out with Bill. I fell asleep for a couple of hours and felt a lot better when I woke up. I swore I'd never drink orange juice again.

I met Arthur the following week as I was walking past Woolworth's, and he asked if I was feeling better. I told him to get lost! I didn't want to speak to him.

"What did I do?" he asked. "I stood at the top of those toilets for about ten minutes; it was freezing! I shouted down to you that I was going home; there was nothing else I could do."

"You could have gone and got one of those women from the party to come and help me!" I said. "I was there all night; I nearly froze to death!"

He said he was sorry, and added, "But at least I got you away from the house. So let's start again. Will you come and have a cup of tea with me?"

So I went with him to a café and that was the start of my life with Arthur.

It was my eighteenth birthday on February the 18th 1957. I started to see Arthur at the weekends. He was eight years older than me so when we went out it was always to a Pub, or a Workingmen's Club. I started to drink lemonade; he said I was cheap to take out, but he would drink loads of pints of beer. Then he'd get up on stage and start singing! I got embarrassed because I was left sitting on my own and didn't know where to look or what to do, although he had quite a good voice. He always had lots to drink before he could build up the courage to go on stage and then it was a job trying to get him off! One of the committee men would keep saying, "Right, Arthur, make that your last song, there's other people waiting to sing."

Once a week he came to our house and seemed a different person. He hardly ever spoke and never stayed long. One day after he'd left I asked Mam what she thought of him. She said she didn't like him. "He's quiet when he comes here because he's not had any beer, and he'd have spent all his money over the weekend—so he comes down here. If he had money, you wouldn't see him at all. I've heard all about him, so if I were you I'd get rid of him."

That did it! I was going to look for a job with more money so that I could go and find my own flat.

I managed to find a job at the Harrogate Hospital as a ward maid and after a couple of weeks I found a bed-sitting room.

After going home and packing all my clothes I was ready to move out. I took my suitcase down to the bottom of the stairs and left it in the hall and went to say goodbye to my mother. I said, "I'm going now. I'm only fifteen minutes away if you need me at any time. I'll always be there for you."

"I've said all I want to say about that man," she said. "You'll be sorry!"

I left the house and got the bus to town without looking back. That was me—off to start my new life and live it the way I thought it should be.

Postscript
(by Jane McGregor, Muriel's daughter)

MY mum died on 3rd March 2005 and never got to finish her book. Chapter 37 was actually the start of the next book.
We are all very proud of her, and we love and miss her so much.

Hindsight is a wonderful thing. Muriel married Arthur in 1958 and had five children: Alan, Kim (who, to add further heartbreak, died when only a few days old), Wayne, Peter and Jane. After the break-up of her marriage to Arthur in 1973, she remained in York, England, until she finally got the one chance that few of us are lucky enough to get... she met her true soul mate, Alan Hall.

They moved to Scotland in 1980, where they were married in 1983, and where she spent the years from then until her passing in 2005, being shown the love and respect she always craved and finally found with her husband Alan. Not only was he a wonderful husband but also a wonderful father and grandfather.

Alan remains today a central part of all our lives and will always be cherished!

Starting from left to right, Wayne, myself (Jane) my Mam Muriel, step dad Alan,Alan and peter

THE END